ENDORSEMENTS FOR KEEPING UP WITH GOD

Taken from the pages of Colorado's historic economic housing crisis, this book will encourage you, even when certain stories don't have a "happily ever after" ending. Each story will remind you that God is in every story.

Connie Zimmerman and Donnetta Wilhelm use many stories to tell one really BIG story of God's faithfulness in KEEPING UP WITH GOD.

When things seemed impossible, Connie found ways to provide housing and support services for countless families. Through partnerships with God, government agencies, funding sources, and people who cared enough to faithfully provide financial support and get involved, the lives of people were changed forever. Families worked hard to make a better life for themselves and their children. They developed solid life skills. In the process, many also found God.

— Vicky Reier
President of the Board | BeyondHome |
Retired Assistant City Manager for the City of Arvada

God stories are my favorite stories. It was the God stories of generations past that made me see more of who God is and how He works through His people. What TRAMP FOR THE LORD by Corrie ten Boom and GOD'S SMUGGLER by Brother Andrew did for me, I hope KEEPING UP WITH GOD will do for the next generation.

This is the story of one woman who refused to take "no" for an answer when she knew her God was saying "yes".

Connie Zimmerman's memoir tells how God built Colorado Homeless Families (CHF) out of nothing in 1987 and used it to house more than 500 families and counting is the story of one miracle after another. It is the story of how God invites each of us into His greater story for the good of all people and for His glory.

It was such a privilege to be chosen by Connie to continue the work of CHF upon her retirement. I will be forever thankful for the hard work she endured for almost thirty years to create the stable, debt free organization that we have today. I know it is Connie's hope and mine that CHF (now BeyondHome) will continue to be led and used by God to help hundreds and even thousands of vulnerable families in the future. You can check out what we are up to now at beyondhomeonline.org.

I hope you enjoy reading KEEPING UP WITH GOD, and I hope you keep your eyes and ears open for what God might be inviting you to do. God is continually inviting His people into His greater story. As the pages of KEEPING UP WITH GOD demonstrate, God stories are always the best stories.

— Karen R. Allen, M.A. Executive Director of
Colorado Homeless Families dba BeyondHome

Back in 1987, when God gave me a front-row seat as an eyewitness to many of the miracles recorded in this book, it was breathtaking.

This book will capture your heart and challenge your faith with its recounting of incredible times! I am *out-of-this-world* humbled to have watched and supported the birth of a mission that would change the lives of hundreds, then thousands, of people through transitional housing.

Every reader will find it inspiring and life changing. God moved Connie Zimmerman to selflessly give her life to serve people needing sustainable housing through Colorado Homeless Families.

— Dr. Kim Skattum Retired Pastor | Crossroads Church | Colorado

For any person seeking to launch a parachurch or mission organization, this book will serve as a perfect blueprint for ministry success. "The Lord himself goes before you and will be with you; he will never leave you nor forsake you. Do not be afraid; do not be discouraged" (Deuteronomy 31:8). If ever a book exemplifies this verse, KEEPING UP WITH GOD unquestionably does. Connie Zimmerman and Colorado Homeless Families provide compelling accounts of what it means to be led by the Lord to "bind up the broken hearted" (Isaiah 61:1) and provide hope for hundreds of homeless individuals and families. These miraculous testimonies will install in each reader how faith in action and prayer can surely move mountains in all our lives.

— Reverend Evelyn E. Bodett, MA
| Pastoral Counselor | Former Adjunct Professor, Denver Seminary

Keeping up with God

Thirty Years and Running with Colorado Homeless Families

Donnetta Wilhelm with Connie Zimmerman

Publisher's Cataloging-in-Publication (Provided by Cassidy Cataloguing Services, Inc.)
Names: Wilhelm, Donnetta, author. | Zimmerman, Connie, author.
Title: Keeping up with God : [Colorado homeless families (1987-2016)] / Donnetta Wilhelm with Connie Zimmerman.
Description: Littleton, CO : Capture Books, [2022] | Subtitle: Thirty Years and Running with Colorado Homeless Families | Includes bibliographical references and index.
Identifiers: ISBN: 978-1-7324457-4-1 (paperback) | 978-1-7324457-6-5 (ePub) | 978-1-7324457-5-8 (Kindle)
Subjects: LCSH: Zimmerman, Connie. | Women--Colorado--Biography. | Homeless persons--Housing--Colorado. | Low-income housing--Colorado. | Nonprofit organizations--Colorado. | Trust in God--Christianity. | LCGFT: Biographies.
Classification: LCC: F784.D453 W55 2022 | DDC: 305.420978883--dc23

This book is the official memoir of Connie Zimmerman. It is a work of narrative non-fiction. Some personal identifiers have been changed to protect participants in the program.

Credit for the running legs frontispiece: Shutterstock.com/Aleksandr Pasenchnik

Published in the United States by Capture Books
lb.capturebooks@aol.com
Editor: Crystal Schwartzkopf
crystalschwartzkopfi@gmail.com
5856 S. Lowell Blvd. Ste. 32-202
Littleton, CO 80123
978-1-7324457-4-1 paperback
978-1-7324457-5-8 Kindle

With honor, gratitude, and appreciation I dedicate this book to the single parent moms who face many trials and tribulations raising their children; first, to my daughter Jennifer, my sister Carin, and to the single parent moms who lived at CHF and to those single parent moms who are now living at Beyond Home.

Dear Ruth,
    You have the gift of
hospitality + love. The Lord
sees your heart and He is
with you.
    Many blessing to you
Connie Zimmerman
8/1/22

Table of Contents

Disclaimer

The specifics of a person's life in crisis are never indeed known or details understood. To keep the identities of Colorado Homeless Families' clients protected and private, creative license was required with each family story, i.e., "When God…"

Stories are based on actual families that Colorado Homeless Families helped, yet names, identifying characteristics, and most recognizing details have been changed. Although confidentiality agreements were not signed as part of the Colorado Homeless Families legal documents, nor were releases obtained from every family, we respect the privacy of those who diligently worked to change their lives from homelessness to successful, self-sufficient families. Neither the authors nor publisher is responsible for any errors or omissions, and this print information does not replace the advice of experts.

FOREWARD

Every once in awhile, you encounter someone driven by a true mission and vision for their life and you realize that you can help them accomplish their mission. You also realize that it is no accident that you are placed at this juncture with them, but that God is guiding you both. That is the story of Connie Zimmerman and Colorado Homeless Families.

When I started my speaking, training, and consulting firm in 1999, I knew that tithing 10% of my new earnings as an entrepreneur was important if my firm was to succeed. I was also aware that God wanted more than my money. He wanted my time. So, I looked at a 40-hour work week, and decided a tithe of 4 hours was in keeping with that 10%. I offered to teach English as a second language for Colorado Homeless Families (CHF) one night a week while I built my business. Classes were about 2 hours, and the preparation and travel time made up the 4 hours+ that I wanted to contribute. I had taught English as a second language in the language schools in Washington D.C. during the de-escalation of the Vietnam war, and had experience, resources, and interest. I knew that is what God wanted me to do. The result was a chance to contribute to CHF and the students, and a side benefit was that my business was blessed and started to grow. As I became more successful and started to travel, I couldn't commit to the weekly classes anymore, but my connections with the speaking community had also grown. CHF needed educational seminars, put on by experts, and I knew who they were. I contacted speakers to come to CHF, did some of the seminars myself, and insisted my speaker colleagues volunteer their time. I reminded them of the principal of tithing and giving back, and they stepped in the gap. One speaker shared her expertise with nutrition and meal planning and at the end of her talk gave away a week's worth of healthy food to a deserving family. Each program blessed CHF and each speaker was blessed in return. It was a true win-win. God works when you are willing to stand in the gap and share your gifts with those who need them most.

For the last 25 years, I have traveled the world speaking and training. I have flown over the North Pole, walked barefoot through the monasteries of Myanmar, and sat on ancient Viking stones. I have seen what Connie Zimmerman saw years ago – we are all just people, who sometimes need a little help to become the man or woman God wants us to be. Thank you, Connie, for allowing me to be part of your vision. You have left a lasting legacy for all of us.

— Christie Ward,
Certified Speaking Professional (CSP) | The Impact Institute |
Thornton, Colorado

PREFACE

"Welcome to Colorful Colorado," the hospitable sign greets travelers at the Colorado state lines.

Inspiring songs have been composed echoing the majestic mountains, pictures painted reflecting the exquisite colors of the state, and books written regarding the magnificent land. But Colorful Colorado has a dark side.

The 1980s was considered the second worst economic period in Colorado's history, trailing only the Great Depression. From 1982 to 1984, nearly 50,000 people lost their jobs. By 1985, Colorado was the nation's top state for business failures.[1] Economists saw the bottom fall out in 1987, with unemployment reaching a high of 9.1%.[2] Much of the blame was placed on energy industries: oil, gas, and mining. However, manufacturing, airlines, construction, banking, and real estate contributed to the fall as they all took heavy economic hits. 14,000 U.S. Department of Housing and Urban Development (HUD) homes sat vacant[3] as the economy, and worse, its people, crumbled.

One of the greatest biblical stories of rebuilding a crumbled culture is found in the Old Testament book of Nehemiah. Nehemiah was tasked with rebuilding the broken-down walls of Jerusalem. Nehemiah exhibited unequaled leadership and organization skills through this God-appointed task while consistently demonstrating humility, integrity, patriotism, energy, piety, and selflessness.

Like Nehemiah, a Colorado woman named Connie Zimmerman was deeply troubled at seeing the rubble of people's lives on a daily basis. Her heart especially was burdened for families with children who are forced to live on the streets.

Also like Nehemiah, Connie's deep distress led her to ask the Lord to help her fellow people. And, as God does, He did send

15

help in the form of the least expected person: He sent Connie Zimmerman herself in 1986. Perhaps because she was a married woman who also juggled the costs and responsibilities of raising a family, Connie felt the dire feelings of homeless people in a deeply personal way. Any person who lost a home would find it incredibly difficult to rebuild on their own. She knew these people needed someone to be beside them, to encourage and guide them back into a home with an assurance of hope.

First, with just a few people and then with team development, Connie, running after God with every step, built a nonprofit organization that worked tirelessly—and faithfully—to rebuild the rubble of lives created by homelessness.

Faced with everything from ridicule and taunts to threats, physical attacks, internal disagreements, false rumors, and enemies scheming to kill them, Nehemiah's task to complete the wall was finished in only 52 days. Though this wall has experienced many changes, it stands today. Colorado Homeless Families nonprofit organization was not built in 52 days, but through miraculous years of development, it also stands today after Connie's 2016 retirement.

Whatever the task, a thankful heart is vital for all He has done, personally, and through someone who walks the deep and fulfilling journey with God. It is important to tell of our Lord's goodness of the journey to rebuild, renew, and restore.

This is the story of Colorado Homeless Families, one woman's heart for God and His people, and how God is present in each story.

1986

WHEN GOD CALLS YOU

Responding to the Call

Taking the same route today as always, thirty-nine-year-old Connie Zimmerman drove to The Villas at Sunny Acres, an exclusive senior living community, in her 1972 Monte Carlo. Located on 64 idyllic campus acres, one could enjoy the majestic Rocky Mountain panorama of the Colorado front range. A supervisor now, Connie often thanked God for this dream job.

She was responsible, as resident manager of the Towers Building, for the overall care and transportation of the residents and overseeing the maintenance of the 85 apartments. Connie loved the people she came into contact with daily, enjoyed serving them, and delving into the details of her job. She found it rewarding and her friends there were inspirational. She tried to speak to and encourage as many as she could each day, several of whom she helped come along to know Jesus Christ in the seven years she had been employed there.

A giant radio billboard read "KBPI Rrrrrrrrocks the Rrrockies!" which greeted her day after day on her morning drive to Thornton from Westminster.

This morning, she saw the homeless man holding his ragged and torn cardboard sign like a label dangling from the string around his neck, pleading for money to help feed and shelter his wife and two young children. The same red Denver Bears baseball cap perched on his head and the same torn blue jeans that she'd seen him wearing every day.

She prayed the prayer she did each day when she saw this gentleman and the many others just like him, *"Lord, please bring*

17

someone to help these homeless families. Help these parents care for their young children."

Local news reports about the economic problem weighed on her spirit as she drove on. She knew it was a growing problem in Colorado, but like many people, she thought these people were lazy and didn't want to work, so she didn't give much attention to it. She and her husband of 17 years, Larry, had been watching the local news in the evenings over the last few months.

Repeated reports claimed a Colorado Coalition for the Homeless study showed that 9,500 to 11,000 people, including 1,500 children, were currently homeless in Colorado. The homeless population was rising quickly.

Many homeless families were back and forth continually from transitional homes to the streets because few social services were available to help them maintain a stable way of life. There was insufficient public housing, and more than 1,500 families were waiting for rent-subsidized apartments at the Denver Housing Authority. In Aurora, the largest suburb, the waiting list for housing aid was over 1,700 families long.

This reflection of the news reports led Connie to her second prayer, a prayer of relief, *"Thank you, Lord Jesus, for my family, for our jobs, and our home."* Married since 1971, Connie and Larry had two children, Jennifer and Jason. Their family lived a typical suburban life with two busy careers to make ends meet. Their children were healthy and lively. The family also enjoyed spiritually captivating programs offered at Crossroads Church led by Pastor Roland Taylor and his wife, Gayle.

The Zimmermans were active church members. Connie served on the Board of Trustees during the building program, and for five of the six years as Chairman overseeing a yearly budget of over $420,000. During that time, she also served four years as the coordinator for Operation Blessing and diaconate member. Larry served on the diaconate board for more than fifteen years and was chairperson for nine of those years.

Today, especially, as she passed the familiar homeless man, she felt a deep stirring, a growing burden that was becoming too difficult and too heart-wrenching to ignore. Connie knew that the burden on her spirit was from God. He often seemed to highlight needs to make His will known and to bring about each believer's cooperation with Him to achieve His purpose. Connie strongly sensed the Lord was telling her, *"I love the homeless. I care for the homeless. I am looking for people who are listening. I am looking for people who are obedient. I am looking for people through whom I can do exceedingly abundant things."*

Over the course of the next few weeks, Connie would wake up at 3:00 am with thoughts of the homeless, and her questions began to receive answers.

"Lord, I don't know what to do, nor do I even begin to know what they would need!" To which He answered, *"My grace is sufficient for you, for my power is made perfect in weakness. Therefore, I will boast all the more gladly about my weaknesses so that Christ's power may rest on me"* [2 Corinthians 12:9].

"But, God," Connie asked, *"How can one woman make a difference when there are so many families needing help? I'm just a regular person, nor do I have the skills or knowledge to help these people. I wouldn't know how to go about this."* The Lord answered her, *"If any of you lacks wisdom, you should ask God, who gives generously to all without finding fault, and it will be given to you."* [James 1:5].

She continued asking, *"God, how am I supposed to help these families? I already work so many hours. If I try to do both, I can tell right now that I'd be useless to my own family. If I quit my job to do this work, how will I support my family? We don't have any extra money, and we barely make it by!"* To which He replied, *"every animal of the forest is mine, and the cattle on a thousand hills"* [Psalm 50:10].

"This is unreal, Lord! Are you telling me to start a program to help homeless people? Well, Lord, You helped David. You helped all

19

the people we read about in the bible. If this is really You keeping me awake, this could be fun. This could be great, but if it's not you, Lord, I could be in so much trouble!" And His response, *"Remember: I can do all this through Christ who gives me strength"* [Philippians 4:13].

Connie knew that this invigorating and powerful conversation with the almighty Father had changed her small view of the possibilities for, as the Bible said, "all things are possible with God," and, "if God be for me, who can be against me?" She suddenly saw the greatness of God with new direction and compassion. Connie sensed a deep love and vision to work alongside God almighty. Connie put herself behind her leader, this God she said she trusted. *"Lord, I choose to believe You. You have chosen me. Help my unbelief. I am willing to serve You."*

Even so, she opted not to speak to anyone about it.

She continued to ask for confirmation, and the more time that passed, the more excited she got about the idea. A thought continued to seed in her spirit, *"Doesn't God have the power to do all things? When we believe Him enough to act, won't we see His name is 'Almighty?'"*

She began to confide this oyster of an idea to a few close friends, including Pastor Taylor who exclaimed, *"That's a wonderful idea to help homeless families!"* Connie decided to tell her dad, who abruptly took the pragmatic voice that this was not something his ultra-feminine daughter could manage. He warned, she could get into a lot of trouble. He was concerned for her safety. On the other hand, Connie's mother believed that if God was leading her, He would keep her safe.

Connie continued to walk in faith that God was leading her into His will to help the homeless. Knowing that it is vital to walk in agreement not only with Him, but with her husband, she told Larry what had been placed on her heart, the prayers she had offered, and the confirmations she had received.

Larry didn't offer enthusiastic encouragement like Pastor Taylor, but neither did he dissuade her from doing what was so obviously God's will. Connie knew that Larry would take any of his concerns before the Lord.

She moved forward praying, *"Lord, give me the faith I need to proceed. Help me to hear Your voice so that I will stay close to You and not get off the path You want me to follow."*

The weight of the burden was no longer there. God had spoken to Connie Zimmerman. She relied on His word as true and trustworthy, and He had confirmed His calling. He had answered her prayer to find His purpose and plan for her life. Now, she was excited and full of joy to see what He would do and where He would lead her.

The next day, as Connie walked over the ice from the Sunny Acres parking lot to her warm office, she knew without a doubt that God was calling her to do something to make a difference in the lives of homeless families, but questions again began to rise.

Staring out her office window, lost in the question, *"How do I even start something like this? Can one woman make a difference when there are so many families needing help? Maybe I'll just help a few families..."* a knock at her door brought her out of this deep contemplation.

One of Connie's favorite employees, William Bridges, stood in the doorway in his dark blue Sunny Acres uniform, his hat in one hand and a slip of paper in the other. Bill had been one of Connie's transportation drivers employed by Sunny Acres for the past five years. As he gently placed the paper on Connie's desk, she noticed it was a form for change of address and phone number. This was the third change request he had submitted in as many months.

"Why do you keep changing your address and phone number, Bill?" Connie asked.

Bill sat down across from Connie's desk, with sagging shoulders, a hanging head, and a sadness that permeated her office.

Connie was stunned as she listened to Bill tell his story, and the love of God for the homeless filled her heart. As he left and quietly closed her office door, she knew that he was the first person she wanted to help.

With complete conviction and renewed determination, she prayed, *"God, if I'm supposed to help people who are homeless, I want to help Bill. This is the guy. I want to help him now. I don't know how to help all of them, but let's start with him."* Connie *knew* that Matthew 11:30 says, *"For my yoke is easy and my burden is light,"* and that taking the first small step to help just one friend was the beginning of the race. Once a person begins to cooperate with God, the burden on the spirit finds wings of joy and is lifted.

She made a list of names and began calling several of her friends at church excited to explain how she was going to start a program to help this man, and as the Lord provided, the homeless. Would they consider being part of this effort, perhaps on a board of directors? Everyone she spoke to offered ideas and most said they would be willing to help.

Connie didn't know, and would quickly learn, that she would need to lace on her best pair of running shoes because, in only a short time, she would be trying to keep up with God.

Finding the Forerunner

Connie Louise Armstrong was born in the small eastern Colorado town of Stratton in 1949. In 1953, her family moved to a farm in Olathe on the western slope of Colorado, where they lived on a family farm and ranch with three different homes with many aunts, uncles, cousins, and grandparents, and three younger sisters and two brothers. The 248-acre farm allowed them space, but the relationships were close as they worked and played together. This is where her desire to help others took root.

The Protestant family attended a country church, but Connie never felt comfortable. She heard many stories about God and His son Jesus, but the stories didn't translate to reality for her. It was the family closeness that taught her everyone is a contributor, and everyone lends a hand to anyone who needs it.

In search of better-paying jobs, Connie's parents moved the family to Denver in 1961 where she quickly found herself lonely and sad. Both of her parents were working long hours, nights, and weekends to provide for their family. She found herself displaced from a small close-knit town where she was surrounded by grandparents, many relatives, and numerous friends to a large city where she had no friends and no extended family. This was an overwhelming change for Connie.

Connie began to ask God if He cared about her, if He was really alive, to please show her. In 1965, sixteen-year-old Connie was invited by an acquaintance to attend a church camp called Camp Id-Ra-Ha-Je. The Christian youth camp was not far from her home, located a short hour into the mountains west of Denver, in Bailey, Colorado. Id-Ra-Ha-Je was founded in 1948 by Paul Eiselstein and was growing to be a year-round children and youth ministry. What an opportunity to camp in the mountains with teens her age.

She didn't know that "I'd Rather Have Jesus Than Anything!" are the words of the theme song for which Id-Ra-Ha-Je is named. Connie rode to camp in a car packed with strangers, not yet friends, talking about Jesus as though they were all family. They sounded excited about camp and enthusiastic in telling their stories about Jesus and spoke of Him as if they personally knew Him. She began to regret going on the trip because she felt strange and uncomfortably exposed without her own stories. She thought she would not fit into this crowd.

One evening, lagging behind the campers, Connie followed the group hiking further up the mountain to listen to a speaker named Jim Groen, who was director of the organization Youth for Christ. This man talked about having a personal Savior and about knowing Jesus personally. His message was clear: we are all made

23

for God, and without Him, our lives will be empty. Jesus loves us and wants to fill our lives with joy and purpose.

Acres of evergreen vistas, the wonderful air smelling of pinecones and bonfire, engaged new mindful thoughts; thoughts of nature and purpose and belonging. The hiking event had Connie contemplating that there really was a purposeful Creator who loved everyone sitting around her. That this Creator had sent this speaker into her own life to explain answers to her prayer on whether there was a God and whether He noticed or cared about her. The speaker was now asking if anyone needed to receive God's love and wanted to know Jesus. Connie raised her hand. It was as though God saw her heart before the speaker did as she felt God's Spirit come into her being, bring her spirit to life, and filled her with His presence and love. She felt at peace and knew instantly that she was a different person from that moment forward.

Connie's father picked her up at the end of the week. She told him that she felt she had a new purpose and a new servant's heart. She began doing her chores without complaining and was willing to do more. As Connie shared her experience with her mother, brother, and younger sisters, each one eventually gave their lives to Jesus.

After her graduation from Abraham Lincoln High school in 1967, most women in Connie's circle of attractive friends married immediately after high school. Connie didn't desire this direction, but rather, was more encouraged to seek a meaningful career that would require a higher level of education.

Connie began attending Metropolitan State College in Denver as a music major. After deciding music wasn't quite the career path she wanted, she changed her major to art. It didn't take long to decide that was not the path that she wanted either. After a couple of years, she was becoming bored with her life and her college goals. She didn't have a clear direction.

In one "light bulb moment," she thought, "*I'm going to ask God what to do. After all, He made me.*" Afraid He would send her to Africa to be a missionary, she waited to ask Him. Entering her third year of college and not liking anything she was doing, she finally decided to pray with the thought of, "*Okay God, if You want me to go to Africa, I will*".

The answer was undoubtedly not what she expected. "Social Worker" was the phrase that dropped into her mind.

The next semester she focused on sociology classes—loving it. Her courses focused on poverty, homelessness, the needy, and many different social cultures. She found that writing research papers on aspects of poverty were what she enjoyed the most. Her laboratory work helped her begin to understand what social work entailed.

Experiencing real-world examples was much different than classroom education. She found that there are many differing backgrounds, cultures, ways, class structures, etc., in the real world. One of the areas that interested her was learning about the structures of the poor. She began to understand those groups and how they related to society.

Group One was considered the new poor. They were educated, had skills and training, dreams, and goals, and could easily transition back into society, the workplace, and self-sufficiency. Group Two was called the working poor. They were people who had little to no education or training who worked low-paying jobs that could barely make ends meet and lived day to day bordering on self-sufficiency. Group Three were refugees and immigrants who required assistance with legal paperwork, had to learn the language, and may have had education, skills, or training that may not translate to America. Finally, Connie learned that Group Four was commonly known as "street people," those who came out of a variety of bad situations, some with mental or emotional disabilities, drug or alcohol problems, physical disabilities, etc.

Uncertain of where she would use her education, Connie graduated from Metropolitan State College in 1972 with a BA in Sociology and a minor in music.

Knowing it was important that she marry a Christian man, Connie married Larry Gene Zimmerman in 1971. He was employed by the county, and together, they started as volunteer youth leaders at Far Horizons Baptist Church. As a child, Connie was raised in a family who had a deep desire to help others; as an adult, this is where Connie began to take an active interest in those who were suffering and hurting. Connie served as a mentor to several young girls in pain, and she and Larry fostered runaway girls for a period of time.

Caring for the vulnerable and wanting to make sure they were nurtured and encouraged became part of Connie's fiber. At the same time, her career provided her a solid foundation for managing many aspects of a successful business. It wasn't known at the time, but both of these opportunities were preparing Connie for the many hats she would need to wear when God would lead her to create Colorado Homeless Families.

Four years after marrying, Larry and Connie started their own family. Connie's days were full working both outside the home and nurturing her family. Raising her children was Connie's favorite job and brought her enormous joy and contentment. Her desire was to be with them full time, but that didn't help to pay their bills. Like most young married couples with children, her income was necessary to make ends meets.

When their car broke down and there was no money for repairs, Connie wanted to better understand what living as a Christian really meant. She didn't understand why they were worrying about bills and various needs, and seeking God was the only way she was going to get answers for her life. Connie prayed, *"I wish I could have an office meeting with You Lord, because You are the One who said You would provide for us, Your children, in*

Matthew 6:25-34, and I don't see You keeping Your word. We just don't have the money to take care of our needs."

In that moment, the Lord placed His thoughts into Connie saying, *"You can have a meeting with Me. Arrange a time."* Connie looked at her calendar and picked out 1:00 pm the following Wednesday. This was a time when the children would be taking naps, and it would also give her three days to fast and pray. Continuing to seek answers from Him in preparation for her office meeting with God, she understood that her life was not independent of God; her true purpose could only come from Him.

On the appointed day, she fed her children, put them down to nap, opened her Bible to Matthew 6, and began asking her questions. Immediately, the Lord showed her the verse, *"Seek first the kingdom of God and all these things shall be added to you."* The Lord explained to her that just being a child of God was not what this verse meant. What it meant was that she should promote the kingdom of God and serve its needs. She was to advance and honor the kingdom in any position He gave her, and wherever she found herself serving.

There was silence as she soaked in the message. Then she said, *"I did not think about it that way. I thought I could believe in You but do my own thing without a thought about requirements or stipulations for Your promises."* Connie knew that this office meeting was special. She felt the love and kindness of God, and He didn't push or pressure her into a decision.

Connie knew that God would love her regardless of her choice, but to work alongside a Great King and God of the Universe, to promote justice and mercy, serving and caring for others, included wonderful blessings. She told the Lord that she agreed to seek the good of His kingdom first, and then said, *"If I could have other meetings like this with You, that would be very special."*

Cleaning off a dresser one day, thinking that God would be putting her to work soon in some department of government

27

social work, she saw an article in World Vision Magazine about a young girl in Thailand who had been sold into prostitution by her father to make money for their low-income family. As a prostitute, one of her "Johns" was found stabbed to death. This young girl was blamed for the crime and was imprisoned. Innocent yet imprisoned, this young girl held no hope for her life until the World Vision missionaries found her and told her about Jesus. World Vision helped prove her innocent of the crime, freed her from prison, and even helped her secure employment.

After reading this article, the Lord spoke to Connie's heart and said He wanted her to work with those who were locked up. Taking this to mean imprisoned people, she contacted the Denver Police Department and asked about ministering to prisoners. They suggested she contact the Jefferson County Juvenile Center as they needed volunteers. It wasn't long until Connie and her two friends from church, Gaye Andersen and Gayle Taylor, were distributing tracts and giving testimonies. Connie spoke of being a young woman saved from her discontentment with life and lack of vision into a life of purpose, kingdom goals, and life adventures. Connie and her small team prayed for the juveniles and helped them come to know Jesus.

After two years, the Jefferson County Juvenile Center decided they wanted only Youth for Christ volunteers to speak to the juvenile offenders. Connie felt she had faithfully served for two years and believed a new season would begin.

Within a week, Connie was offered a job working at Park Avenue Nursing Home. She worked two evenings as the night shift secretary, and then as a guard until midnight. She patrolled the premises, checking the building, mechanical rooms, and various spaces. Connie's varied work also had her scheduled for two additional days in the office keeping meticulous medical records.

One night while on security, the Lord told Connie that someone was in the boiler room. Immediately Connie prayed, *"Lord, You have to come with me and protect me,"* as she went to investigate. She turned on the lights, and descended the steps, but didn't find anything. Reviewing the security camera footage later, it showed a man running from the boiler room. Connie had not encountered him, but it was likely a homeless person looking for a warm place to sleep. This job taught Connie to be aware of everything in and around the facility, and to carefully guard and not become complacent. She knew that in all situations, she needed to listen to God, seek Him in all things, and rely on Him as the Protector.

When Park Avenue Nursing Home offered Connie a take-it-or-leave option with a full-time position of nights and weekends 3:00 pm to midnight, she was hesitant. She didn't want to abandon her family with her children in school and weekend family activities. It was a difficult schedule for a young mom. Her life felt like a theme song she was piecing together in different keys and different meters, running all over the place. She knew she had to find her focus. She brought this before the Lord and asked for another opportunity somewhere. *"Lord, if you enable me to have my own company, I will always make sure to be flexible with the mothers so they can take care of their children."*

As she was looking through the help wanted ads praying for God's guidance, she saw an advertisement for Sunny Acres. They needed a manager for their 5-story building and a coordinator for all the resident transportation. Not wanting to misrepresent herself, she asked her supervisor in medical records if she could learn and perform some of the other tasks required at Sunny Acres so that she might include them on her resume.

Whatever job Connie worked, management appreciated all her efforts, and she found favor in everything she set her hand to do. Connie believed she'd finally found her life's work helping at Park Avenue and soon, Sunny Acres. This, however, would not be her last stop. Connie was further being prepared for her calling at Colorado Homeless Families through every opportunity presented to her.

1987 – 1992

Do Not Despise These Small Beginnings

A New Thing Springs Forth

Unbeknown to Connie, her beloved career at Sunny Acres was preparing her in many ways for another calling. She was already framing the model of her new nonprofit to help the homeless on what she observed working at Sunny Acres. This included allowing residents to live independently in whatever type of home best fit their needs: cottages or apartments. There was a central community area for meals, meetings, group get-togethers, games, and fellowship.

What Sunny Acres also incorporated, central to their success was resident volunteers. These resident committee volunteers worked at the community grocery store, in the community garden, or within a variety of resident activities. Each day, Connie saw how grateful the residents were for the assistance they received, but also the opportunity to give back through volunteering. Operating with resident volunteers was an important puzzle piece in itself. It created a physiological and psychological shift from the temptation to live as a hapless victim. Giving to others as a life-style habit creates a sense of responsibility that translates to purposeful living and thriving. The receiving *and* the giving made the daily lives better for each resident, gave them a better sense of community, and allowed them to get to know and help one another.

Connie was blessed with the opportunity to observe and gain knowledge from the retired professional residents living at Sunny Acres, and those who were running small businesses within the retirement community. This gave her many ideas on how to organize homeless families to work and support one another.

If Connie didn't know something, she did know who to turn to: God Himself would help her if she asked. To begin her nonprofit entity to help the homeless, Connie filled out the necessary forms to establish the organization, however the necessary forms for the tax exemptions were difficult.

Connie completed as much of the forms as possible, then prayed, "*Lord if this is what you want me to do, send someone to help me figure this out. Please bring someone to my house and help me.*"

A friend who she had once volunteered with at Jefferson County Detention Center called her one day unexpectedly. His name was Frank Trueblood, and he told Connie, "I've had you on my mind and wondered what you were up to." She explained her current situation trying to start a nonprofit organization to help with the homeless crises and the problems she encountered with all the forms.

"Hey, I know how to do that," Frank told her, "I'd be happy to come over and help you."

The next day, he arrived at Connie's house, and together they completed all the tax-exempt forms. He provided information and assistance with her bylaws as well.

Connie decided to call her nonprofit "RB Ranch," respectfully named after her cousin. He shared many ideas on how a farm and ranch community could provide food resources for homeless families. RB was his agricultural livestock brand, to which Connie paid tribute.

After the paperwork was filed, Connie began calling all her friends at church and proclaimed RB Ranch the official name of her nonprofit organization. She was excited to call it official. These decisions would bring people together to focus on God's aim for housing the Colorado homeless.

Prayers and volunteers were needed to help the homeless in RB Ranch. She also told trusted friends that she was looking for people interested in serving on the first Board of Directors of this new nonprofit. Some were hesitant, so she assured them there would not be much work for them. She would be the point person, herself, the worker bee.

Due to years of Connie and Larry's faithfulness in serving on various boards and committees at Crossroads Baptist Church, six people offered to serve on the new non-profit Board of Directors, each one donating $50.00 to open a bank account.

With $300 dollars in a bank account, she took a moment to thank the Lord for this small beginning. The groundwork for what appeared to be an official nonprofit business was laid.

Second Step, HUD Homes

Putting legs to a vision is the biggest hurdle to gaining the ability to run and jump. Connie didn't know where to begin. Driving home one day from work, God gave Connie the thought, *"call HUD about transitional housing."*

She inquired of HUD and found out that the United States Department of Housing and Urban Development had just begun a program that allowed nonprofits to rent foreclosed homes for a $1-a-year-lease-program. For a new nonprofit like RB Ranch, this was an amazing opportunity, and HUD was looking for directors like Connie Zimmerman and RB Ranch. An application was all that HUD required, and the nonprofit would be responsible for the cost of taxes, insurance, and any repairs to the property.

Of course, she asked for the application and obediently submitted it, attaching the financial account history. The RB Ranch bank statement balance proved it was a little over $300 from the six board members and a few small donations.

In short order, HUD notified her that her application was denied due to insufficient funds to cover taxes and repairs. Hanging up the phone, Connie immediately prayed, *"Ok, God, this* *was Your idea, not mine. You are going to have to change this man's mind. In Proverbs 21:1, You say that You can change the mind of a king. So, You will have to change HUD's mind because we need these $1-a-year-lease-program properties."*

Over that weekend, the Lord placed on Connie's heart to "have a sponsor for each family." Someone who would adopt each homeless family, including helping with the taxes and repairs of the vacant home.

On Monday morning, Connie called the HUD representative and explained the idea of having a sponsor for each homeless family, assuring the representative that sponsors would cover the costs, security deposit, taxes, and some maintenance and repair. HUD was amenable to this plan, and the representative told Connie to come to the HUD office and get her master keys to the foreclosed HUD properties.

Eventually, HUD properties owned by the federal government became exempt from property taxes under CGS § 12-81(1), regardless of who manages the property for charitable or non-profit purposes.

Getting the first HUD home was a little challenging, but Connie kept yielding to whatever God opened up for her. There began to be success after success. Connie could look at two homes, one being a former parsonage. After carting her children to school one morning, she headed out to meet her new inspector at the homesites.

Connie's near-homeless friend, Bill, from Sunny Acres, inspected both homes, and after the inspection, Connie signed the contract on the parsonage. It needed the least amount of repair. Later, when Bill turned on the water, he called Connie and told her, "The plumbing pipes are bad, and some are even rusted together." Bill said he could fix them for her, but being borderline homeless himself, he didn't have the money to pay for the supplies, and he knew Connie didn't have the money for the supplies either. She told him that she would call him back.

Again, Connie prayed, *"God, this is not my problem, this is your problem. What do I need to do?"* Connie remembered a hardware store near the parsonage house and called the owner. She explained that she needed supplies to fix the home's pipes because she was helping the homeless. After just two phone calls, the owner agreed to provide the needed pipes and fittings. Bill fixed the plumbing, and he and his family moved in. Connie praised the Lord, and everyone gave glory to God for the completion of this first small step.

Whenever Connie worked with a homeless family, she told them they needed a sponsor in order to enter the program. Many families found their sponsors from churches, their employers, family members, and various organizations. Crossroads Baptist Church, Connie's home church, also sponsored many of the families.

RB Ranch held their first fundraiser at Crossroads Baptist Church where one of the new board members spoke to attendees about the first miracles of Connie's obedience to God's will in helping the homeless and the creation of RB Ranch. Everyone prayed and thanked the Lord for His faithfulness. The spaghetti dinner raised over 800 dollars.

With the fundraiser money safely deposited, Connie had seed money of over 1,000 dollars to begin leasing more HUD homes, and the fundraiser had allowed them to acquire several more potential sponsors.

While she continued her Sunny Acres employment that was needed to help support their family, Connie and her husband Larry would spend their spare time during nights and weekends taking care of the newly acquired houses that needed repairs: plumbing, furnace, and general repair for privacy and safety issues. RB Ranch continued to grow, accumulating HUD homes for the homeless to live in. Sponsorship was growing which helped with the resources to make repairs and to sponsor families. Connie was also recognizing that she would soon need to hire support staff as she was wearing too many hats, and the volunteer bookkeeper was also leaving.

Accumulating HUD properties in Arvada and Wheat Ridge (Jefferson County), and Westminster (Adams County), Connie learned all she could about guidelines, codes, and available grants. She learned that since some of the HUD homes were in Westminster, the City of Westminster offered a grant program to hire personnel. Connie applied and was given a $7,000 grant to hire a semi-retired woman as a part-time bookkeeper.

Supplying Every Need

Providing every new CHF family with a clean and safe home to live in was only the beginning. One of the obstacles each homeless family faced moving into a HUD home was that they had no personal belongings or furniture to fill it with, and some had little more than the clothes on their backs. Many had either walked away from what they owned or sold what they owned to pay bills and buy food.

Connie also found how long it could take for families to receive food stamps, so while they were waiting for support programs to take effect, they required access to a food bank. As a young mother herself, Connie's heart twisted for the plight of homeless mothers with children. Learning the homeless problem was so much more complex than she originally dreamed, she needed to provide more than just a roof over a family's head.

Connie collected donations from her church, friends, and neighbors. Donated items such as furniture, clothing, household goods, and food could be used to supplement the needs of these families.

However, storage of these items quickly became problematic for her own small house as Connie found both her basement and garage were now stuffed full of donations. Also, not all donations were in the best condition. One donation of several mattresses turned out to be malodorous, and Connie had to remove them from her house to the trash. Providing for the homeless was a learning process.

Eventually, there were so many donations moving in and out of her residence with the use of a borrowed pickup truck, she prayed, *"Lord, we need a truck to move all this stuff out of our home and to where it can serve others best! I am borrowing our assistant pastor's truck, but I can't continue to do that. A truck is what we need."*

Connie began listing scriptures and reading them out loud:

"You are the God who helps the homeless but whoever has the world's goods and sees his brother in need and closes his heart against him, how does the love of God abide in him?" (John 3:17-18).

"Let us love in deed and truth. This is your organization, Lord. Your word will not return void. You, Lord, hear the voices that ask for help," she prayed.

Within the week, a woman from Ohio called Connie and said she had heard about her organization helping homeless families. The caller said her family had a small foundation, and she wanted to ask Connie some questions about her nonprofit organization. Connie patiently answered the woman's questions, and the woman finally asked how much money they had.

Connie told her they currently had $500 in the organization's bank account.

The woman paused, then asked Connie what they needed most at that moment in time. Connie replied, "A pickup truck." The woman's foundation sent $6,000 to purchase a 6-cylinder pickup truck with an 8-foot bed perfect for hauling furniture and household items. It served the ministry for all future years, needing very little mechanical repair.

Also problematic was that all the activity in Connie's quiet residential neighborhood was beginning to cause problems for her neighbors with the increased traffic and the concern about so many strangers coming and going in the community. After many considerable donations, including a generous donation of 16 mattresses, Connie decided that she needed to find a big, centralized warehouse to store all the donated furniture, appliances, and clothing.

Connie contacted a gentleman who owned a string of warehouses and asked if she could rent one of his warehouses for $150 per month to store all the donated furniture and clothing. She explained to the man why she needed it and what she was doing, and he willingly agreed because he liked the idea of what Connie was doing for the homeless. However, he countered her offer for a warehouse for only $50 per month and gave her one of his largest warehouses central to the HUD homes temporarily. Unfortunately, if a customer needed to rent a large warehouse, Connie's organizational donations would be relocated to another of his warehouses. After several relocations, the donation placement warehouse was finally established permanently.

Some people are just the answer to what others pray for. Connie always prayed that God would specially bless those people who donated to the work of caring for the homeless.

The warehouse for donations exists even today and is housed in a 1,500 square foot space for a fixed price and the original warehouse owner's family continues to work generously with the homeless program.

New families entering the CHF program were escorted to the warehouse to select the items they needed. They would tag the items with their name. The following day the maintenance staff would pick up the items at the warehouse and deliver them to the family's home. Current transitional families in the program had access to the warehouse from 10:00 am-2:00 pm every other Saturday.

The warehouse was initially staffed by CHF families fulfilling their volunteer agreement. Unfortunately, Connie discovered that some volunteers were taking items from the warehouse and selling them to pocket the money. Disappointed that some were stealing from the hand that fed them, all families were given new regulations. Connie put a church volunteer husband-and-wife team, Linda and Don, in place as staff managers for the furniture, clothing, and household goods availability on Saturdays.

The managers became responsible for overseeing the warehouse, locking and unlocking the doors, checking all items taken by families, assigning duties, and supervising the family volunteers. The new managers were kindhearted and encouraging of the families in the program.

Family volunteers enjoyed fulfilling their hours at the warehouse by sorting and organizing the donations and cleaning the warehouse, but Connie's big lesson was that not all areas of CHF could be handled by volunteers, so staff supervision was necessary. To avoid family volunteers picking through the best items first, volunteers were only allowed to make their selections after 1:30 pm on the days they volunteered at the warehouse.

All furniture, clothing, and household goods selected for use by each family became theirs to keep permanently, so they would not have to start all over again with nothing when they graduated from college or tech school and moved out of the program. Families were never allowed to bring friends, guests, or relatives to the warehouse, and the Executive Director approved all large furniture and appliance needs. That approval was provided to the warehouse staff before removal.

Many families were overwhelmed with the generosity of donations. In turn, they wanted to eagerly give back a portion of what they had received by volunteering at the warehouse and continuing to donate after their graduation.

Douglas Miller sat at his gray, metal, industrial desk in cubicle 425 in Denver's United States Department of Housing and Urban Development offices. He stared at the photo of his young family and reflected on his career goals. Working at HUD was not his plan when he graduated from the University of Northern Colorado in Greeley several years earlier in 1982. The economy and his pregnant wife pressed him to take this job. Graduate school would have to wait.

The stacks of dingy brown files seemed to scream at him. Stacks everywhere. Piles on the desk. Stacks on top of the filing cabinet. Now piles on the visitor's chair. One stack on the floor was so tall it had begun to fall over into the aisle. He dreaded hearing Arthur's mail cart whine its way down the corridor each day, groaning under the weight of new files and incoming mail.

With the newest national program, the Stewart B. McKinney Homeless Assistance Act of 1987[4], Douglas hoped that the stacks of files might begin to recede.

The bulk of his job with HUD was to authorize funds to state and local governments and nonprofit organizations to assist homeless individuals and families. Although this was not his desired career path, he always believed, in some small way, he was assisting the community to help the homeless move from the streets to temporary shelter, to supportive housing, and ultimately back to the mainstream of life. Decidedly different, the widespread economic downturn seemed dire.

Middle-class families like his own were being pushed out of their homes as the economy began to look bleak, and unemployment increased dramatically in the Denver area. At last week's staff meeting, his supervisor reported that there were currently 14,000 vacant HUD homes in Denver because people could not pay their mortgages. Sadly, most of these homeowners were hard-working, skilled, and educated people who lost their jobs.

Lately, he had increasingly been hearing the term "new poor."

In a recent training, he and his colleagues learned that the Denver community was changing rapidly. Oil companies were leaving, Savings & Loan Banks were beginning to collapse, and many manufacturing jobs were being outsourced to foreign countries. Older workers who lacked computer skills were being replaced as technology quickly changed. Hard-working Coloradans were suddenly becoming jobless and, by extension, homeless.

Looking at the stack in front of him, Douglas said, "I'm only one guy," pushing back wearily.

Added to these files were the layers upon layers of Federal bureaucracy in which he had to operate. As he opened the top folder, his phone rang. *"Hello, my name is Connie Zimmerman, and I started a nonprofit called RB Ranch to help with the homeless situation in Denver. I want to use some of the locked houses, the ones no one lives in, for some of them. After all, the windows are being broken out; people are getting in there, the plumbing is falling apart. I'm a nonprofit, and I want to help the homeless and put people back in there, so they won't be homeless anymore,"* the woman said. Bright, cheery, and...bold, Douglas thought.

Douglas explained a current HUD program simply referred to as the "$1-a-year-lease-program for transitional housing." If she represented a nonprofit, he would send her an application, and if her nonprofit qualified, she could rent boarded-up houses for one dollar per year to help the homeless.

The woman didn't question the highly unusual opportunity he outlined, but matter-of-factly stated that yes, she would like to fill out that application and provided her contact information.

Douglas prepared the application and contract packet and mailed it to the address she provided. He sent multiple applications out each day, but many of those returned did not qualify.

Nonprofits were required to pay home and liability insurance, annual taxes, and perform all the necessary repairs needed in the home such as broken windows, frozen pipes, break-in damage, painting or graffiti removal, etc. To his dismay, he had seen multitudes of applications rejected. Douglas thought it was too bad, as people were willing to help with the homeless population, but much of the bureaucracy just did not allow ordinary people to assist in this manner. His job, he realized, was beginning to depress him.

Friday morning, Douglas heard the squeaky mail cart make its way down the aisle. "Mail call!" Arthur heaped the mail in the already over-burdened inbox.

"Have a great weekend, Arthur," Douglas replied as the top envelope slid off the pile onto the floor. As he reached to pick it up, he noticed a completed application packet. He opened it and saw that it was from the woman from RB Ranch. He was too curious and opened the envelope immediately. After a quick review, however, he realized the costs would disqualify RB Ranch.

With great sadness he called Connie to explain that her nonprofit did not qualify because they only showed $300 in the bank account, and this amount did not qualify to pay the taxes and insurance, as well as perform the needed repairs on any of the vacant homes. As he explained the denial, he couldn't help but groan. "A bummer of a start to the weekend. Something needs to change."

Douglas trudged back to his cubicle on the dreary Monday morning after, balancing his jacket, briefcase, and his morning coffee. He could hear his phone ringing. It was the woman from RB Ranch, Connie Zimmerman. She was calling to ask about rescuing the deal with a creative option.

"If each homeless family had a sponsor who would pledge to take the financial responsibility for the taxes and repairs of the vacant homes, would HUD re-consider the application? *Please?*"

The clouds seemed to part, streaming a light of hope he so desperately wanted to see. "Okay, Mrs. Zimmerman, there are two homes you can pick from. Come and get the keys and choose your first house."

William Bridges liked his job at Sunny Acres.

He considered himself a "people person" and was employed as a transportation driver. He took residents of the upscale retirement village to doctor appointments, social outings, the grocery store, or on errands, and he genuinely enjoyed getting to know each resident. He remembered them all by name after just one conversation and would even help them out if they needed something done outside the scope of his "driver" responsibilities. He especially liked it if they needed something done in their cottage or apartment. This was the job of maintenance, but Bill, being a contractor by trade, could build or fix anything they needed.

This was not Bill's ideal job, though. He used to own his own construction company, but due to the downturn of the construction industry in Colorado, he was devastated when he had to lay off his most trusted and skilled workers.

In the end, Bill lost his entire company anyway, and there were not any construction jobs to be found. He took the first job that paid a decent wage and had some benefits.

He and his wife, Claire, had seven children, and after the loss of his business, they were only able to sustain their house payments for another six months. Eventually, they had to sell their home because of their financial difficulties. It broke his heart to see Claire removing pictures from the wall and packing her grandmother's precious china. Although he knew it wasn't his fault, he felt like an utter failure of a man. He felt responsible for ruining his wife's safety and comfort and for breaking her heart.

He, Claire, and four of their seven children were able to move into a mobile home rented to them by the landlord of an acquaintance. After arriving home one evening from visiting their eldest married daughter, they found the mobile home had caught fire. There wasn't much salvageable, and they had to vacate immediately. In that moment, despair reigned.

The six of them, desperate, moved in with one of his daughters in the home she was renting with her husband. It was a tight fit, and it wasn't long before the landlord told them they would need to leave because the house had legally been rented to his daughter for single-family use. The landlord said he would let them slide another thirty days, but he showed Bill the lease where it specifically detailed additional occupants were prohibited. If additional occupants were living in the house, all parties could face eviction. Bill contacted the pastor of their church for a recommendation, and the pastor said he would get back to him.

At the end of the week, the pastor called and said that a woman from the church had offered her basement to his family. She could not make it a permanent dwelling for them, but they were welcome to it on a short-term, temporary basis. She inquired whether Bill would be able to paint the interior and exterior of her house in exchange for free rent, and he agreed. She said they could live there until the spring, but once all the painting was complete, they would need to find somewhere else to go. Her Homeowner Association (HOA) just did not allow for multiple families over many months, and she apologized.

This past weekend, Bill had finished painting Mrs. Samuelson's house. She had found several other jobs for him to do to lengthen their time, but then those were completed, and he and Claire knew they would need to move along by the end of the month. This time, he had nowhere to go with his family.

It was nearly impossible to find homeless shelters that could keep a family of six, so Bill began to send his children to various homes of family and friends.

Every time he moved, he had to notify his Sunny Acres supervisor, Mrs. Zimmerman. Her face would light up every time he knocked on her door. Today, he once again stood in the doorway in his navy-blue Sunny Acres uniform, his hat in one hand and a slip of paper in the other.

He handed Connie the paper, and she noticed it was a change of address and phone number form. Again. This was the third or fourth change request he had given her in as many months, and she jokingly asked him, "Why do you keep changing your address and phone number, Bill?"

Sitting down across from Connie's desk, Bill told her his story. Connie was stunned and saddened. She came around the desk, hugged him, and said she wanted to help him if he would let her. She told Bill that she was in the process of putting together a nonprofit organization that was going to help the homeless.

Bill left her office with sure hope, understanding that she would be looking to him for some assistance using his construction experience, just as soon as Connie had more information. For today, Bill was scheduled to drive Mrs. Tucker to her doctor's appointment, pick up Mr. Ochoa from physical therapy, and repair Mr. Carson's bookcase. As Bill stepped out into the spring sunshine, the scripture message from Sunday flooded into his heart: *"So don't be anxious about tomorrow. God will take care of your tomorrow too. Live one day at a time,"* [Matthew 6:34].

"Hey, it's Bert and Ernie!" the group laughed in friendly welcome for their newest members, Beatrice and Ernest Moore. The Moores were growing closer to the Lord each day, so when an opening became available to join a small group from their new church, they took it. Wednesday night's Bible study was something the couple now looked forward to. These were their new friends.

The group was currently studying Colossians, the New Testament book of Christ's supremacy, and how Christians are to live in the world and before God. This study was quickly changing their hearts, and both "Bert & Ernie" believed this small group was exactly where they belonged.

"Safe" was how Bert & Ernie had lived their lives. Ernie had a great-paying job that was secure in good or bad economic conditions. Beatrice, or "Bert" as she had been known to her family and in school, focused on making their home comfortable, their landscape beautiful, kept the household running smoothly, and joined some social clubs that were of interest to her.

Several weeks into the book, they studied Colossians 3:12: *"Therefore, as God's chosen people, holy and dearly loved, clothe yourselves with compassion, kindness, humility, gentleness, and patience."* Both felt the jolt of the Lord's conviction during the study and throughout the following week. Beatrice even reached out to a couple of her new study friends and asked for prayer. They continued to talk about this "conviction" they both received and what it meant practically for their life together.

Ernie gave to United Way through payroll deduction, and they made sure to give a little something to most any charity that knocked at the door or that bothered to send a mailer. Anything they no longer wanted, and decided to replace in their home, was given to Goodwill. And they made sure to make annual donations to the Denver Museum of Natural History, Center for the Arts,

Ronald McDonald House, and even PBS. So, what did this new conviction mean?

As Ernest neared an early retirement, they began to sense that something about their giving was missing. Something was off. Their lives were not exactly...genuine. The "clothe yourselves with..." part of the Colossians verse hit somewhere deep inside, causing a conviction. Where was their true compassion, true kindness, humility, gentleness, or patience described by the verse? One evening, this especially came to light as they drove home from a local fundraiser for homelessness in Colorado. Their hearts had been genuinely moved on behalf of Colorado's new poor. The stories of real people grasping for a safe place to land their families couldn't be shaken.

A gentleman, who was formerly homeless, was the guest speaker at the fundraiser, and he talked about the plight of homelessness for him. He told his story of becoming homeless almost overnight, even though he had a stable job, a college education, and a willingness to work hard.

He lost everything in the blink of an eye: his career and profession, his money, his home, and nearly all their belongings. It took him a long time to find *any* job, and eventually, he became a custodian, and his wife worked 12-hour shifts at Kmart.

They lived in a homeless shelter, and each day he and his wife wished someone would do something about the homeless situation facing Colorado. Yet, nothing got better. He told his story through tears as he explained that this was a debilitating situation he never imagined could happen to his own family.

After shelter-hopping for eight months, he was able to get his life back on track and find a good job, although it was not in his chosen profession. What this man expressed was what hit home with the couple: "None of us are immune from homelessness."

Wasn't homelessness due to poor choices, addiction, lack of education, being lazy, or a deep unwillingness to work?

"Judgmental" encapsulated the attitude Bert and Ernie had when it came to the homeless.

They always felt that if someone was homeless, he lacked integrity, or she was lazy. Perhaps they'd chosen bad friends and got addicted to alcohol or drugs, or maybe they were not responsible for anyone else to require them to stay employed. Many of the homeless appeared to be immigrants. Why shouldn't they go back to where they came from? Neither Bert nor Ernie ever felt like they were responsible for helping a homeless person, especially an immigrant. They were all freeloaders.

The meeting and the stories left them stunned and more than a little curious. They learned that the circumstance of sudden illness or ongoing disability brought some people down. Some were fleeing persecution, others with small children were abandoned by their spouses, and for others, the lack of hope had broken down their walls.

After the close of the fundraiser, Bert and Ernie approached the information table. They found a lot of literature on helping the homeless in different ways. A variety of homeless shelters seemed available, but what drew their attention was a "Sponsorship Form" for a new nonprofit organization, RB Ranch, which helped the homeless by leasing empty HUD homes. They each took the information they were drawn to, placed it in their Bibles, and prayed about it for the next couple of weeks.

Ernie had been giving the same begging man at the corner by his office a dollar each day for months not realizing that by doing so he wasn't helping the man at all. Giving him a dollar just made Ernie feel less guilty about having to see this man each day.

Since the fundraiser, Ernie began to take the man breakfast food, lunch, and some money. He learned the man's name was Tony, and both Tony and his wife had been laid off from their manufacturing jobs which were outsourced to China. After selling their furniture and cars, they ultimately lost their home, too. Tony cried that the heartbreaking thing was they had to sell or leave most of their family mementos behind, including his children's favorite toys.

While Tony begged for money, his wife had been staying back at a pay-by-day motel with their two young sons. That didn't last long. Now she was looking for a homeless shelter for them or aimlessly riding the RTD bus during frigid days to keep their little boys warm. Ernie, though he found Tony's story to be gut-wrenching, found he had nothing more to offer the family. Every day, he had to walk away again.

In the following weeks, after hearing the formerly homeless man speak at the fundraiser and praying about the RB Ranch sponsorship form, Bert and Ernie began to find that their "conviction" about the homeless was about a change in their education and gut attitude. They realized there were many misconceptions they had.

It was shocking to learn that most people were only two paychecks away from homelessness. Homelessness does not mean "criminal" and can be caused by personal tragedy, abuse, fire, illness, or even death. And with the current economic crisis, a large percentage of self-sufficient families were finding themselves homeless for the first time.

As the Colossians Bible study closed for the evening, they asked the group to pray with them about the sponsorship form. As the group prayed, the desire to help the homeless became stronger and stronger, knowing that it was time to step out of their safe giving and really "clothe themselves" in helping the homeless. After a joyful ride home, Bert & Ernie's prayers were answered.

When Ernie took Tony his breakfast and some cash early the next day, he also took the applications for this new nonprofit transitional housing program. The night before, Ernie had called the woman, Connie Zimmerman, who was named on the form. She explained the application process while Ernie told her they would be sponsoring this family and wanted to get them into a home as soon as possible.

Ernie invited Tony to sit in his warm car. They completed the application for Tony and his family together. Ernie showed Tony the notarized sponsorship form he and Bert had completed that morning to sponsor Tony and his family.

Bert and Ernie helped Tony and his family move into their HUD home the following weekend. As qualified sponsors, Beatrice and Ernest agreed to provide personal support and financial assistance. Finally, to the surprise of Tony and his family, they presented the young boys with some new toys to replace those left behind.

Katy Lewis was grateful. With the recent downturn in the economy, her real estate business had slowed but had not suffered as much as others she knew. "Thank you, Lord," she said as she drove to her second showing that day.

The house was an easy sell, and this showing was the second time these buyers wanted to look. She was incredibly grateful to the Lord Who had always provided for her as a single mother caring for her four daughters and Who still provided. Now that her daughters were all grown and moved on with their own lives, she was thankful that her career was fulfilling, and she could look forward to thinking about retirement—maybe.

As she drove through the neighborhood, however, she noticed yet another empty house and another foreclosure sign that constantly reminded her of the many people who lost their homes in the economic downturn and were now camping out somewhere in the elements. The plight of the homeless was one of the biggest reasons she accepted the opportunity to sit as a board member of a local nonprofit called RB Ranch DBA Colorado Homeless Families. Katy had known Connie Zimmerman for years. They attended the same local church when Connie was a youth leader. Katy had witnessed firsthand the strong leadership, determination, and love for people that God had placed in Connie.

In 1997, when Connie approached her about becoming a board member, Katy believed that the Lord urged her to accept. She had been wanting to get involved in some area helping people, and she knew Connie's character was trustworthy.

Connie approached others from the church, telling them, "You'd be excellent, and I do need board members." Katy reflected that Connie would ask, but she always allowed the Lord to stir their hearts to accept and act on behalf of the organization's needs. The Lord did stir Katy's heart, and after she donated $50.00

to help maintain the nonprofit's checking account, she replaced a board member who was moving away.

Katy liked helping people in any way she could, but even more, she liked seeing God move in the most surprising ways. These timely surprises always felt miraculous. In the five board meetings held per year, board members would pray about the many projects that Connie would bring to the table for review. Within the next six months, the board grew from six members to nine, allowing for more diversity of expertise. Katy liked all the board members she served with and became close with a couple from India who were quick to pray about everything.

In its infancy, some board members had been vocal in expressing their concerns that things were moving too fast. Nevertheless, Connie was faithful. She believed whatever the Lord indicated for her to do at any time. She would assure board members that, "Jesus can do anything." The board, "shouldn't worry about anything." Katy remembered from those early board meetings, that Connie had to declare repeatedly and firmly, "Colorado Homeless Families was His idea, not mine, so we are meant to trust Him and make sure He said it – then He can work miracles."

Katy had seen Colorado Homeless Families grow and multiply in just a short time since its launch. Connie was emphatic about getting the assistance of community and governmental agencies to support the solutions for homelessness, and she was creative about getting local businesses to work with Colorado Homeless Families and their many projects. Connie was clear that the board should practice with the higher fiscal responsibility and duty of care to those most vulnerable. Board members were first to trust God, then maintain the nonprofit's best interests in all decisions.

Even though board meetings were a 45-minute drive for her, Katy always looked forward to the meetings. She enjoyed the collaboration and listening to Connie's ideas as the board prayerfully considered each of them. Discussions were never contentious because members listened and waited on the Lord's timing and provision if things were to move forward. Additional input and the tweaking of ideas was encouraged. Sometimes their brainstorming sessions turned into the most successful projects.

The building projects were the most interesting developments as those were never a small undertaking. Connie, having no experience with civil engineering or architecture, would simply tell the board, "We are to do these things to proclaim all the good deeds of the Lord." Everyone would pray about the project and the financing, and by the next board meeting, there would be an announcement about breaking ground, new funding, new personnel, or additional housing. Katy knew that miracles are not synonymous with being instantaneous, but God came through again and again, and it always seemed rather quickly.

As Katy pulled up to her open house, she saw that she was 45 minutes early. She noticed the most recent CHF newsletter sat on her passenger seat in her pile of mail, so she read it. What amazed and delighted her this time was seeing the testimonies of those in the Colorado Homeless Families program who had experienced a complete life change under this system.

This month's testimony touched her as a husband and wife spoke about the process of becoming self-sufficient again. They especially thrived under the participatory nature of the program, where the husband helped with the groundskeeping and his wife volunteered in the food bank. They were with the program for the entire two years typically allotted for each family. Upon leaving, they were re-trained and gainfully employed in stable jobs, able to purchase their own home again. They had become new Christians and were helping in their local church serving the underprivileged. Their children were thriving, and they owed it all to the help that Colorado Homeless Families gave them.

Their ending statement, "Colorado Homeless Families helped us get our lives back," brought tears to Katy's eyes. She smiled and wondered what God would do next at tonight's board meeting. It seemed they were constantly keeping up with God.

Curmudgeon. That's what many people called him. "Tightwad." "*Mingy*," now, that was a good one. His old friend Joe had to explain that one to him. Half mean, half stingy. None of those names ever bothered Mac. Nope. He worked hard. Born during the Dust Bowl and living through the Great Depression, Mac knew how to work and worked himself right into owning his very own profitable hardware store in Colorado.

Olson's Hardware on 90th in Westminster had been a mainstay for many years, and Mac enjoyed personally helping each customer that came into his store. He let the high school seniors paint the windows for their homecoming contest every year.

He let the Girl Scout Troop set up a table for their annual cookie sale each February and allowed the local 4-H Club to have a fundraising table before the yearly fair. His buddies pushed him to be more a part of the community and give more, but Mac knew that a good businessman couldn't "give away the farm" and expect to make a profit. Still, he had made a good living, saved enough to send both his sons to college, and pay off the mortgage of the home his wife, Scarlett, loved so much. They were secure. No matter what anyone said about him, he felt good about his accomplishments.

As Mac walked to the local diner to have lunch with his buddies like he did each Tuesday, he thought about Scarlett meeting with her church friends at their home. Scarlett loved hosting the Tuesday Bible study. He didn't understand it, nor did he understand her wanting to always volunteer at the local church. He also knew that she would take portions of the shopping money and donate it to what she thought were "good Christian causes."

He would sometimes go with Scarlett to church, but he didn't understand this God that everyone sang to and talked about. He prayed anyway, just in case. Maybe his heart was just too hard after everything he'd seen and lived through. After the way Mac grew up, he didn't mind helping anybody out, but he just did not want it to cost him anything.

Something stuck in his craw today.

A woman called his store last week. Said her name was Connie Z-something-or-other, and she was looking for donations for some community do-good thing she was involved in. She was helping the homeless and whatnot.

Shoot, Mac knew from his background that if you worked hard enough, you'd never be homeless. She was nice enough, he supposed, but he told her what he told anyone looking for handouts: "I'm busy, call back next week." This was Mac's gruff way of kicking the can down the street, and it worked because most of them never called back. This one was different.

He knew she was going to be one of those who kept calling. She said she would call Tuesday, which was today, and there was adamancy in her tone.

As he walked to the local diner, he found himself hoping that he would be with a customer when she called back so Frank would just have to tell Connie Z-what's-her-name to call another time.

Mac enjoyed Tuesday lunches with his buddies. They had been friends forever through thick and thin and served in the Army together. Helping each other with whatever was needed, they had each other's backs. Mac even hired several of them over the years for part-time work when they were down on their luck. That was as far as he went when it came to handouts; "no such thing as a free lunch," he thought, so even his friends didn't get handouts.

During lunch, though, Cecil asked him if he was doing okay. "You seem quiet today," Cecil said, and the rest of his buddies nodded.

He skipped the apple pie and slowly walked back to the hardware store. Mac could not get out of his mind what this woman had said to him last week. Maybe that's why he was a little too quiet at lunch. Wanting to reflect on the phone conversation, Mac walked back to the store the long way.

"Hello, Mr. Olson. My name is Connie Zimmerman. I've started a nonprofit that helps the homeless in Colorado."

He wanted to end the conversation right there, but she continued, *"I've been able to purchase an older brick house, a parsonage, actually, in Westminster that has been vacant for several years. I have a near-homeless friend, who is a contractor, and he is willing to do the work to make the house livable for a homeless family."*

Mac knew that the downturn in the economy had indeed hit all walks of life including his own neighborhood, like it was some kind of dart board. Some contractors coming into the store for supplies were singing the blues about losing business. It no longer felt like a song and dance.

"What we would like to ask is if you would be willing to donate the supplies needed to repair our first house. We need some plumbing supplies and electrical supplies."

Mac knew from his financials that his store was doing okay, and there was nothing to worry about. He just didn't believe in giving things away, so he offered her a discount.

"Mr. Olson, don't you want to help the homeless?" She was gutsy, he'd give her that.

"So, I suppose you want me to fix the whole thing?" Mac replied. His crusty tone usually turned people away, which generally worked for him.

"Yes! We all need to work together in the community to fix this homeless problem." The woman seemed relentless.

Time to kick the can, Mac thought. He told her he was busy. Maybe she could call back next week. She thanked him and told him she would call back on Tuesday.

Arriving back at the store after lunch, Mac went to his office. Something stirred deep in his heart as he sat down—something the woman said, or how she said it. There was love in her tone;

authority in her words. He didn't know what that piercing feeling was as he had never sensed it before, but it felt like a softening.

Surely, he wasn't getting soft!

He would see the homeless people on his way to work, with their cardboard signs asking for money. It made him feel uncomfortable. He always hoped that he wouldn't get stuck at the stoplight where he'd have no choice but to stare into the sorrowful eyes of one of them. His own Scarlett had told him last month their neighbors across the street had just lost their home, and he wondered what was going on over there. What were they going to do with their three small children? Lost in reverie at his desk, Frank buzzed him on the intercom. "Phone call, Mac."

Mac picked up the phone and said hello.

"Hello, Mr. Olson. This is Connie Zimmerman. We spoke last week when I asked if you would donate supplies to repair...." The softened-by-God heart in Mac didn't even let her finish her sentence when he instructed her to make a detailed list of everything needed to repair the house. He would gather all the supplies together himself and have them waiting the next day for pickup. He donated everything she requested, everything her nonprofit needed.

Autumn breezes blew through the open window and fluttered the pages of a John Deere 1990 calendar hanging on a nail on the wall. Opal Levine Bensinger and Ruby Levine Arnett sat at the kitchen table working as the sun set over the Ohio cornfields.

Enjoying a cup of coffee and Ruby's blue ribbon apple pie straight from Grandma Levine's secret recipe box, they shuffled through papers stacked in front of them. A stack of 25 proposals was a daunting read. It was time to pick one candidate from these proposals collected throughout the quarter.

Since 1950, after their parents died, they habitually met to do this task four times a year.

Mama and Daddy Levine had worked hard their entire lives. The Ohio cornfields had blessed them for returns. You would never find two people who worked better with one another coupled with a virtuous work ethic. Mama and Daddy always said they couldn't live without the other, and true to their word, in 1950, they died within three days of each other, Mama going first.

Most surprising to their 35-year-old twin daughters, Opal and Ruby, was their parent's Last Will and Testament. Besides leaving the family farm to be shared between their daughters, Mama and Daddy left a trust to be used to create a family foundation in their name. Their parent's directive was to provide grants for charitable purposes for education, religion, or the less fortunate families living in the margins and struggling daily. Mama and Daddy's Trust put hands and feet to their belief in the Ohio state motto, *"With God, all things are possible."*

Mama's family staunchly believed in *tzedakah*, the Hebrew word meaning "righteousness," but commonly used to indicate charity.

As Mama explained to the twins at a young age, the Hebrew word for this kind of charity was different from what most people defined as charity. Charity had become more about a random act of goodwill or generosity, like throwing a coin in the Salvation Army bucket, or tossing a bill in the church offering baskets, or hauling your used items off to the local thrift store and seeing "Good Willy" smile back at you from the postcard handed back.

In the purest definition, Mama explained, tzedakah is an *ethical* obligation. Mama wanted to make sure that all they had worked hard for became useful to others and made life better for struggling families.

The Levine Foundation was not a household name, and very few people outside of their town knew what these two 75-year-old women were up to, since they were the only two board members. This family foundation operated quietly and generously, just as Mama and Daddy had lived their lives.

Holding to the foundation's directive, Opal and Ruby sat down four times a year to sift through the various requests. They always picked one they believed could put the money to the best use. The amount of the request didn't matter as much as how the request would be used.

"Let's just draw one from the pile this time," Opal finally said. "No," replied Ruby, "we're going to do what we always do and read each one of these. And don't forget, we always start with prayer." So, they held each other's left hands and placed their right hands on the pile of papers.

"Father God, Your word says if we lack wisdom, we should ask, and You will give generously of Your wisdom. We come together in prayer intending to make another big decision and so we are asking for Your guidance. Father God, we come before You today to ask You for wisdom. Lead us in the way that we should go to bring glory to Your holy name. In the mighty name of Jesus. Amen."

Getting down to business, the first thing they did was sort out the requests, brochures, letters and remove anything unrelated to the foundation's directive. It was an informal way of doing things, which is likely why so little was known about the foundation. That was the way the sisters preferred to keep it. Most requests came through word of mouth, or family members would pick up brochures or information sheets from their travels. Sometimes one sister or the other would see a newspaper or magazine article and save it for their once-per-quarter meetings. After each sister finished reading, each would place her top two or three picks in the middle of the table. They would then discuss each one.

"I like this one," Opal began. "RB Ranch in Colorado. I think Martin brought this home after they took the kids on summer vacation to Colorado. They stayed with Donna's sister and went to church with them. They found this brochure on the church bulletin board. It says they help homeless families and only work with those who are serious about getting back on their feet."

Ruby agreed she liked that one also. There was something about helping people who wanted to help themselves, knowing they just couldn't do it alone for reasons beyond their control.

"I wonder how much they need," wondered Ruby. "I'm going to call them." After a 20-minute telephone conversation, Ruby hung up. "They need a pickup truck. The woman has food, furniture, and clothes to distribute freely to the homeless families that have qualified for transitional homes. RB Ranch has been borrowing a pickup truck for hauling these things. What they need most immediately is a pickup truck. I wrote down all her information." She pointed to her notes on the piece of paper.

Ruby and Opal signed the $6,000 check and addressed it to Mrs. Connie Zimmerman at RB Ranch. Placing their hands on the check before they mailed it, they bowed their heads in prayer:

"Lord, thank You that your promises are sure, You are faithful, and we can rely on You. Your word says that we will find joy in offering our time, talents, and money to meet the needs of others. Help us to give freely and cheerfully towards the work of Your kingdom. May You cause the seeds that we sow to grow into well-watered, fruitful trees of life. Lord, bless this organization, keep them, and make Your face shine upon them. Through Jesus Christ, our Lord, Amen."

Norman Wilson had never cried in his life. People called him many things, but soft, emotional, or a weeper was not one of them. He blew his nose in his tattered red handkerchief, wiped the moisture from his eyes, got in his 1969 Ford Ranger F100 pickup, and drove away. He glanced in the rearview mirror and saw the banker lock the door and walk to his car. He had one stop to make. Helen was home packing the last of the boxes, and he hoped there was room in the rented trailer for what they were taking.

Norman and Helen were high school sweethearts. She asked him to dance, while his buddies chuckled. Her brown tendrils wrapped around his heart leading him to the dance floor. Her pretty brown hair, big blue eyes, and broad smile were ribbons on the package of love as Bing Crosby sang "Pennies from Heaven" through the dance hall speakers. The next dance where they embraced was to a song by the Nat King Cole Trio. They continued twirling through the rest of the night until the dance was over.

The following weekend, April 18, 1936, Norman took Helen to see *Mr. Deeds Goes to Town* with Gary Cooper and Jean Arthur. Tickets were a quarter, but he had to borrow a little extra from his father.

After the movie, they stopped at the soda shop where Norman told Helen that his favorite line of the film was when Longfellow Deeds said, *"People here are funny. They work so hard at living they forget how to live."* Norman walked Helen home and surprised himself when he told her he loved her. She said she loved him, too. They were married two years later and vowed never to be apart, for better, for worse, for richer, for poorer, and they would never "work so hard at living they forget how to live."

By the end of 1938, Norman and Helen had settled into married life as she pursued her goal of becoming a teacher, and Norman had finished his training at the police officer training school. He began teaching a highway and driver safety education program, and the police department bought several new 1940 white sedans for $515 each. The sedans came with a loudspeaker on the roof designed to publicly embarrass drivers into better habits.[5] Norman liked his job, but by 1941, he had set his sights on Federal law enforcement.

The draft announcement of December 1941 changed everything. Now known as the Greatest Generation, Norman and Helen's lives quickly turned to war consciousness. Norman had to leave his bride to serve in the military, fighting in World War II from 1942 to 1945. Many of Norman's police friends became soldiers, sailors, marines, and airmen.[6]

Norman returned from the war a changed man. Still, with Helen's love and support and the Servicemen's Readjustment Act, Norman was ready to anchor his identity in American strength after World War II. He did so by becoming a capable husband and earning a living to support the family he hoped to start.[7] If nothing else, being a soldier made Norman a proud man.

In 1946, Norman took a job with the Colorado State Corrections Department (CSCD). Between his police training and military service, he certainly qualified for this governmental agency. The CSCD was tasked with overseeing at least a dozen facilities of incarcerated criminals statewide. He began in security, and over his 30-year career, he worked as a correctional officer, supervisor, jail captain, deputy warden, warden, and finally retired in 1976 as an executive director. It was a stable career with a good income to support his family.

After retirement, Norman and Helen decided to move to the foothills west of Denver. Not ones to sit around in rocking chairs, they found their town and neighboring areas needed food services. Both Norman and Helen had loved to cook and bake in their spare time, so several years after retirement, they put together a solid business plan and picked their location to start a bakery business. It was hard work but enjoyable.

The first several years gave them a sharp learning curve, but eventually, they hit their stride. The business became successful. However, by the late 1980s, with the economy in a spiral, they kept assuring each other that tough times were temporary. Growing up in the hard years of the Great Depression had taught them to hold on. Rather than scale down, Norman and Helen chose to expand their business from retail to include wholesale.

The widespread economic tragedy continued, and by the start of the new decade, they faced the fact that their business had been losing money for several years.

Making matters worse, they had tied up their home in their business, so they found themselves not only losing their business, but also their home, their savings, and they were in debt more than $300,000. Helen sobbed when the bank foreclosed on the bakery and their home.

On their last day at the bakery, a long-time customer and friend, Harvey, pulled Norman aside and told him about a nonprofit organization that helped people get back on their feet after experiencing hard times. He handed Norman the phone number and shook his hand, telling Norman that if they needed a sponsor, to put Harvey's name down.

Norman turned his eyes to the road ahead and drove away from the business that was no longer theirs and drove to the home that was also no longer theirs.

For several days, Norman stared at the phone number, and no longer able to bear Helen's tears. With homelessness ringing their doorbell, he finally decided to call. He spoke with Connie Zimmerman, the Director, and made an appointment for the end of the week. With great trepidation, Norman met with Connie. He told her that he was a proud man and had never depended on anyone in his entire life. Norman felt humiliated by this experience. It was difficult for him to ask for any kind of help. Connie, however, was kind and compassionate explaining that she had heard many similar stories. She told him that her nonprofit was started to help people just like Norman and Helen, who are not generally associated with homelessness. She told him that their program had helped bankers, real estate professionals, managers, and even state officials who were all fighting to keep their chin above the rough waters. Connie assured Norman that many of the people she placed in HUD homes are just like him, individuals who needed some encouragement and support for a couple of years until they were back on their feet. Norman closed his eyes and could hear Helen's sobs ringing in his ears. He agreed to accept assistance and Connie had him complete the paperwork.

RB Ranch notified Norman and Helen that a HUD house had become available in Westminster, only 35 miles from their lovely foothills community. They loaded their boxes and what furniture they decided to keep into the rented trailer and made their way to the city. Pleasantly surprised at how large and nice their new home appeared, Norman and Helen settled in by the end of the day.

Norman and Helen began their required search for new work. Though they were each 76-years-old, they were now bound to actively look for employment, proving at least three to five contacts each week. It wasn't easy to do. They feared no one would want to hire older individuals. Within a short time, each of them found gainful employment, jobs they enjoyed, and responsibilities that were perfectly suited to their age, work experience, and personalities.

While they worked to become self-sufficient over the next two years, they discovered they were more relaxed than they had been in years without the financial worries and burdens of owning their own business. They enjoyed their work, appreciated their home, and best of all, they were back to their marriage vow to not *work so hard at living they forget how to live.*

Lina could not stop talking about the United States. For months after returning, she would look at photo after photo of her trip and at the myriad of books she brought back with her.

As part of a three-week trip to learn more about the U.S. education system, this young, privileged, and enthusiastic educator from a private Soviet Union high school had traveled with a delegation who, accompanied by translators, visited a variety of universities and schools in the United States.

Lina, with the other delegates, came to the United States through a program based in San Francisco.[8] Their three weeks were spent in the state of Utah, where Lina was thrilled at the beautiful landscape, the freedoms granted to citizens, the beautiful homes they lived in, the kindness shown by Americans, and the whole general experience of freedom in American culture for the first time.

After her return from the United States, Lina Glazkov had changed. She and her husband Stepan were exhausted with the chaos and upheaval of their country. They were young, married, and had great hopes for a more stable life with a freedom to make choices for the direction of their own lives. From the time they met, they dreamed of going to the United States to see the Statue of Liberty.

Returning to the United States was all Lina talked about after she returned. Stepan began feeling the desire to go as well.

Stepan and Lina were present as young adults for the fall of the Berlin Wall in November of 1989. It was a surreal and chaotic event that they knew would forever change their country of citizenship.

In December of 1991, just days after Lina returned from the United States, the KGB was officially dissolved and succeeded by the Foreign Intelligence Service (SVR). Later that month, on

On December 25, Mikhail Sergeyevich Gorbachev resigned as president and left the Kremlin. The Soviet flag was lowered, and the State Anthem of the Soviet Union was played for the last time. Then the Russian tricolor flag was raised in its place, and Boris Yeltsin became president of the newly independent Russian state.

Within hours, the dissolution of the Soviet Union marked the end of the Cold War.

With so many changes happening so quickly, there is always the potential for instability and chaos in a country. Stepan and Lina knew many people who were leaving Russia for a variety of reasons: poverty, economic collapse, the disastrous state of public health care, and the absence of housing. Many Russians were trying to emigrate because of the abysmal standard of living, even after the collapse of communism. Russia's people were left among the poorest of modern empires. Not much was going to change for them.

Compared to the average American, they learned, an average Russian citizen had to work ten to twelve times longer to buy meat. Russians worked eighteen to twenty times longer to buy poultry, three times longer for milk, seven times longer for butter, fifteen times longer for eggs, and two to eight times longer to buy bread.

While 65 percent of Americans own homes, every third Russian citizen, or more than 100 million people, had less living space than the meager Soviet minimum of nine square meters, or 97 square feet, per person. By contrast, households classified as "poor" by the U.S. government had 405 square feet per person.[9]

In 1991, the Soviets recognized the right of all citizens to travel, which eliminated restrictions on leaving the country.

To settle legally in the United States, Lina and Stepan would need to be granted refugee status or admitted as an immigrant. They were not considered refugees, so they decided to enter as immigrants. To become a lawful permanent resident of the United States, obtaining a Green Card was required first. Most immigrants did so through employment, through family sponsorship, or by being an immediate relative of a U.S. citizen.

Lina sought out the diplomat program based in San Francisco to help. Through a translator, she asked for information and guidance to obtain what she and Stepan needed to gain employment.

Coming to the United States as immigrants, they left what little they owned behind.

They could gain help through contacts they found in a California Russian Orthodox church and made more contacts while staying there.[10]

After weeks of learning how to become American citizens, they decided to travel along with an immigrant family leaving for Denver, Colorado. They were able to stay a short time in a Russian Orthodox church in Denver, and the translators helped them contact Colorado Homeless Families and submit an application. Stepan and Lina yearned after the American dream of individual dignity and prosperity and were tenacious to do whatever it required.

Arriving at Colorado Homeless Families with only a few changes of clothes, they were accepted into the program, with a faithful parishioner from the Russian Orthodox church agreeing to sponsor them. Executive Director Connie Zimmerman showed them to their 1,800 square foot home and made the furniture, clothing, and food banks available. The Glazkov's were also provided small appliances to help them complete the set-up of their new home, and their sponsor helped with transportation as needed.

Stepan and Lina began attending ESL classes at a local community college to help improve their English while looking for work.

Stepan had been trained as an electrician in Russia and wanted to become an electrician again in the United States. The local electrical workers union offered training programs to apprentices with the opportunity to earn excellent wages with good benefits as they learned the skills needed to be a successful electrician. Stepan found he simply had to adapt what he learned in Russia to the American codes, theories, and supplies. Still, he was required to begin as an apprentice performing 8,000 hours of on-the-job training and at least 288 hours of classroom instruction which would take about four years to complete. Then he could take the state journeyman exam. The pay, even for an apprentice, was remarkable.

Lina also began her journey to find work. She reached out to the teaching community and was hired as a teacher's assistant for a private elementary school.

Stepan and Lina soon realized that earning good wages enabled them to buy what they needed and save some of their earnings. They realized they would achieve the very dream that they could have never achieved in Russia.

The Glazkov's made good friends by helping other CHF families living in HUD homes. Stepan volunteered his electrical and maintenance skills to other families living in the HUD homes. Lina helped the families by cleaning and painting, and she brought them baked goods of Russia's most beloved desserts, ptichye, moloko, pirozhki, or vatrushka.

Stepan and Lina exceeded their volunteer requirements with joy. They worked hard to become United Stated citizens and became fast friends with the neighbors in their community.

When they graduated from the Colorado Homeless Families programs, they were honored to buy the HUD home they lived in. They hung the American flag beside their front door and made plans to take their first vacation as Americans to see the Statue of Liberty in New York. They longed to see the broken chain that sat at Libertas's feet, the very iconic symbol of freedom that they enjoyed.

Ask any eighth grader what their least favorite subject is, and the likely answer would be poetry.

Trying to teach personifications, alliterations, metaphors, stanzas, or onomatopoeia, Maggie Quinn would persist, even when she would see their eyelids droop, but Maggie enjoyed poetry best. She tried to teach her students that poetry uses sounds and images to express feelings and ideas. One of her favorite quotes was from the words of Robert Frost, "Poetry is when an emotion has found its thought, and thought has found words."[11]

Being a teacher, Maggie Quinn's favorite subject was poetry, and as she reflected on her life, she found poems that perfectly summed up each season of her life. From 1982 until 1991, her season of life poem was *The Forsaken* by William Wordsworth:

The peace which others seek they find;
The heaviest storms not longest last;
Heaven grants even to the guiltiest mind
An amnesty for what is past;
When will my sentence be reversed?
I only pray to know the worst;
And wish as if my heart would burst.

O weary struggle! silent year
Tell seemingly no doubtful tale;
And yet they leave it short, and fear
And hopes are strong and will prevail.
My calmest faith escapes not pain;
And, feeling that the hope in vain,
I think that He will come again.[12]

69

In the early 1980s, Maggie had begun having breathing problems, and a series of tests finally revealed what she feared most: they had found cancer in one of her lungs. Having many options available, the doctors recommended that the best course of treatment was to completely remove her lung, known as a pneumonectomy. The surgery had risks, but they assured her it was possible to live and function without one lung and live a relatively normal life. They did caution her that without full lung capacity, she would need to learn to slow down and adapt to this change.

Unfortunately, Maggie developed severe asthma following surgery and could not return to her job as a teacher, putting another level of stress on their family.

Her husband, a law enforcement officer, had always been a social drinker. After her diagnosis, his drinking became more frequent, and soon, she realized his excessive drinking was his way to cope with the stress and anxiety. After several years of increased drinking, he became unstable in his employment and was soon unable to pay the rent.

Angry and humiliated by his loss of work, he moved out. Their marriage hit the rocks. Still unable to teach, Maggie and her two sons, Nicolas and Noel, lived on child-support payments, food stamp programs, and hand-outs from parishioners at their church.

This gloom quickly became despondency when their oldest son was given a physical for school sports and was found to have a cancerous tumor in his chest.

Crying out in despair, Maggie thought God had forsaken her.

She had never felt so crushed emotionally, mentally, and even spiritually than she was by her son's diagnosis—until several months later when the landlord sold the home they were renting out from under the family, leaving them nowhere to go.

Geena Smith was a teacher who worked with Maggie in the same school and heard of her health problems, but when Maggie disappeared from school one day, she realized it must be an extremely serious situation. Geena went looking for Maggie but couldn't find her.

With growing concern for this missing family, Geena and her husband launched a search and found Maggie and her sons living in their car at a local park near a public bathroom. When Geena asked Connie Zimmerman for help, Colorado Homeless Families had a home available for them, and the pastor and his wife paid the security deposit to become the sponsors of Maggie's family. Eventually, Geena became the President of the Board of Directors of Colorado Homeless Families, serving for two years.

Maggie's church, her former school, and both boys' schools were asked to donate furnishings and necessities for the family. Colorado Homeless Families also supplied food and miscellaneous provisions, allowing Maggie to focus on her son's cancer treatment.

While Maggie's son underwent treatment, medical and health care staff encouraged her to attend their free support groups and continue attending her church to participate in the support and outreach programs offered by the hospital and by the church.

Maggie eventually found a job as a telemarketer, which allowed her flexible hours to work and to also help her son recover from his treatments. On their last visit to the oncologist, Nicolas was cleared, and the cancer was in total remission.

Through the housing and donations provided by Colorado Homeless Families, a group of supportive teachers, and Crossroads Baptist Church, Maggie and her sons could enter a place of peace and healing, both physically and relationally.

Unbeknownst to them, Maggie's ex-husband had been seeking alcoholism treatment and had also returned to the church. After successful counseling and continuing in his Alcoholics Anonymous (AA) support groups, he asked Maggie and their sons for forgiveness and hoped to reconcile their family.

The Quinn family found an extensive support system within the Colorado Homeless Families community and worked together to rebuild and restore their relationships while enjoying the volunteer opportunities of giving back and helping other families.

Ongoing marriage counseling by their church, church support, and AA, Al-Anon and Alateen helped the family reconcile and regain their self-sufficiency.

Within two years and dedication, Maggie's family was on solid footing and were able to buy their own home after graduating from the Colorado Homeless Families program.

Maggie continued to enjoy poetry, and the Wordsworth poem expressed how lonely she had felt in this long season of her life, her challenges to overcome, and represented where she had been left and let down.

Maggie understood that it was not by her own strength that she prevailed. She never gave up, and she continued to learn of this higher faith placed in Someone Who did not forsake her:

And hopes are strong and will prevail
My calmest faith escapes not pain
And, feeling that the hope in vain
I think that He will come again.

Sometimes your past follows you wherever you go, but Douglas Martin knew that the Lord can, *and will*, show a person a new path, cleared of the dust from the past.

Douglas and his wife, Coryn, would say they had a nice life. They were considered living as the upper-middle class and enjoyed the lovely things that money could buy. Nice house, new cars, vacations, savings, and investments; Coryn did not have to work, which was the case with a lot of upper-middle class married couples. They enjoyed friends, family, and many church relationships.

Douglas held his head high, not from pride, but from studying hard to get a good education, by being a diligent worker, and being honest. Douglas was a true believer and man of faith. He agreed with Proverbs 22:1, "*A good reputation and respect are worth much more than silver and gold.*"

Douglas' job as Division Director of six Savings and Loans in Colorado was what many people called, "a cushy job." He was respectful of his superiors, fair with all his employees, got along well with the other directors, and was judicious in his daily decisions. With an education in finance, Douglas knew that Savings and Loans (S&Ls) were initially established for the social good of individuals pursuing homeownership. Year after year, he knew there was nothing better than seeing a family move into their own home.

However, overnight, Douglas found himself unemployed along with many other bank employees. Well respected banks were being bought out and reconfigured throughout the metro area or simply shut down. Though his situation was due to S&L policies gone wrong, he was still one of the hundreds of bank employee casualties.

For Douglas in particular, knowing that his reputation would quickly become as *others* perceived him, not the true reflection of who he really was, caused anxiety. This would become a black spot on a resume, no matter how innocent he was. Being a director of an S&L did not scream "respectability," and the constant words in the media like "scandal," "crisis," "disaster," "debacle," and "fraud" were non-stop. The shadowy word "failure" was something he felt personally, and it rocked him.

Douglas knew that while several factors contributed to the S&L losses, one of the most important was the structure of the deposit insurance system, along with a policy that allowed insolvent and poorly capitalized institutions to remain in operation.

The S&L industry where Douglas was employed was hit with several upsets, including sharply rising interest rates and increased competition. These upsets, in turn, weakened the financial stability of many S&Ls. At that point, the S&Ls had little to lose and potentially much to gain by taking significant risks—employing a "go for broke" strategy of investing in riskier projects, hoping they would pay off in higher returns. These risks resulted in compounding the losses, especially the losses to the federal deposit insurance system.

Congress reacted to these staggering losses in 1989. Several reforms were addressed and enacted. Two regulating boards were abolished: the Federal Home Loan Bank Board and the bankrupt Federal Savings and Loan Insurance Corporation.

The Resolution Trust Corporation (RTC) was subsequently established and funded to resolve the remaining troubled S&Ls.

The RTC closed 747 S&Ls, and after the RTC resolved the S&L crisis, it closed on December 31, 1995.

The ultimate cost to taxpayers was estimated to be as high as $124 billion.[13] The mass failure of the S&Ls was terrible enough, but investigators also found rampant fraud. It was discovered that some S&Ls knew of and allowed fraudulent transactions to happen. Although the fraud practices were difficult to quantify and assess, fraud was not a significant cause of the S&L's failures.[14]

Overall, 1,043 out of 3,234 Savings and Loan Associations collapsed. This was considered one of the most devastating failures of the banking industry in the United States after the Great Depression.[15] Being a Division Director in the Savings and Loan industry, Douglas knew the word "fraud" and "failure" would be the dark shadow that would follow him around like a wolf stalking prey in his professional career.

For the next year, Douglas and his wife spent all their savings trying to make house and car payments and buying only necessities until he could find a new job. Week after week, month after month, he could not find any new job in his field, even though he had a college education and many years of professional experience. It was the dark shadow looming over him.

Both Douglas and Coryn worked, he selling burial insurance through a funeral home, and she working at a nearby discount store. They both worked 12-hour days trying to make ends meet.

Eventually, they were forced to sell their house, having exhausted all their savings, their investments, and even selling most of their belongings. Humiliated, they eventually moved in with their son and daughter-in-law, living in a two-bedroom apartment. When a new grandchild was born, although it was a joyful event, it made the two-bedroom apartment impossible to continue to occupy.

With nowhere to turn, the name of Colorado Homeless Families came up time and again through their church, where Executive Director Connie Zimmerman also attended. Douglas sadly told Connie that this was a situation he never imagined would happen to him, but he now understood that no one is immune from the possibility of becoming homeless.

Douglas and Coryn entered the program, moving into a HUD home that Connie had acquired through a $1-a-year-lease-program. It was a beautiful house, and whoever had owned it prior had taken excellent care of the property. Douglas found it ironic that they lost their home, became homeless, and then moved into a house that someone else had lost through the same difficulties Douglas and his wife had faced.

From the start, Douglas and Coryn enthusiastically volunteered wherever their skills and help where needed.

Douglas helped select the appropriate computer and printing system for CHF, then he set it up for the office and trained Connie on the new system.

Connie knew they would not require long-term assistance with Douglas's solid work history, college education, and a sincere desire to get back on their feet quickly. Douglas was soon hired as a manager for a national moving equipment and storage rental company overseeing 80 employees. Douglas and Coryn lived at Colorado Homeless Families for only a year before they were able to resume a new life—and one free from the dark shadow of the past.

1992 – 1995

SEASONS OF CHANGE

Obeying God Rather Than Men

One of the biggest hurdles of the HUD $1-a-year-lease-program proved to be the guidelines only allowed for a two-year maximum of a tenant's lease. Many homeless people, now tenants furthering their educations, needed longer than 24 months. Connie knew one of these families well.

A widow with three children had lost her firefighter husband through difficult circumstances. She sought help to alleviate their homelessness, and the woman rented one of the HUD properties from Connie. She faithfully worked part-time and attended school to become a math teacher. During the two years of college, she had earned straight A's in all her coursework. After two years, however, the agreement with HUD meant that she could no longer live in the home that had been provided to her. She would need to leave.

Not having yet completed college, the woman was ineligible for her teaching degree, and Connie found this situation frustrating and untenable as she could not set better guidelines to help those in transitional housing without more time to meet the educational needs in a meaningful way.

HUD was a good organization, and Connie had learned a lot from them about establishing requirements, setting up proper files, and the application process. Though she had facilitated a host of other administrative and programmatic HUD guidelines, there was something important these HUD guidelines could not address.

Due to the inflexibility of HUD's program, Connie began to pray, asking God for another practical source of hope, another arrangement for this woman, and many like her. She knew God's compassion and purposes were not limited to any program devised by humans.

Connie prayed, *"Lord, this woman needs to become a teacher! If she cannot earn a higher wage, she will not make enough money to support her family. Please help me obtain some properties that would allow me to set my own rules for special circumstances."*

Connie knew some individuals needed more time to stand on their own, especially single parents who both worked and sought to complete a college education.

Stepping into the Gap: Resolution Trust Corporation

At the time of Connie's prayers, the newly created RTC (Resolution Trust Corporation), whose motto was "Resolving the crisis, restoring the confidence," had just undergone one of its most significant undertakings: the selling of a nonperforming loan for a single-room-occupancy hotel in New York.

This historical and fashionable hotel, named The Times Square, was built in 1923 and comprised of 1,000 units, eventually became overrun by vagrants. Due to the loan default, the building now housed vagrants, vandals, and drug dealers. However, a nonprofit named, Common Ground, turned the historic building into 652 affordable housing units, with tenant support, such as medical services, job counseling, community facilities, and even several commercial spaces. When Common Ground purchased the building from RTC for 9.5 million dollars, and turned the investment around, "The Times Square" project was applauded and honored with special recognition for, "endurance, tenacity, and courage," and for working with federal agencies to help not only preserve the landmark building but simultaneously help low-income workers and the formerly homeless.[16]

Within a week of Connie's prayer for God's direction and help regarding this single woman's housing, Connie received a brochure entitled: "RTC Foreclosed Properties Available for Nonprofits." RTC made many properties available for thirty days to nonprofit organizations before becoming open to the general public. Connie attended the informational seminar, which the RTC Asset Director arranged for nonprofits like RB Ranch in Denver, Colorado to attend.

After the seminar, attendees were supplied a lengthy list of foreclosed properties for sale at a discounted rate to nonprofits. Carefully reviewing the list, Connie found that most were one or two individual homes or townhomes spread across larger rental areas. Connie kept looking for something with greater potential. Having learned this lesson from her job at Sunny Acres, she was looking specifically for homes grouped together to complete her vision of tenants sharing life in a community. A community where families could help other families and not be isolated or spread over a large area might be a better situation than the 20 HUD homes she was currently leasing.

One of the listings caught her eye. An area showed that ten properties were offered together for sale. She immediately drove to Arvada to view the property. Having difficulty locating the address, she considered the isolation an asset for safety given the fact that so many children would be housed there. She finally found the address with a great realization of hope: the entire property of 10 townhomes was foreclosed, and the properties were all located together. In the middle was a play area for children, and the entire grouping sat on about one acre.

Connie prayed at once, *"Lord, this property is exactly what I am looking for. And if this is what You want me to have, then I pray Deuteronomy 31:8: The Lord himself goes before you and will be with you; he will never leave you nor forsake you. Do not be afraid; do not be discouraged."*

With $5,000 in the RB Ranch bank account and Connie's unquestioning faith, she called the RTC representative and made an appointment to purchase the properties listed at $42,000 each, for a total of $420,000 for all ten. The RTC representative told Connie that RTC would work with Connie if the nonprofit could provide a solid plan.

Sitting down at her kitchen table that night, Connie worked in prayer while doing her best to formulate a plan. She added up what her tenants could realistically pay. She determined not to offer something that could fall apart later because of unreasonable payments. The appointment was scheduled for the following week, and Connie had not yet talked to the board of directors. Not to worry, she knew that she could sign contracts and conduct other necessary and immediate business with the clause, "contingent on the board of directors approval."

Throughout the week, Connie was given the wisdom to investigate the details of this property. She wanted to make sure there was nothing wrong with them. Not knowing an inspection professional, Connie prayed, *"Lord, please send someone that can help me. I need someone to look at the properties and let me know if these are worth purchasing or if they need major repairs."*

That very night, Connie received a phone call from a man named Steve, who said he was a contractor and a real estate broker. He explained that he had been contacted by someone from her organization asking for donations, but he told her that he would prefer to donate his time or skill if needed. He told her if there was anything he could do for her to please let him know. Thanking the Lord, she asked if he could meet her at the properties that she was considering buying to perform a cursory inspection.

Connie and Steve met the following day at 10:00 am, and they went through each property. Steve's inspection was thorough, and he found them to be in good shape and to also be an excellent purchase at the asking price of $420,000.

She told him what was in her heart, that she would offer $180,000 for the entire property based on her financial plan. Steve volunteered to be her buyer's agent and represent her at her meeting with RTC the following week.

With shoes of peace and a shield of faith, Connie ran forward. She arrived at her meeting with RTC knowing that God was with her. She and Steve sat at a table with the RTC staff, and one of them mentioned what a great deal she was getting for a price of $420,000.

Connie explained her nonprofit status and told them she would be offering $180,000 for the property. She felt the weight of scoffing and mocking from the RTC staff when they instantly declined her offer. Steve interrupted the meeting and reminded them that by law they were required to consider every offer made. Connie, Steve, and the RTC staff spent the next two hours on the details of her offer and completed the required paperwork. Connie put down $1,000 earnest money, and she left the meeting feeling the sting of rejection, but with peace and expectation in her heart that God was involved in this business transaction.

RTC contacted Connie with their counteroffer of $280,000. Connie had the spiritual knowledge from her budget that their counteroffer was too high to accept. Connie didn't know if God would supply the additional funds, or if He would change their minds. She knew, by faith, she was to stay the course.

She asked that a 60-day contingency clause be added giving RB Ranch the right to back out of the contract if they could not secure financing. While signing the contract, Connie began to pray, *"Lord, You said You would help me. This is important, and I can only see that we can afford the $180,000. You'll go before me, Lord, that I know."*

Connie spent the weekend in prayer asking God for wisdom and direction. On Sunday afternoon, God began sharing His thoughts with her. He would go before her, however, she needed to contact the RTC Asset Director in Texas, who had given the seminar she had attended.

After she found the number in the brochure, Connie called in the early morning and reminded the woman that RTC said they would work with Connie on this purchase. Connie told her this had not been the case. She told the Asset Director that she had, in good faith, offered $180,000 to buy the properties but instead of accepting it, the offer was met by a counteroffer more than CHF could afford.

The RTC Asset Director assured Connie that she would accept the $180,000 offer and put the original documents through. She would disregard the second contract. Within hours, Connie received a phone call from the local RTC office asking to make an appointment to sign the documents to purchase the ten homes on a well-hidden acre of land for $180,000.

With purchase documents in hand, Connie had 60 days to acquire financing.

Two days later, Connie received a call from Blake Chambliss, the RTC Housing Coordinator. This individual served as a nonprofit advisor to find community-based solutions to housing and services. His advice was to offer to purchase the properties for cash, as RTC would give a discount on the purchase price for cash offers.

Amazed that such a discount could become available, Connie took his advice, called RTC and told them that her nonprofit planned to pay cash. The purchase price was indeed discounted and dropped to $146,000—a nearly 20% discount.

A monthly board meeting for RB Ranch/Colorado Homeless Families was set, and there Connie found a complete agreement by all members, including overcoming the hurdles of financing.

A conditional commitment for tax-exempt permanent financing came from Colorado Housing and Finance Authority (CHFA). However, CHFA would take almost two months for the permanent financing of the properties, and in the meantime,

Connie needed a bridge loan for a down payment to buy the properties.

While trying to secure funding, the RTC thirty-day offer to nonprofit organizations had expired, and properties were being made available to the general public. Several individuals, companies, and other investors were trying to infringe on Connie's offer, going so far as to offer full price, and telling the remaining tenants under contract with the previous owner that they were the new owners. RTC came to Connie's aid and dismissed the poachers.

This 60-day lag time waiting for the CHFA loan forced Connie to contact numerous banks to inquire about a bridge loan. After rejection from most of the banks due to Colorado Homeless Families being a nonprofit with very little money, a bridge loan was finally offered through a new bank that had only established itself in Colorado in 1989. The closing was scheduled, only to have the bank representative fail to show up for the closing. After waiting for an hour, Connie prayed all the way to the closer's office, where she confronted him to honor his word.

Since starting RB Ranch, Connie became well-versed in applying for grants. While waiting for the bridge loan, she applied for a $10,000 grant for the down payment and won the grant provided by the Arthur H. And Helen K. Johnson Foundation. With this, a new closing was scheduled, the bridge loan was secured, and Colorado Homeless Families obtained the 10-unit property.

Connie also applied for other grants and was awarded a $10,000 Coors Foundation grant for minor repair work to some of the units.

By purchasing RTC's affordable housing in bulk, Connie suddenly found she had more significant operating and program flexibility to serve the homeless and near homeless with transitional housing.

Bearing Fruit in Every Good Work

As Connie designed the systems needed to attain the community vision at RB Ranch for her homeless families, she was still working her full-time job at Sunny Acres Assisted Living. This newest purchase made her even busier.

Then, she learned the news that her dream job of being the Director of Resident Services at Sunny Acres was becoming available, and she was being considered for that position. As much as she had always longed to grow into this position, her experience and time were no longer available to Sunny Acres. She had to commit to the project of RB Ranch at hand in order to shape its community and help it thrive.

Connie found when she reflected on the blessings of this project given the open doors and a cleared path, that her confidence had grown, that God had sent her to build out RB Ranch as fully as He purposed for her, whatever that looked like. She also discovered that God had changed her heart to have an excitement and deep, burning desire to fulfill her calling to the homeless.

Connie prayed: *"Lord, You are going to have to do something here. I need the money if they offer me the Director's job. If You don't want me to take it, You will need to open a different door for me. You know I need a salary in order to work full time as the Director of RB Ranch."*

A local team-based fundraising program contacted Connie. They suggested working together to raise funding for RB Ranch. Their program would place the phone calls for donations, in which the program would retain fifty percent of the donations for their company and employees, and the other fifty percent would go to RB Ranch. The Board of Directors approved this program, and in the first 30 days, they had raised $5,000.

After the first month, the manager of the fundraising program contacted Connie. He told her she should seriously consider changing the name of RB Ranch. Connie quietly listened as he said to her that the fundraising might be hindered as their fundraisers spent a lot of time explaining RB Ranch, what it is, and how it ties to helping homeless families.

Connie knew that Proverbs 19:20 warns us to, *"Listen to advice and accept instruction, that you may gain wisdom in the future."* Although she was hesitant to change as everything she had done so far was in the name "RB Ranch," she sought counsel and found that she could easily change the name to RB Ranch doing business as (DBA) Colorado Homeless Families. This name clearly explained who they were and their mission, and it provided a more straightforward conversation for fundraising.

Listening to this advice began to increase fundraising and make grant writing easier.

Ultimately, the dream job of being the Sunny Acres Director of Resident Services had changed. After watching God bring a stream of steady donations to the new nonprofit, Connie submitted her resignation letter to Sunny Acres and began working at RB Ranch helping the homeless full-time. The board of directors agreed on her humble salary of $10.00 per hour, but it was enough to allow Connie to commit 100% of her time towards managing the ministry to Colorado's homeless.

As Far as Possible, Dwell in Peace with All

Upon purchasing the RTC townhomes, there were still tenants from the previous owner still living on site. As leases expired, the newly named Colorado Homeless Families put in their own residents.

It wasn't long before Colorado Homeless Families was able to help up to 30 families at a time; twenty families were still in outlying HUD homes, and families began to move into the recently purchased townhomes, referred to as RG1.

Working from her home, Connie continued to accept food, furniture, and clothing donations and stored them in her basement and garage, as getting a storage facility had not yet become a reality. New Colorado Homeless Families' tenants were encouraged to come to her house to obtain what they needed from the supply. All the activity in Connie's quiet residential neighborhood was beginning to cause problems for her neighbors. Between working out of her house and the donation drop-offs and pick-ups, it made for a busy street, and her neighbors were also concerned about all the strangers showing up in their community.

One of Connie's neighbors suggested she use one of the newly purchased ten units for her office. She knew this was a promising idea, as she could better centralize the operation and help further develop the sense of community by being on site and readily accessible.

Connie consulted the board of directors and they agreed she should use one of the ten townhome units as the CHF Office.

As with the HUD home communities, the new CHF townhome residents were required to commit to a minimum of five hours per month per adult of community work. The volunteer commitment could be served in a variety of ways, such as perform maintenance and repairs to the buildings and grounds, help other tenants with personal services, exchange childcare services, or tutoring. Connie knew that helping others in the community builds a sense of personal worth. She also knew that in order for families to become successful and graduate from the Colorado Homeless Families program, each family needed to help others build personal independence.

Many families were reserved when they first arrived, but eventually, most began to understand that hiding inside their home and being isolated from the community rarely leads to success or independence. Connie began to assign volunteer tasks to each family in order to assist them with getting out of their homes, be seen in their community, to help neighbors, and to build relationships. She knew that growth in these areas would also grow respect and honor among families.

With the purchase of the townhomes, Connie no longer had to follow the 24-month resident limit of the HUD guidelines. She selected families who showed themselves to be good contributors, had initiative towards self-sufficiency, and a desire for education. She found the attributes of these types of families fit well into the CHF community. Once in the community, many needed time to process who they were, explore their dreams and goals, and set a plan to attain to be who they wanted to become.

After working with some new families, Connie began to realize that there were those who really wanted to move forward but did not have the confidence necessary to do so. Many individuals had been beaten down and abused mentally, physically, or emotionally. Some individuals had been programed to think that they were worthless, had no value, and would never be able to do anything worthwhile. Seeing this trauma, Connie deeply felt God's love for these individuals. She prayed for love and discernment of their spirits and intentions and created an environment to encourage and build them up. CHF worked with the residents to discover their gifts and talents and recognized any small step forward an individual made. It was a daily exercise that CHF acknowledged improvements to build a person's confidence.

The educational seminars, support groups, case management and counseling were used to build up their value and self-worth. Connie desired that the families living at CHF have valuable opportunities and blessings and live in a safe community where everyone works together and respects each other. What God placed in Connie's heart was to teach those who were struggling or abused to 1) learn to love themselves as they loved others, and 2) set healthy boundaries to keep themselves and their children safe from influences that were trying to control or take advantage of them.

The long road to self-sufficiency was made longer when abused and mistreated families could only see the dark walls of the deep hole that they were in. It was difficult for these individuals to have goals, dreams, and a vision for their future. Many were ready to give up as they didn't know how to follow the requirements of the program, many thinking they couldn't do what was expected to stay in the program. Connie was exceedingly patient with these individuals. She explained that the CHF program may not be for them and urged them to look for another homeless program that may better fit their needs. She knew that she didn't want to waste time and resources being supportive of those only looking for a handout. CHF operated on a month-to-month basis, and Connie emphasized that while they were there, they needed to follow the guidelines. However, if they chose to leave and enter a different program, they would be granted a release from the CHF requirements and they would be free to leave at the end of the month with a good reference from CHF. Individuals who sought a different or better program generally returned to CHF seeing the benefits of the supportive environment that Connie offered them. In other programs, they didn't find what CHF offered: dwelling in peace with everyone, a win-win situation while working towards self-sufficiency, and to always part on good terms. These individuals would ultimately decide to move forward staying with CHF and began setting goals, making even small, but good changes and confident choices. Connie and her team were patient and gave them time and encouragement to heal.

Not always was patience and dwelling in unity the best road to take. With the ability to draft her own guidelines and for the safety of the CHF community, Connie could quickly remove those who were associated with dangerous behavior, physically abusive to others, abused alcohol, or took drugs.

Connie's goal and vision for CHF was to help the newly homeless and working poor. These families generally had some social ties, hearts with hope, and self-dignity to aid in their road to self-sufficiency. However, many families who had a history of being poor and experienced many hardships–but were still fighting hard to succeed and to make a positive difference in their lives–were also selected for the program. Connie found that refugees from many countries usually possessed a lot of drive and initiative as they were grateful for the opportunity to come to America. They wanted a better life and now had the opportunity for freedoms and education.

With the growing problem of homelessness and poverty, Connie began to use stricter guidelines and new interviewing techniques to screen families. Those who qualified for revolving HUD placements received them. Those selected for the newly acquired townhomes were people with difficult medical issues, vulnerabilities, or educational needs who may need more time to get on their feet. Connie knew starting small was vital to test her faithfulness. As Luke 16:10 reminded her, "*Whoever can be trusted with very little can also be trusted with much, and whoever is dishonest with very little will also be dishonest with much.*"

With the new office space established among the homes, Connie now had the space to hire staff. As she progressed in her hiring, she found that most of her employees were retired or part-time helpers passionate about the cause.

Colorado Homeless Families started to develop wings.

Photo: Steve and Promise Phan. This young woman used her natural gifts and talents with courage and personality to become a successful YouTube makeup artist. Promise spent several of her formative adolescent years living at Colorado Homeless Families.

Photo: Volunteers,. Stephanie Parmley,(left) Food Bank Manager and part time case manager, Yulia Graham helper (center), 3rd lady a resident volunteer.

Bontu Desta sat on the front porch of the townhouse at the Colorado Homeless Families complex. He'd been there eight months enjoying Colorado sunsets. He wasn't much for the winters, but overall, he liked Denver since immigrating in 1989 from Ethiopia. Admittedly, things were very different from home.

Bontu was a non-refugee immigrant, which are individuals who do not arrive via the refugee process.

Immigrants come to Colorado for various reasons including joining family, finding economic opportunities, and building careers. Although they may not have refugee status, many immigrants are similarly escaping difficult situations in their home country. Non-refugee immigrants who are living in the U.S. with legal status are unable to apply for public benefits for the first five years of their residency.

His childhood friend had gotten word to him that Colorado in the United States was a good place to live, so, at first chance, he fled Ethiopia. The first six months were difficult because his official language was Amharic, and he was a lazy student learning English. Bontu preferred to ride the coattails of his friends.

Bontu bounced around in Colorado for his first couple of years. He worked odd jobs in construction and other physically demanding jobs, but they were too difficult for him. He always found himself short of money and unable to pay rent, so he would find a comfortable place on the street for a while. He would lie and steal to get things that made the street living more secure. When the weather turned cold, he would call the local homeless shelters home for a while. That is where he met his old lady. She was at the homeless shelter with two kids and she was working at a local restaurant. They got married because she wanted the stability of having a husband and family. He would even go to church with her sometimes just to appease her, but she was more into being married than he was. He found work when he wanted to, but often, street corner begging would supply enough for his minimal needs. If begging didn't provide him enough money, he'd sometimes sneak a little money from his wife's purse to buy something at the liquor store. The last time he had snuck $2, she had caught him and scolded him. A quick backhand was all it took to shut her up.

He found a flyer at the local homeless shelter. "Colorado Homeless Families" was what a friend had interpreted for him. He could only read a little English. That's how he ended up sitting on the porch of the townhouse.

Bontu always knew he was on the lazy side. "The easier, the better" was his motto. When he was required to have a job to live here, he looked up an old contact who worked in landscaping. Some of the work was difficult, but he always made sure to get the easiest tasks. Raking leaves was the plum job. He could go slow as he watched the world hurry by, take frequent breaks, stretch out the days. Colorado Homeless Families also required tenants to volunteer, and since he was working for a landscape company, he offered to weed the landscape beds. He also knew that this work was effortless. He could do very little and still stretch out the time. He would bide his time until the local bars opened and would then disappear to meet up with friends.

As he sat on the porch steps today, he was disturbed. The last few months, he had been drinking more than usual, and some of the punks at the bar were harassing him and some of the others there. Several fights ensued, leaving him to work with a black eye and bruises. His boss at the landscaping company didn't care. In fact, many of the guys showed up on Monday with leftovers of Friday and Saturday night trouble. The lady that runs the housing place, Connie Zimmerman, was beginning to ask questions. She would seek him out and see if he was okay, and he was finding that he didn't want her kindness and concern.

Two weeks prior, Bontu decided to please his wife and took her and the children to the church she had been wanting to attend. His wife was happy attending as a family, and they were surprised to see Connie in the entryway as they were leaving. Neither he nor his wife knew Connie attended this church. He remembered thinking that he was glad Connie greeted them. Maybe this would appear that he was trying to improve his life.

The following week at the required CHF educational meeting, Connie mentioned how glad she was to see their family at church and mentioned some of the other programs at the church such as a great children's ministry, a wonderful women's bible study, and Promise Keepers, which was a supportive men's ministry.

Maybe it was just his hangover today, but he was hoping that staying at CHF was not contingent upon doing anything additional. It was bad enough he had to have a job and do volunteer work. He drew the line at Promise Keepers. Never. Going. To. Happen.

At work on Monday, Bontu saw the man leaving the office complex. He had seen him before, many times, leaving the building in his stylish suit, pricey shoes, and an expensive briefcase. A couple of the other workers knew him to be an attorney, t'ebek'a in Amharic. That day, Bontu dropped his rake and grabbed the chance to ask the man for his business card. After a brief conversation, it turned out the attorney had been born in a city near to Bontu's small village, and the attorney was interested in more of what Bontu had to say.

After a week of telephone calls, Bontu was told by the attorney that if attending church and joining Promise Keepers was a requirement, then he had a case against Colorado Homeless Families for violating his rights. The attorney explained that the Fair Housing Act of 1968 protects people from discrimination of race, color, national origin, religion, sex, familial status, and disability. "Discrimination" was the only word that Bontu wanted to hear, and quickly pushed the attorney in that direction. Colorado Homeless Families and Mrs. Zimmerman would subsequently be served with the complaint.

Bontu remembered he had been elated after speaking with the attorney. This seemed to be the answer, as the attorney was optimistic that a lawsuit might follow. Bontu hoped that he could make enough money from a lawsuit to find his own place and be able to find a job that was more suitable to him. The dismay he felt today came from the phone call he had just received from the attorney. Expecting good news, the attorney said that the complaint was dropped. Somehow it was rejected in the system and would not be moving forward. The attorney promised to investigate it further, but this rejection seemed to come from a high place and was final with no prospect to re-visit. "Inexplicable" was the word the attorney used. As Bontu hung up the phone, he felt that same "shrinking" that resulted when Mrs. Zimmerman would seek him out. He didn't understand it, but he knew that shortly his life was going to look different.

For the part of Colorado Homeless Families, after receiving a complaint about discrimination, Connie was told that since the nonprofit had less than nine employees and was a small business, she could not be sued at a federal level, but they could bring suit at a state level. The complaint was that a tenant was suing her because she was making him attend church, and the resident believed that continuing to receive housing from CHF was contingent upon him joining Promise Keepers, a religious organization. Connie found that the time and attorney fees to address this situation was proving to be difficult, and as she was reading her Bible, she found the verse in Proverbs 16:7, *"When a man's ways please the LORD, He makes even his enemies to be at peace with him."* She prayed, *"Okay, Lord, is there anything that needs to change? Is there anything I've done wrong? I'll take care of it, just tell me. Show me any areas of my life that are not pleasing to You so I can immediately correct them."* Connie knew the promise of Proverbs 16:7 was hers, and this verse was meant for her at this exact time. Within several days, she received a phone call saying the case had been dropped.

Surrounded by boxes and waiting for the knock on the door, Chloe Fisher sat on the sofa in their townhome at Colorado Homeless Families watching her two sons play on the carpet with a set of Lincoln Logs. It was a welcomed surprise to recently find the toy set at a local thrift store. Her memory flooded with warm thoughts of playing with Lincoln Logs with her brother, Gage, as children. As with most of their toys, their momma had bought the set by collecting S&H Green Stamps. Momma had finally saved enough to purchase the Lincoln Logs set and bought them at the local S&H Stamp Discount Store by their house. It had cost her one and three-quarter stamp books.

Her husband, Mark, was in the bedroom. He rarely came out to be with his family and when he did emerge, his mood was foul, and his words were angry and bitter. Their two sons were beginning to show fear when Mark raised his voice. Their older son was at a tender age of wanting daddy's approval, but when it went unnoticed by Mark, he would act out.

Chloe Parker met Mark Fisher during winter break at Sun Valley Ski Resort. She would graduate in the spring from Boise State University and he from Boise Bible College. It was love at first sight, and the more they got to know each other, the more they fell in love. During finals, Mark was offered a youth pastor position at a new church in Denver beginning in the fall, so by late summer they married in a small ceremony at Mark's church in Boise and had their large reception at the private country club where Mark's parents were members. As Chloe reflected on that day, she remembered being so full of hope and excitement for their future together.

They both loved Denver, and the enjoyment of downhill and cross-country skiing was something they had in common.

Mark began his job as a youth pastor, and he loved it. Moreover, the youth community loved him. He was energetic, active, and caring. The trait she knew all the youth loved most about Mark was that he listened. Mark had a way of making everyone around him feel special and heard. He remembered your name and details of your life, and he was always interested in not only *what* you were doing, but *how* you were doing. His wisdom, gentle guidance, and patience were the trademarks of a good youth pastor. He always made sure to engage the youth in the scriptures where help, love, and guidance could always be found. Mark and Chloe's nights and weekends were filled with numerous youth activities organized by Mark's department.

By the new year, Chloe was pregnant with their first son. It was sooner than they both wanted but they happily accepted this gift and joyfully prepared to begin their family. Chloe's degree in art kept her busy and fulfilled as a freelance artist, but becoming a mother had her yearning to expand into illustrations and artwork for children's books. Her pregnancy was easy, and the labor and delivery were equally stress free. By Christmas, their tiny apartment was filled with all things baby, and after Mark's parents left, the apartment was bursting at the seams with all the Christmas gifts bestowed upon them.

Mark continued to mature in his role as a youth pastor and was further developing the youth curriculum, organizing retreats and summer camps, and expanding the Youth Ministries team. He was also beginning to assist in the family counseling center where problems with youth were negatively affecting the harmony in homes. Although his passion was to teach and train youth into a deeply enriching faith experience, he told Chloe that he was prayerfully considering returning to school to get his master's degree in counseling.

During endless summer activities, Chloe learned she was pregnant again. By the time the tulips and the daffodils pushed up in the spring, they had another son, and summer found them looking for a larger apartment, preferably with a pool and a playground. They found the perfect place close to Mark's work at the church. Mark was still considering expanding his education to counseling, and Chloe was busy with various lucrative art projects.

November and December arrived with record snowfall. Mark and Chloe decided to take a weekend ski trip while Mark's parents enthusiastically offered to babysit their grandsons. Driving through the mountains, Chloe relaxed on the beautiful drive, and began silently reciting verses from her favorite book of Psalms and the words that were written about the mountains:

- Psalm 36:6 Your righteousness is like the highest mountains, your justice like the great deep. You, Lord, preserve both people and animals.
- Psalm 50:11 I know every bird in the mountains, and the insects in the fields are mine.
- Psalm 90:2 Before the mountains were born or you brought forth the whole world, from everlasting to everlasting you are God.
- Psalm 98:8 Let the rivers clap their hands, let the mountains sing together for joy.
- Psalm 121:1 I lift up my eyes to the mountains—where does my help come from?
- Psalm 125:2 As the mountains surround Jerusalem, so the Lord surrounds his people both now and forevermore.

They checked into their condo and hit the slopes. They skied together the first day, had a nice dinner and sat by the fireplace before going to bed. The second day they skied together in the morning, but after lunch when Mark took to the black diamonds, Chloe opted to exercise caution and stay on the blue squares.

Ski Patrol found Chloe at the lodge as she was removing her boots. She had a wonderful afternoon but was finished for the day and wanted to curl up by the fireplace and enjoy a good book. Instead, a resort van ushered her to the hospital where she found hustling emergency room staff hurriedly tending to Mark. There were so many medical staff around him, she couldn't get to his side.

Frantically finding a nurse, Chloe was told that Mark had been cut off by a snowboarder and crashed into a tree. Although he was awake and talking, he did not currently have feeling in the lower extremities. Chloe nearly fainted at the news, and at the first opening in the medical staff, she rushed to his side.

Since 1956, Craig Hospital in Denver has been a world-renowned rehabilitation hospital that exclusively specializes in the neurorehabilitation and research of patients with spinal cord and brain injuries.

Mark Fisher, a 28-year-old male, was transferred to Craig Hospital seven days after a skiing accident that resulted in a paraplegia spinal injury. The local mountain hospital had exhausted their treatment for Mark in the intensive care unit and completed their findings using all the diagnostic tools available: CT scans, MRIs, X-rays, and evoked potential tests. There was nothing more they could do but to transfer Mark to the inpatient program at Craig Hospital for his injury treatments and rehabilitation. Mark Fisher would begin to learn to concentrate on learning about his new life in a wheelchair, and months of intensive physical therapy would help strengthen muscles and nerve connections.

Everyone in Mark and Chloe's world rallied around them with encouragement and lifting them up in prayer. As the weeks progressed, Chloe began to see the change in Mark's eyes. A menacing darkness began to descend, and Chloe was quick to pray God's light into it. She stayed in constant contact with the church, and the pastors from the church rotated days visiting Mark and Chloe and agreed in prayer for healing over Mark.

Chloe was certain that given Mark's competitive ways, optimistic attitude, active lifestyle, and his deep and unshakeable faith, that this darkness would be temporary, and Mark would not let this injury stop him from living life. After being discharged from inpatient rehabilitation, however, Mark sunk lower and became withdrawn and sullen. Both of their boys had missed their daddy, and they were so excited that he was home. Mark simply just held them for a few minutes, gave them back to Chloe, and turned his back on them to stare at the television.

In the ensuing weeks, Chloe did everything she could to help bring Mark out of the darkness he was in. His parents offered support and to purchase anything they needed, and the pastors of the church would constantly visit. Families of Mark's youth congregation would bring food and stay to visit, but Mark would barely notice them and rarely speak.

Mark continued with long-term outpatient rehabilitation, but when they arrived home after those appointments, he would go directly to bed and sleep. Chloe understood the exertion of physical therapy, but she knew this was more than being tired. She held out hope that it would turn around soon, and the Mark she fell in love with would return.

The other big concern of Chloe's was their rent. With a limited income, and she unable to work because her time was spent with Mark, rent was due and there was no way to pay it. She talked with the apartment management, but their grace period was over, and the goodwill had run out.

She approached the lead pastor, and he asked for a couple of days to look into some options for them. He finally notified her that he was able to secure a place for them at Colorado Homeless Families in Arvada. He had worked with the Executive Director Connie Zimmerman on several occasions, and they had an ADA accessible place right next door to their offices and would be happy to take in the family until life stabilized for them. He explained the CHF program guidelines to Chloe, and he also told her that the church paid the security deposit for them. The youth group and church members had amassed a large team of volunteers to help box up their belongings to get them moved and settled in the following week. Tears of relief washed over Chloe.

Chloe loved living at CHF. The staff was exceptionally caring and understanding, and several families volunteered to watch their sons while she took Mark to rehabilitation. Mark's parents were supportive and helped with whatever equipment Mark needed to aid in his recovery. The darkness remained, and the moodiness turned to anger, which turned to hostility.

One sunny summer day, she answered a knock at the door to find a van parked outside their townhome. The church had been having fundraisers and was finally able to purchase a wheelchair accessible van so Mark could freely get around. The crowd was joyful, and the environment was celebratory. Mark thanked everyone and even got in and waved from the driver's seat. After the supporters prayed for their family and departed, Mark wheeled back into their townhome, into the bedroom, and slammed the door.

Heart-to-heart talks with Mark were impossible. The hostility and resentment boiled over, and it hurt her heart to look at the man that sat before her. One night as she sat on the couch and prayed, she tried to identify this feeling that she had never felt before in her entire life. Desperation. Fear. She was afraid she was losing her husband and their marriage. She was afraid their sons were losing their father. Although his doctors said he was rehabilitating well, she was afraid there would be no recovering from the emotional and mental trauma. She knew that God was bigger than everything she was facing, but she couldn't do anything herself to fix it.

Mark made little effort in anything other than the rehabilitation appointments. He would not participate in any family activities and didn't even want to watch his sons on the playground. Their friends from church would visit and tell them how much they missed seeing him at services, but Mark was unmoved. It was a requirement that they attend certain classes at

CHF, but Mark went through the motions, and remained glum throughout. Finally, crying and begging, Chloe convinced him to attend counseling, but he barely spoke to the counselor and proceeded to be angry at her the rest of the week. While at Mark's rehabilitation one day, Chloe picked up some information on Craig Hospital's integrative and comprehensive psychological services for patients and their families, and they began counseling there as well. Mark was his usual miserable self, but Chloe found their sessions enlightening and helpful.

Nothing worked to improve their life, and Chloe found herself living with the ghost of Mark. He was there but wasn't present. Mark was sacrificing his family on behalf of his resentment. He lashed out at everything, and his words became vile. She knew he lived in fear and pain, having given up his faith and joy. He focused on his inadequacies and became more bitter each day. He was refusing to engage in life—his own or his family's.

The time to leave CHF was quickly approaching, and there were no goals, no job, no transition to a new beginning that CHF offered. Counseling and case management had not helped, and for as grateful as Chloe was to CHF for the assistance, encouragement, and support, for Mark it went unappreciated.

Mark's parents had visited last month and while Mark stayed in the bedroom, they took the boys to the park to play. His parents told her they had arranged to purchase an ADA accessible home in Denver for them to move to. They believed that Mark's ties to their church, the many friends he had made, and the youth he had impacted, would be a hopeful reason for their family to stay in Denver rather than return to Boise.

Chloe was overcome with gratitude, but also told them that she was beginning to pray about her and the boy's future with Mark. She would never make any decision without hearing directly from the Lord, and she would always be obedient to how He guided her. Yet, Mark's bitterness and inability to re-engage in life at any level was deeply hurting her and causing behavioral issues with their boys.

The knock on the door came and she stepped over her sons playing with the Lincoln Logs to answer it. Mark's parents and several church friends were there with a moving truck to load their boxes and take them to their new home. She had seen the house and it was very nice. The school that the boys would one day attend was nearby, and it even had a basement for her to work. Everything was set up to be wheelchair accessible. They would have a nice backyard for the boys and since Mark used to love being outside, there was a place for vegetables with wheelchair accessible elevated garden beds.

Everyone made quick work of putting their belongings in the truck, and soon they were loaded up and ready to go. As Chloe stayed behind and finished the cleaning, she drank in the quiet atmosphere and took a long look around at the place that had given her support, encouragement, counsel, love, and hope. Colorado Homeless Families provided everything they needed to help them stabilize their life and improve their circumstances. Yet they weren't leaving CHF as a success story. Chloe knew that Mark felt broken, crushed, and depressed which led him to give up and stop trying.

CHF Executive Director Connie Zimmerman reminded CHF families that Jesus Christ knows our troubles, temptations, and sorrows and He meets the deepest needs of broken people. He gives them joy and peace (Romans 15:13) and He heals the brokenhearted and binds up their wounds (Psalm 147:3).

Newlyweds Greg and Rachel Stewart were happily settling into their life together. They had been back from their honeymoon a short time, not all the wedding gifts had even been opened when Greg was in a car accident and seriously injured his back.

Having always been a car enthusiast, Greg worked as a Rail Car Unloader and enjoyed taking special care to unload automobiles from rail cars. Not only did he get to see a lot of interesting shipments, but Greg liked rules – and there were lots of them set in place by the American Association of Railroads (AAR) that purposed to safely ship this precious freight. Greg even saw how to make some improvements and had given his ideas in writing to the AAR, the governing body for railroads. It was a physical job that kept him moving but also required attention to detail.

Greg had always been a quick healer when he was injured as a kid and even with playing sports in high school. So given his young age and being physically fit, the doctors thought a quick recovery was certain and without the need for surgery. He had been in debilitating pain for three months, and further tests revealed his pain was occurring as a condition of the spinal discs. Surgery would be necessary as well as many months of recovery and rehabilitation.

They knew that they would need to move out of their wonderful first apartment. He was not able to return to his job, and Rachel was newly pregnant and only finding part-time work. With nowhere to go, they moved into his parent's basement. This move was a last resort, as Greg's sister and her family had also been living with his parents for the past year. This put a strain on the household, and Greg was having a tough time navigating the narrow steps up and down to the basement.

The surgeons told Greg and Rachel that his back surgery was a success, but it would be a while before he was fully recovered and hopefully pain-free.

As soon as Greg began walking, he told Rachel he planned to get them out of the basement. With time on his hands in recovery, Greg read all the newspapers. One article caught his eye about a new organization called Colorado Homeless Families. They helped homeless people get back on their feet, but CHF would only consider hard-working families who were dedicated to becoming self-sufficient. When families were accepted, they also had to commit to functioning as a part of the community and helping each other in whatever way possible.

He contacted Colorado Homeless Families for more details and learned that at least one family member had to be working, which Rachel was still working part-time. He also learned that each family needed a sponsor: either an individual or organization that would pay a $250 deposit on the HUD home. The sponsor also had to commit to providing financial assistance if the family continued to have trouble. The families or their sponsors were required to pay taxes, maintenance, and any other required fees on the property they occupied. Greg asked his parents to sponsor him and Rachel, and they agreed.

By summer, with the help of his parents and his sister and her husband, Greg and Rachel moved into a three-bedroom townhouse in Westminster. The townhome was beautiful and spacious, it was close to his rehabilitation center, and it was timely as their daughter was born in late August.

Within a couple of months, Greg began to move around, and his rehabilitation was going well. He knew that all he needed was a little time to get back on his feet. Stopping by the CHF offices to meet with the case manager and shop the clothing bank for his daughter, Greg told Connie Zimmerman, the Executive Director of Colorado Homeless Families, that he was doing well and wanted to know what he could do to help any of the other families. Connie found out that Greg had an aptitude for cars and was, in fact, an expert mechanic. Greg immediately went to work on a few of the lesser physically demanding jobs. It wasn't long before Greg had repaired dozens of cars for others at CHF.

The first snow of the season revealed that Greg and Rachel's townhome roof was leaking, and Greg received a phone call one afternoon from a man living at CHF who wanted to come by and fix their roof to re-pay the work Greg had done on his car and for Rachel driving his wife to some appointments.

Celebrating their first Christmas in their home with their new daughter, Greg and Rachel found themselves to be exceptionally grateful. Greg was healing well, and because he was such a diligent worker and prized contributor, his job wanted him back as soon as he received a release from the doctor. Rachel worked with their case manager on her education and career goals and together, they mapped out a plan, including a plan for applying for financial aid to begin paralegal school.

With tears in her eyes, she watched their daughter play with a glittery bow on her Christmas gift, Rachel told Greg that she had a new Christmas wish: she hoped that they would be able to buy their lovely townhome someday.

Danny Garcia looked through bleary eyes at the dark highway ahead. *Denver - 551 miles* was what the last highway mileage sign indicated. There was not much to see in Billings, Montana, in the dark of night, but even less so once he got outside the city lights. Since graduating from high school in Denver, Danny had made several steps into adulthood.

He went to training and became an over-the-road truck driver.

He and his high school sweetheart, Rhonda, got married, and their first son was born before they were 20 years old. That active, happy baby boy was the light of their life, and within a couple of years, they were blessed with their second beautiful baby boy. Danny had always yearned for higher education, but with a bride and two young boys, he took the job he could get that would pay him a reasonable wage without any college requirement.

Over-the-road trucking paid decently and allowed Rhonda to work a few hours each week and go to school part-time. It was essential to both Danny and Rhonda that at least one of them be at home always to be present with the children. Steering their boys in the right direction was vital because Danny and Rhonda personally knew the effect of absent parents and lack of guidance had played in each of their lives. They wanted to break that cycle. Only because they were high school sweethearts did they confide their needs and questions to each other, and they helped rescue one another to grow in the right direction as teenagers.

Raising their boys to be strong, capable, stable men of honor and dignity was important to both of them.

It was during these late-night long-haul travels that worry and fear crept into Danny's thoughts. He had not wanted to ask for more routes as he was already sacrificing time away from his family and had a deep desire to be a present father and husband. He had left Rhonda crying over the bills when he took to the road for this haul. It broke his heart. He felt like a failure. Things were not looking up, especially since the rising cost of education and the lack of ability to be in more than one place at a time forced Rhonda to quit school.

"How are you going to make it?" and, "Those doctor's bills are past due!" were the voices that Danny heard when the night was dark, and the road was long.

The last time he'd been home, he and Rhonda listed their income and bills into columns and the bills, with the children's medical needs, far outweighed the resources. This was deeply distressing. That's why he asked his boss for extra routes, but his boss shook his head and simply said, "Get in line, Danny."

Although his insurance, through the trucking company, paid for some of the unexpected medical bills, they still had a significant portion to pay, and these parents soon realized that they could no longer afford to live where they were located. Rhonda asked a couple of family members for help, but these dark economic times stretched everyone to their limits. No one had any "rainy-day savings," especially not to hand out to others.

Danny knew something had to change. He placed a call to Rhonda from the payphone in Cody, Wyoming. That call alerted him that things needed to change sooner than later as Rhonda told him the landlord would not allow any more late or extended rent payments from them. They would have to move—and Danny had no idea where they could safely land.

Rhonda mentioned that one of their friends at church on Sunday had heard Connie Zimmerman talking to a group about her organization called Colorado Homeless Families. Rhonda had called CHF earlier that day and inquired about their program. "We'll begin the application process when I get home from this haul," Danny told her. Now, driving through the dark towards Denver, "homeless" is all Danny could think about. *Jesus, we need a direction,"* Danny prayed. For as hard as Danny worked, and his deep loyalty to his family's success and happiness, he could not believe they might actually be homeless in such a short time.

When Danny found his family living at the Colorado Homeless Families complex, he discovered the educational seminars on finances and budgeting were helpful to them, as were the support group meetings.

Danny and Rhonda realized that they were not the only ones who were not making ends meet, no matter how hard they worked at their current jobs. There was a name put to their scenario. They were part of "the working poor." They listened and learned that the working poor had little or no post-high school education or training, causing them to work at lower-paying jobs that would barely make ends meet, especially in economic downturns. This opportunity at CHF was God's answer to help them step out of the downward spiral.

Upon applying to Colorado Homeless Families, Danny and Rhonda happily signed the contract to attend a trade school, college, or university and apply for PELL grants for financial aid. Through counseling and working with their case manager, they realized they needed a master plan rather than a "work hard just to get by" plan. Rhonda also decided to return to school, and together she and Danny decided to pursue nursing degrees.

Danny changed his OTR trucking job to a local delivery job to be home more with his family, but they found it would be more cost-effective to attend school together where they could support one another, take the same courses, and share the textbooks. Danny's new job closer to home was not his ideal position, but it did pay more than his trucking job. Danny and Rhonda found that using the Colorado Homeless Families' food, clothing, and furniture bank helped them supplement their household resources and lessened their expenses. This allowed them to pay off the unexpected debt that had been mounting.

One day, as Danny watched his two energetic, happy boys play with other children on the Colorado Homeless Families playground, he reflected on their new path. He realized a correlation that road maps were an important tool in his trucking job and were vital for direction. The road map of life requires different navigation to get from Point A to Point B.

Working harder to catch up is like driving faster on a pitted road. It isn't the best way to the intended destination. Rather, having a bigger, more educated understanding of what is happening around you is the way to go.

For Daniel, his family, and having the ability to reach out and help others, Colorado Homeless Families taught the way to salvation.

He enjoyed living at Colorado Homeless Families. When he and Rhonda sat down and listed their income and bills into columns, they saw that self-sufficiency and homeownership would soon become their destination. They prayed over their papers from Psalm 32:8, "*I will guide you along the best pathway for your life. I will advise you and watch over you.*"

The cancer diagnosis was overwhelming. This was a life-changing diagnosis. Doctors discussed all the treatment options, and which would work best for this tumor. Surgery was their first option so they could remove as much of the tumor as possible.

While in surgery, the doctors planned to give radiation directly to the cancer cells without going through the skin. However, there was little success with the surgical removal, and the intraoperative radiation therapy did not shrink the tumor as expected. Sofie Watts had just finished her last round of chemotherapy, and it left her in a weakened condition. Chemo had severely compromised her body.

A multitude of tests, CT scans, MRIs, and X-rays would tell the doctors if the cancer was growing again. And it was. Aggressively growing at that.

Donny and Brenda Watts sobbed when they learned the results of their four-year-old daughter's latest tests. Sofie was so weak, and the last year of her short life had been filled with pain and suffering.

After Sofie's initial diagnosis, Donny and Brenda decided Donny should quit his job. His job offered no insurance and very few benefits; one of them had to be with Sofie for every appointment. For some of the experimental treatments, travel to other states was necessary, and lengthy hospitalizations also required that one of her parents be with her all the time. It made sense that it be Donny so Brenda could work and keep their insurance. They gave a lot of attention to coordinating schedules so their two other children would be cared for. Brenda's sister, who also worked full time, took care of babysitting, feeding the kids, homework, cleaning their house, making sure they had groceries, and the laundry done. She was an angel, and Brenda did not know what she would have done without her help.

After blood transfusions, bone-marrow extractions, and antibody injections, the doctors could do no more for this relentless and ruthless disease. No human should ever have to endure this, let alone a four-year-old. Within two weeks, Sofie gave up her year-long fight and died peacefully with her mom, dad, and her beloved life-sized teddy bear "Lucky" by her side.

Family, friends, classmates, their parents, neighbors, and parishioners from their church all came to mourn Sofie's loss. Healing was not going to come quickly as pain from the loss of a child is incomprehensible. It shattered their hearts and left their family—and the soul of them all—horrifically empty. Every motion or any need beyond the basics of breathing seemed impossible.

Donny and Brenda held their other two crying children each night and cried with them. Suffering did not even begin to describe the effect of Sofie's loss. Knowing they had to try to make life as "normal" as they could for their other two young children, day by day, they began to put one foot in front of the other, doing whatever seemed necessary.

While mourning Sofie, Donny and Brenda began to receive another source of devastation in the form of medical bills. The treatments and medical costs that were not covered by insurance were quickly climbing to over $100,000. Some of Sofie's latest treatments had been experimental, and those costs were not covered at all by Brenda's insurance.

As medical bills came due during the last year of Sophie's treatment, Brenda would use their savings, credit cards, and finally, a second mortgage was taken on their home. She reasoned, "When your child needs help, you will do anything." They were fortunate to receive donations from their church friends, and Brenda's company also held fundraisers to help offset the growing medical bills. People were kind, but as Sofie's death began to sink in, so did the reality of medical bills.

Out of hope and without any other options, their bank began to foreclose on their home. Brenda's sister offered to house them all at her home. Donny began working again and even got an additional job on evenings and weekends to make a more significant dent in their debt.

One late-night conversation took a gloomy turn. Bankruptcy might be their only option. Brenda had begun to research bankruptcy and found that medical debt is considered a non-priority unsecured debt, so it could be discharged, partially forgiven, or even restructured with medical providers. They hoped it would not come to bankruptcy. They would want to buy another home one day. After the past year, their credit deteriorated, and bankruptcy could not help their credit score stay afloat. The idea of owning their home was lost in quicksand. They also knew they couldn't keep leaning on Brenda's sister after everything she had already done for them. Her house was small and bursting at the seams.

A friend told them about Colorado Homeless Families and explained it was an organization helping families get back on their feet after financial crisis.

Donny and Brenda were able to complete the application and meet with management. The Watts family soon joined the CHF program. They were provided a house that, thankfully, happened to be in the same school district where their children already attended, and it was close to Brenda's sister. They saw flickers of hope.

Though heartbroken to have left the home behind where Sofie had lived, and though it was a difficult move to the temporary CHF house, Donny and Brenda were able to restructure their debt. Colorado Homeless Families helped them with grief counseling and attending educational seminars. The couple was on their way to rebuilding their finances.

A case manager helped them identify goals to enable them to get back on their feet within two years. It seemed impossible, but as they took small steps and continued to focus on their healing, emotionally and financially, they stepped up and stepped again onto solid ground.

Brenda received a promotion at her job, and Donny found a better job with higher pay and benefits. He also took advantage of the reeducation program by attending the university at night. In short order, he was able to finish the degree program he had started years before.

One summer afternoon, the family painted their new picnic table Sofie's favorite color. As their children laughed and began painting each other's faces and arms, Donny and Brenda realized that the emptiness of their souls was slowly transforming into fullness of life.

Staff L to R: Andrey Russ, maintenance, Bonnie Russel, bookkeeper, Virginia Furry, managed the women's housing unit, Jamie Parmley, full time supervisor of maintenance, buildings and property upkeep, Elaine Nava, office manager, Kirsten Baynham, part time case manager Norm Strasheim part time senior case manager, a volunteer resident couple is in the back.

As the noisy city bus rumbled down the street to its next stop, Abigail Donnelly closed her eyes and tried to think back to a time when she felt safe. Or loved. Or accepted. Even wanted. Memories and feelings such as these evaded her.

Abigail had always felt alone and had lived more than half her life that way.

She never knew her father, and the woman who gave birth to her was unable—or unwilling—to care for Abigail. One morning when Abigail was eight years old, her mother dropped her off at a distant relative's house with a small suitcase and a secondhand Cabbage Patch doll. The relative, whom Abigail had never met and never even heard of couldn't care for her, so the child welfare caseworker showed up at her door and ushered Abigail away to foster home one. That is how Abigail thought of them: foster home one through eight.

Within four years, foster home one quickly turned into two, three, and four. Shuffled continuously from home to home, school to school, Abigail's grades worsened with each move.

Foster home five lasted the longest by keeping her stable physically for two long years. Abigail never felt she belonged at any foster home or at school. Teased at home and bullied at school, Abigail didn't fit in or bond with anything or anyone. One of her teachers, Mrs. Johnson, felt sorry for her and let Abigail eat lunch in her classroom and read quietly after school so that she did not have to go home right away and walk in front of the bullies.

Foster home five was also where she found herself pregnant. Mr. and Mrs. Five did not want to foster a kid with a kid, so nine months later, Abigail gave birth to a baby boy in a shelter for pregnant teens.

It was understood from the beginning that foster home six took her in strictly for the money each month—all $516 of it and some added money thrown in for Abigail's baby boy.

Foster home seven lasted three months when someone at child welfare realized they had hired former criminals as foster parents in this particular home. That explained a lot. The one thing that all the foster homes had in common: they all treated Abigail like she would never amount to anything. Even as life grew more complex and Abigail's body and mind grew, the foster homes provided her with only the basic needs of food and shelter, but that was it. She learned not to expect any more.

Heaven forbid at this stage that she allow herself to dream of one day being adopted. That dream was dashed with the baby.

She was writing a paper for school one day in the library when she looked up to see the word "foster" defined: to promote the growth or development of; to further; encourage; to care for or cherish. Boy, was *foster home* the wrong phrase.

Finally, she was transferred from the care of criminals into foster home eight, simply the stopgap until she "aged out." She would be born out into the world entirely on her own without money, a job, babysitting, no spouse, and no help or support. There would no longer be even the record keepers of the foster system to keep track of her. How was a newborn baby expected to walk, talk, and fend for itself when it leaves the womb? Just turned out and expected to survive in a strange, friendless world, figuring out life?

At 18-years-old, Abigail aged out of the foster care system lugging a couple of suitcases from a thrift store, a few hundred dollars in her purse, and a reliable used car she had found through a school acquaintance. Thankfully, the acquaintance felt generous in the car department because he had received a new one for a high school graduation gift.

Not understanding the impossibility of her situation, having a baby made Abigail determined to gain stability and a better life.

She knew it would be difficult, but undeterred, she persisted and received the training qualifications she needed to work at a daycare center. However, there existed a much bigger more immediate problem: she couldn't afford a safe place to live. Where was there a safe place for her son to play outside? Abigail knew from experience what kind of evil existed in the world.

Through one of her daycare co-workers, Abigail learned about Colorado Homeless Families. She managed to apply, and although she had no confidence in herself, she went through the interview process and expressed her determination to want a better life for herself and her baby.

Within days of her interview, Abigail received a phone call at work. She had been approved to move into CHF! Abigail felt such a flood of relief. Never before had her outlook for her future taken on this hopeful feeling. She and her son moved into their first real, safe home at Colorado Homeless Families and took advantage of the abundance of choices in resources for clothes, food, and furniture.

One of the programs at Colorado Homeless Families taught Abigail to set goals. Determination was good, but having goals helped her stay on target for something specific. She charted a course.

Sitting with her case manager, Abigail set her very first goal: to continue her education to become a social worker. Her case manager helped her with the education decisions. She found that the city bus lines conveniently ran from CHF to Front Range Community College, Red Rocks Community College, and the universities in downtown Denver.

For the first time in her life, Abigail found her own confident legs. She enjoyed the encouragement, support for her family unit, and counseling to help her through the dark periods of remembering the crushing feelings of danger, rejection, and being unwanted. Counseling helped her with her poor self-esteem from years of teasing and bullying.

She appreciated learning how to make a budget and manage her finances. The single-parent support groups were helping her cope with loneliness and provided parenting wisdom so she would not repeat the same mistakes that many single parents make. She loved children and performed her volunteer hours helping other single mothers take care of their young children. Each week when she left the support group, she felt better about herself and her situation, and for the first time in her life, Abigail made friends.

The bus jolted to a stop, and Abigail was brought out of her thoughts. She had been thinking back on the times when she had not felt safe, or loved, or accepted, or even wanted. Abigail had felt alone and had lived more than half her life that way. Stepping off the bus with a smile, she felt happy and self-confident. She felt hope.

In a few short weeks, she would graduate with a bachelor's degree in social work, proving that a child from the foster care system could succeed with some assistance and guidance. Applying her lessons from CHF, her next goal was already in place, with the application submitted and accepted: Abigail could live a couple more years in this community, and she gratefully accepted intending to pursue her master's degree in social work. She set her third goal: purchase her first home.

Abigail knew the statistics of people like her. Foster youths of 15-18 years old have a .6% chance of being adopted. Foster youths in Colorado are more likely to be incarcerated than to graduate from high school on time. Foster kids that "age out" of the foster care system are at considerable risk for homelessness, joblessness, problems with physical health, behavioral health, and general well-being. There are always higher risks from a lack of access to health care and the general lack of social connections.[17]

Abigail was determined to choose her life's work that would help kids just like her, giving them hope by showing them that with goals, hard work, and some structured help, they can become

117

great leaders in their communities, have families, and be successful and happy. She didn't have to be defined by her birth family or by the foster system.

CHF taught her about faith in God's good plan for her and that anyone with determination and perseverance could succeed regardless of her past.

On November 29, 1990, United States President George H. W. Bush signed the Immigration Act of 1990. Part of this law was the Diversity Visa program, allowing 55,000* randomly selected individuals to come to the United States from countries that are not widely represented.[18]

Countries not allowed to participate in the Diversity Visa program are Bangladesh, Brazil, Canada, China, Colombia, Dominican Republic, El Salvador, Guatemala, Haiti, India, Jamaica, Mexico, Nigeria, Pakistan, Philippines, South Korea, United Kingdom, and Vietnam.[19]

The Diversity Visa (DV) program, which has come to be commonly referred to as "the lottery," is the responsibility of the State Department to select and notify the 55,000 winners randomly. Even if an individual wins the lottery, there is no guarantee he or she will obtain the United States Permanent Resident Card. There are many steps and personal expenditures to secure immigration to the United States.[20] The State Department chooses approximately 100,000 selectees to yield 55,000 visas because, historically, about half of the selectees do not complete the visa application process by the deadline.[21]

To enter, paper DV entry forms are obtained from the United States Embassy located in the immigrant's home country. The entry forms are handled entirely by mail, and only winners are notified. The entry form paper system moved to an online system in 2005, but winners were still notified by mail. Beginning in 2010, all applicants are able to verify their status online as to whether they are selected. Notification of winners by mail continued until 2011, but the entire process was moved exclusively online in 2012.[22]

Entering the Diversity Visa lottery involves completing a simple form, and there is no cost to enter. Entries are accepted annually from early October through early November. Only one entry per person during each registration period is allowed. Anyone having more than one entry is disqualified.[23]

To qualify, applicants selected by the lottery program must meet simple but strict eligibility requirements. The first requirement is that the applicant must have been born in the country they are entering from. The second requirement is that the applicant must have a 12-year equivalent education *or* at least two years of work experience in the previous five years before completing the application. If the applicant files under the second provision of the second requirement, at least two years of training or experience on the job is also required evidence.[24]

No more than 7% of the 55,000 randomly selected winners are allowed from any one country. All costs and fees after DV selection will vary. Several steps must be followed to prepare for submitting the Immigrant Visa and Alien Registration Application, including collecting and providing all legal documents, medical exams, and vaccinations. Then there is the interview process, Visa, Green Card, and U.S. Citizenship and Immigration Services (USCIS) fees, plus airline tickets, accommodation and living expenses at the destination. The entire process can take over two years, from entering the lottery to actually immigrating to a United States location.

***

As President George H. W. Bush was signing into law The Immigration Act of 1990, 8,000 miles away in the Democratic Republic of Congo, Kem and Dira Banze were getting married. Kem enjoyed his job at one of the largest and busiest airports in the Congo with his degree in Air Traffic Control. Dira was busy with her career using her BA in Accounting. Within a few years, they had two children and hoped for more.

The 1990s were fast becoming one of the Congo's darkest eras. Rebellion against presidential leadership led to riots, violence, and chaos. By 1994, ethnic strife and civil war were overrunning the Congo from neighboring Rwanda, where the Rwandan genocide had forced more than 1.2 million refugees across the Congolese border. The continued instability of leadership launched an armed coup against the government, whereby President Mobutu was overthrown after 32 years in power. This marked the First Congo War, and the Second Congo War began shortly after that, lasting until 2003.[25]

Kem and Dira knew they would be unable to raise a stable family in an unstable country under these dire circumstances, so they applied for a Diversity Visa. They obtained an entry form from the United States Embassy located in Kinshasa. Dira did the math. Approximately 3,900 numbers would be selected for the Congo. With a population of 41.58 million people, millions of people might be entering the lottery. The odds were low.

While waiting to hear if their number was drawn, the country's condition deteriorated. Good news eventually came when they received word that Kem had won the lottery to go to the United States. The immigration process was long and grueling, but both were determined to make a successful transition to living on American soil and making a fresh start. After the birth of their third child, they were finally given their immigration packets and told that it would be best to leave at once.

After entering the lottery, Kem researched the United States and learned that immigrants from a particular origin tended to live in areas where others from the same origin live.[26] Texas, Arizona, Kentucky, Colorado, and New York had the most significant numbers of Congolese immigrants.[27] Wanting the greatest support possible, he and Dira selected Colorado.

The airplane trip was more than 26 hours with two stops in Brussels and New York, and when they finally landed in Denver, they were greeted by a caseworker from the African Community Center (ACC).

Kem and Dira spoke few American phrases, but the ACC caseworker could speak their native language and helped them.

Having hurriedly left the Congo, they had only a few bags of necessities for them and their three children. Starting over includes extreme loss, the deep feeling of helplessness, fear of the unknown, and upheaval of a once familiar life.

They were provided with some helpful contacts but having spent the last of their money on visas, fees, documents, medical fees, and airline tickets, Kem knew that he would need to find work quickly or he would be homeless in a new country.

Kem and Dira quickly learned that there were significant differences between their educations obtained in the Congo and the education provided to those in the United States. Coupled with the language barrier, they were not going to be allowed to continue in their chosen professions.

Rumors soared that many highly educated immigrants, such as doctors and lawyers, were having to take jobs working as janitors. Before long, the rumors turned out not to be true. Proficient English was a necessity, and customs mattered. With all their job possibilities scattered to the wind, they had nowhere to plant themselves.

Someone suggested Colorado Homeless Families and even offered to speak on their behalf. Within a short time, their interpreters and sponsors helped the Banze family move into one of the CHF homes. They used the food, clothing, and furniture bank resources at CHF to help with their immediate basic needs.

It was not easy to adjust to this new country. The language barrier was the most challenging. Undeterred, Kem and Dira threw themselves into English as a Second Language courses (ESL) at CHF to improve their communication and writing skills.

Kem eventually found a job working at a local box company. It was not a high-paying job, nor was it on the public bus line, so Kem walked to and from work daily. Thankful for the opportunity and eager to embrace living in the United States, he made sure to never complain about walking in the snow—something he had never experienced—and always gave thanks for this new opportunity.

Sponsorship and donations helped the Banze family get on their feet. A CHF sponsor offered to pay their rent and utilities until they found work. Another family donated a used van to CHF, and Executive Director Connie Zimmerman gave it to Kem and Dira. They were making excellent use of all the educational resources at CHF, including attending support group meetings. As their language skills improved, they worked with their case manager to develop academic and professional goals.

Kem found he had a high aptitude for business and began pursuing his business degree. Dira found she was well-suited for the American healthcare industry and began pursuing a nursing degree. The Banze family was also blessed with a fourth child while pursuing their degrees.

In their immigration packet was "A Guide for New Immigrants" offered by the United States Citizen & Immigrant Services Office. It helped them better understand American culture and some of the intricacies of being an American citizen. One section genuinely caught their hearts: "As a permanent resident, you have many rights and freedoms. In return, you have some responsibilities. One important responsibility is to get involved in your community."[28] A community of people from the Democratic Republic of Congo and other nearby African countries expressed needs, and Kem and Dira were determined to offer help. They could find markets that sold the foods they were looking for and helped the other immigrants develop a broader sense of community.

Kem and Dira surpassed their volunteer work required by Colorado Homeless Families. They also learned of an organization called Habitat for Humanity. They discovered it was a nonprofit organization that brings people together to build homes, communities, and hope, and they were looking for volunteers. Kem and Dira knew they wanted to give back to the community that had accepted them. Within one year, each had volunteered more than 200 hours to the Habitat for Humanity organization.

As their life in America got better each day, and the riots, violence, and chaos of their life 8,000 miles away finally lay behind them, they received word from Habitat for Humanity that they were eligible to purchase a new home at 0% interest. Upon moving into their new home, they reflected on how alone they had felt during their first few months in the United States, yet they no longer felt helpless.

They sat down and wrote a goodbye letter to Colorado Homeless Families: "Moving from Africa and being brought here to live is like someone reborn. They have to learn to walk, to speak...We thank you so much to the CHF staff with all of our hearts. Your wisdom, willingness to help, and teaching us through the family support group meetings allowed us to learn more and understand differently. May God bless you."

Flashing lights blinded Priscilla Alvarez, and the shrill sirens stabbed her ears. She sat on the curb with an icepack on her arm, a bandage on her head, and a blanket around her shoulders.

Beyond thankful that her six-year-old son, Bryson, wasn't with her, she surveyed the damage to her old 1980s Honda Accord. The drivers of the two other cars involved in the collision seemed to be okay; the paramedics were looking after them just to be sure. As she picked glass shards out of her hair, she compared the wreckage; all three cars looked like they fared about the same, utterly totaled piles of metal.

The police officer had just left her alone after taking the information from her driver's license, registration, and insurance card. Her *expired* insurance card.

Even though the wreck was not her fault, she knew that she was in big trouble over not having current insurance coverage.

The department store where she worked had cut back on her hours, which meant *she* had to cut back on something. Cable television was first to go, then car insurance was the next cut. She realized that you could justify any wrong decision by talking yourself into something: "I've never had an accident. I'm a good driver. I will be extra careful when I drive. I'll reinstate it as soon as I possibly can." And the worst lie she told herself: "It will be okay." Barely a month later, on her way home after the mall closed, she found herself in this three-car accident.

One wrong decision, and she found herself in court being scolded, "If you don't carry car insurance, you could face penalties even if the accident wasn't your fault." She had broken the law. When her name was called, she stood on shaky legs, and with sweating palms, she crossed her fingers. Her only hope was that she would not go to jail. She *could not* go to jail. As it was, her restitution was more than $3,000, but it may as well have been $30,000. She didn't have it. Worse, her mode of transportation was totaled, and her driver's license was suspended until she paid the restitution. "So ordered," as the judge slammed his gavel.

How would she get to work?

Since the accident, she had been begging anyone and everyone for rides. She could not miss any work, or she would lose their apartment. She was even willing to take the bus, but the bus schedules did not start early enough to get Bryson to school and still allow her to get to work on time to open her department. She could not ask her supervisor to change her schedule for fear of him cutting her hours even more. No, somehow, she could make this work. "It will be okay," she thought.

One of the neighbors in the apartment complex watched Bryson on the nights she had to close and thankfully didn't charge her. She was a former teacher, loved kids, and didn't even mind helping him with homework.

Priscilla picked him up, and as they walked across the building complex to their apartment, Bryson asked, "Are we poor?" Someone had said something at the neighbor's house since they didn't have a car and had to ask for rides, take the bus, or walk everywhere.

Her heart hurt when he asked, but she said, "No, honey, we're not poor. Mommy just has some things to figure out."

That night after she put Bryson to bed, she sat on the sofa and stared out the window at a pine tree. The thought that resonated deep within her was, *"It will NOT be okay. Just give up."* She finally admitted to herself that she was overwhelmed with problems. She had no idea how to pay the court-ordered restitution, and even if she didn't, they would begin to garnish her wages. She needed her driver's license returned, and she needed to buy another car and insurance. It was impossible.

Priscilla bummed rides for the next month, and that is exactly how she felt: like a bum. Trying to juggle rides on different days, or a ride wouldn't show up, and she would have to be at the mercy of the bus schedules, she was late for work on several occasions.

Her supervisor had warned her the first two times. On the third time, she was fired. Her rent was paid through to the end of the month, but then they had to vacate.

Bryson's words echoed in her ears: "Are we poor?" The answer now was an undeniable "yes."

Out of desperation, Priscilla contacted her ex-husband's parents and asked for help. They loved Bryson, and she was convinced they would not want to see him homeless. The divorce had been bitter, and they took their son's side.

Some compassion must have convinced them to allow her and Bryson to live in an empty house that they were trying to sell. That was the best they could do, but they let her know that she and Bryson would need to move when the house sold. This arrangement gave her a little reprieve but the uncertainty she felt was just the tongue of the hounding fear nipping at her heels.

Priscilla found another job near her in-law's empty home for sale. Still unable to afford a car, she borrowed a bicycle from a friend. Riding the bike helped get Bryson to the bus stop, and then it was just a quick ride to her new job at a bakery. Her supervisor allowed her to work hours that enabled her to get off work in time to pick up Bryson from the bus stop after school, and she could get home before it got dark. Each day she returned home, she kept her fingers crossed that as she rounded the corner, she would not see the word "sold" on the real estate sign.

Knowing this was a short-term solution, and it would be gone in just a matter of time, she began to search for some more significant help. No longer feeling "all will be okay," Priscilla began to ask people from their church if they knew of any assistance programs. One couple told her about Emergency Family Assistance available through the City of Denver that would help them find a place to live after an eviction, help with the first month's rent and deposit, and help with some utilities.

Priscilla and Bryson arrived home that afternoon from church to find the dreaded "sold" sign, and the following week, with the

Emergency Financial Assistance Program, they moved into a tiny one-bedroom apartment.

Continuing to seek out church members for ideas, she found that most were encouraging, but they all offered her the same advice: search for a better-paying job. Go to school and get some advanced training or broader education. People also provided her with some ideas for resources to sign up for additional aid, food stamps, and help with medical benefits. Nothing seemed to be a permanent solution, and that "temporary" feeling continued to dog her courage.

One Sunday, someone pointed out a woman that she should talk to. Priscilla knocked on the lady's car window, and the woman informed her about an organization called Colorado Homeless Families. The woman gave Priscilla a CHF business card, encouraged her to apply, and offered her and Bryson a ride home.

This program sounded more like what Priscilla was looking for. It seemed to offer a true source of help to get her from where she was to where she wanted to be. Within a month, her church donated a nice, used car to her. She decided to ask the court for mercy and return her driver's license. She explained how she needed to use her car to find a better-paying job. She explained her new opportunity to begin furthering her education so she could begin to make restitution payments. The judge granted her request, but with harsh penalties if she did not start to make good on the restitution. How could she manage a job, coursework, and restitution payments?

Within a few weeks, Priscilla and Bryson were accepted into Colorado Homeless Families. Priscilla attended the educational seminars and the support groups where she found many other families experiencing similar life-threatening situations and worse. One of the best things she did was to use the counseling services to meet with a therapist who helped her work through many unresolved issues. She also learned important life skills that helped her better cope when she became overwhelmed with problems. She realized that "it will be okay" was a mechanism of helplessness and denial—a refusal to accept reality that there was no better plan in place.

Priscilla found the CHF food bank was a terrific bonus when she experienced a gap in the food stamp program she was on.

The case manager was good at helping her think outside the box for problem resolutions. He also encouraged her to push herself, offering helpful advice, and helping her hold herself accountable for her bad decisions.

She found a better-paying job with flexible hours that allowed her to attend art school to pursue a long-dormant passion. Her talent was quickly put to use when she was hired as a work-study intern. She also accepted freelance side jobs that kept her busy and earned her extra income to pay for the court-ordered restitution.

Priscilla and Bryson graduated from the Colorado Homeless Families program. The community's financial and emotional support helped her get out from under the hounding impermanence of her life and gave her confidence to pursue new life goals and trust in her new decision-making skills.

As she and Bryson left CHF for their own home, Priscilla felt excited and scared. Although she felt humbled by the circumstances of her life, she was able to finally understand that "it will be okay" only when you ask, seek, and knock for help.

Jemila Jackson was finally out of prison. Her boyfriend, Antoine, left her holding his drugs and ran off. She served the four-year incarceration instead of him. Loser. She never wanted to see him again, and last she knew, homey had hooked up with at least two other women since she went to prison. She was done with that playa, good riddance.

Jemila wasn't that good in school; they thought it was a learning disorder like dyslexia or something. So, when she didn't graduate, she knew higher education was not in her future. Pregnant with Maya at 19 years old, that baby daddy was quick to get out. Along came Antoine, fine and kickin', and promised to take forever care of her and Maya. Then she saw the blue and red flashing lights and knew it was over. A six-foot by eight-foot cell was opening its door to her future.

Mimmie, Jemila's grandmother, took in little Maya, even though she didn't want to. "I raised my babies already," she said. "It's your turn to raise your own." After crying and pleading, Mimmie took Maya with the understanding that she was never to bring her baby to visit her in prison. Jemila never wanted Maya to see her that way.

As with the rest of her remaining family, Jemila grew up in the Five Points neighborhood of northeast Denver. One of the city's highest crime areas, it was the original seat of the African American community. Many families that settled there stayed there, but there wasn't anyone good left for her to depend on or help her through this.

The prison was a wake-up call for Jemila. One of the teachers was also a literacy specialist and took a particular interest in helping her with her reading problem. After many tests, the teacher discovered it was not dyslexia but a minor SRCD— Specific Reading Comprehension Difficulty. That meant she had poor reading comprehension but had good word-reading skills. With a new curriculum designed to improve Jemila's comprehension, she began reading at the college level after only two years. Once she earned her GED, she began taking college courses. Prison was not going to be a waste of time. Before her release, she had completed two years of general electives.

Wanting to make a better life for herself, Jemila also took as many life skills courses as possible. These courses were non-credit but helped prisoners in many areas such as anger management, overcoming criminal thinking, setting and achieving goals, family responsibilities, healthy relationships, and several substance abuse programs.

Upon release from prison, however, she discovered implementing these life skills wasn't as easy as she thought. Before release, there was an out-processing class available to take. It was optional, but Jemila took it anyway and found that newly released prisoners faced four major challenges: not knowing where to begin, family strain, finding employment, and mental health issues.[29] At the time, it was not yet understood that the social support component was key. One could not just go back into the same environment with the same connections and expect to change their habits without strong outside support.

Mimmie, ever the tough love advocate, refused to allow Jemila to live with her after prison. Maybe there was also some interest in protecting herself from unproven reforms from her granddaughter's criminal friends and activities.

Checking in with her probation officer, Jemila explained she couldn't find a place to live.

With wintry weather approaching, Jemila took her daughter and checked into The Denver Rescue Mission. They offered a transitional program, but Jemila found this was not the best long-term solution. She didn't feel the support she truly desired. Therefore, she found herself being tempted at times to fall back into the life she was working so hard to get free of. Wanting something different with more support, she approached the counselor at The Denver Rescue Mission who suggested she apply to Colorado Homeless Families.

It took several months—and much convincing—but she was finally approved. Her application had been rejected several times, as Colorado Homeless Families did not take applicants who had been incarcerated at any level. Jemila continued to call CHF, provide character references, and even wrote letters about her willingness to improve her life, documenting the many changes she made and the goals she had accomplished while she was still in prison. Now, she wanted the opportunity to continue to improve her life so her daughter would never have to experience the life Jemila had. Her last letter was heartfelt and truthful, and she promised that she intended to keep it if she was just given one chance.

Chance was not something that Colorado Homeless Families messed with. However, opportunities were offered on a regular basis.

Finally, Jemila gained a probational placement with Colorado Homeless Families.

Executive Director Connie Zimmerman made it a point to meet all the applicants to Colorado Homeless Families. She was prayerful. She was mindful of what each individual might need. Several families came to CHF seemingly hesitant to want a new life, or perhaps, they just didn't know where to begin. After living one way your entire life, Connie knew that one answer was to give them time to re-program their mind to a new way of living. She didn't realize how far Jemila had come or how hard she'd worked already. All Connie could see was how far she had to go in her thinking and behavior.

"Lord, how do I help re-program someone's mind?" she asked.

Always faithful, He answered, *"It is important to find something good in each person and tell them about it."* That is exactly where Connie began with Jemila.

"I like the way you are so kind to your child," she said, and, "I like the way you fix your hair." These compliments initiated the re-programming process, providing positive feedback to the things Jemila was doing well. Connie also found other areas to provide positive feedback, "Hey, I hear you do this," or "I hear you can do that, that's terrific!" Before long, Connie found several good things to say to Jemila and she employed this practice with each adult every day.

The genuineness of these words from Connie helped remove Jemila's defensiveness and helped improve her self-esteem.

Another essential part of living at CHF was that it was a community built on supporting one another and offering hope— and help—to every resident. Connie found it beneficial to place new families next to the more successful, mature families so they could start to see the support and healthy growth in process. Then Connie could provide loving guidance with "See, Jane next door is doing great, and her kids are safe and secure," or "Mary on the other side of you is hopeful and working towards her goals with school, and she is always kind and willing to help others." If Connie complimented the neighbors to Jemila, then maybe she was complimenting Jemila to the neighbors.

These compliments helped the community respect one another and feel safe in each other's company.

Connie learned that when she verbally and physically offered support, it was easier and kinder to correct a family's error. There were times when Connie would softly tell a family, "I notice there is a little trash by your front door, can you maybe just tidy that up a bit, please?" Or she would gently say, "I know you are not this way normally, so let's continue to keep the trash cleaned up because the squirrels or animals can get into it and make a mess for everyone."

Some CHF families came from backgrounds where kindness, support, and hope were not offered and were not seen as an important means of communication. When she asked of God, the

Lord led Connie to understand that showing kindness in everything and allowing her residents to see what is good and better for themselves, and for their community, further helped them see outside their neediness and pride.

Once they began to see outside themselves, their thinking was re-programmed, and they began to understand how to live differently.

A particular challenge was the residents' commitment to fulfilling CHF educational classes. After speaking to several of the families and telling them, "It's really important you arrive on time to your education classes. We know you have to ride the bus and feed your children, but if you could try to get here a little earlier, that would be wonderful because then you wouldn't miss some important teaching, and the interruption wouldn't bother the others," there was improvement in punctuality.

Connie would even tell them her own difficulties in being late, understanding that it's a hard thing to learn to be on time. She confided that she decided to make it a priority to honor her commitments and that it became a matter of honor for her. Connie knew that many people were never taught to arrive on time, be respectful of others, or that there was such a thing as honoring your commitments.

It wasn't long before Jemila knew that Colorado Homeless Families was indeed the perfect place for her. She was receiving a genuine support she had never known, and she felt confident when someone complimented her, especially when she did something right. She found that her actions meant more to her than the way she had lived in the past.

Gaining progress in areas that would affect the trajectory of her entire life and the legacy that she wanted to leave for Maya motivated her. She found gainful employment, she excelled in her college courses, and she continued to put her new life skills into practice. Those life skills were ones she was proud to pass on to her daughter.

Daphne tore off the ticket from the take-a-number dispenser and looked down at it in her hand. 190. She looked around the enormous room with the plastic chairs and sighed. *"I'm going to be here all day."*

She currently worked part-time, and her income was barely enough to feed herself and Wyatt, her seven-year-old son. Looking around, she found a seat in the back row and settled into the plastic chair at the unemployment office. Watching the people behind the row of plexiglass windows, she reached for the cross necklace that hung around her neck. She found herself frequently reaching for that necklace the last several months and saying prayers to heaven for *"help."*

This place was depressing. The chairs were depressing. The chipped linoleum floor was depressing, as were the dingy walls and dirty windows.

Worry and depression defined her life, and Daphne was succumbing to the feelings of hopelessness. *"I will never amount to anything"* is what she thought. With Christmas a month behind, she had only purchased Wyatt one used toy from the local Goodwill. Watching him unwrap it Christmas morning made her feel worthless remembering paying the $1.30 to the cashier. Wyatt had asked for three things, of which she could not afford any. Earning $4.75 per hour, her options—and money—were quickly dwindling; a co-worker had graciously let them stay on her sleeper sofa, with the agreement they would need to be gone by February.

The man two chairs away got up and made his way to the long row of windows. He had left a newspaper section on the chair, and Daphne grabbed it hoping to pass the time while she waited for her number to be called. The article at the bottom of the page caught her attention:

"We don't take people who are looking for a free ride," Colorado Homeless Families' Executive Director Connie Zimmerman was quoted. "We look for people who have hopes and dreams and want to get back on their own two feet." Daphne continued to read about this program that provided housing and guidance for those who were homeless for the first time or those who could not keep up with housing costs. She thought as she put the newspaper down, *"they would never take anybody like me."*

The economy had affected both her and her extended family. So, when her sister Phoebe had suggested they move in together and share expenses, Daphne jumped at the opportunity. Daphne also liked that Wyatt would have a male role model in Phoebe's husband. However, within a short time, Phoebe faced a layoff from her job, and Daphne's own blue-collar job reduced her hours to part-time. Phoebe's husband began to drink more, became increasingly resentful, and showed an explosive temper.

After one verbal attack that left her reeling, vulnerable, and threatened, Daphne left with a duffle bag and her son the following morning vowing never to return, which is how she ultimately arrived on her co-worker's sleeper sofa.

Daphne sheepishly looked around the unemployment office and slipped the newspaper article into her purse anyway. Three hours later, her number 190 was finally called. It took only 10 minutes for the unemployment clerk to explain that there was nothing they could do for her.

Digging for quarters in the glove compartment, Daphne stopped to put $2.75 worth of gas in her car, then drove to her co-worker's apartment to call Colorado Homeless Families.

A month later, Daphne and Wyatt moved into the townhome located in Arvada at Colorado Homeless Families. She was assigned a case manager and a counselor and explained the requirements to stay.

One of the more challenging assignments for Daphne was setting career and educational goals. She had come from a long line of relatives who worked blue-collar jobs—and were happy doing so—always working to support their families. No one in her family had furthered their education by attending college or even a trade school, and Daphne had never considered that for her future. Bucking family traditions in ways of custom and thinking had never entered her imagination.

"I will be just like my family and work blue-collar jobs my entire life," is what Daphne did think. Her case manager recommended she attend a free career-counseling seminar held at the local community college. The information provided at the seminar caused her some alarm to learn what she was facing if she didn't change her family custom.

The biggest economic problem faced by blue-collar workers is that eventually, their earnings will peak. At the same time, expenses continue to rise, with the two biggest contributors being inflation and increasing family responsibilities. The economic problems are compounded by lack of status, a feeling of being forgotten among the workforce, which would push workers from the middle class downward to the lower middle class and eventually into the poor and poverty class. If she were asked to repeat what she had heard, she might not have been able to. These thoughts were foreign to her.

Daphne also learned that as the head of a household in a blue-collar job, she should expect to encounter more financial challenges when Wyatt reached his teen years. This is the time when family budgets are most stressed because teenage costs are at their peak. Her blue-collar job earnings would eventually reach a plateau. These plateaus were caused by either not qualifying for a promotion, or her expenses would rise faster than her budget allowed.

She also learned about how inflation intensifies blue-collar job earnings, while another problem would quickly follow: displacement rates were climbing for blue-collar workers. Displacement from job? Sadly, Daphne was faced with the reality that to keep financially afloat in the blue-collar world of work-a-day jobs, she would likely be one of the 6% of blue-collar workers who would need to hold down multiple jobs to meet rising financial obligations even as her body wore out.[30] Family images of these truths wafted through her mind. Why had she never realized the hopelessness of the situation?

Prepared with these sobering facts, she began to understand that she had programmed herself by her family customs. Never thinking she could do better, live better, *be* better than where and how she lived.

This new and illuminating education had something attached to it: hope. Daphne subtly became aware that her thoughts defined her life.

Newly challenged and determined, she thought, "I *will* make a better life for myself and Wyatt, even if my family doesn't get it." With that decision, Daphne underwent career aptitude testing and chose a course for her educational goals. With this new thought, life came boosted confidence, and with confidence came a new set of friends and support system at CHF.

One of Daphne's favorite things was the "giving back" program. She enjoyed her community volunteer service because she helped with children's educational activities, and she routinely contributed more than the required five hours of service. Her son Wyatt made new friends, and she noticed him becoming more outgoing and friendly with his peers and teachers. It was never too early to introduce good and healthy thoughts to a child.

While dressing for her counseling session and case management meeting, Daphne reached for the cross necklace hanging outside of her sweater and said her prayers to heaven, *"Thank you, Lord. With all this new help, I am an overcomer."*

1996

GROWING IN GRACE

Let The Wise Hear

There is a saying that, "a stable Christian is a growing Christian." Connie Zimmerman knew that to help as many homeless as possible, it would come not from planting two feet and holding fast, but from putting one foot in front of the other and moving forward, one step of faith at a time, trusting God and growing in His grace. Connie discovered that helping 30 families gave her the heart to help even more.

Looking out of her office window one day in 1995, she saw a vacant area adjacent to the 10 RG1 townhomes purchased from Resolution Trust Corporation. This vacant area was just a field of weeds, which Colorado Homeless Families would voluntarily cut down. Connie knew that having "homeless" people in a neighborhood may be upsetting for neighbors, so CHF maintained their own property and those of adjacent properties so neighbors would not get upset about having homeless people in their community.

After buying the 10 RTC properties, Connie decided to improve the property to make it as crisp, clean, and beautiful as possible. Knowing there may be resentment from neighbors, the CHF grounds were beautified with flowers and landscaping and were kept well-maintained. CHF hired someone to clean up everything and remove any junk or debris from the lot. This would also give the CHF residents a place to volunteer to help maintain the property.

As Connie stared at the vacant property that CHF had been tending, the Lord put the thought into Connie's mind to "*purchase that property*." She had no idea who owned it and had never seen or spoken to the owner. After much research, she found it was foreclosed and had a contact name. It was listed for $75,000, and further research unearthed that it had been already zoned for the same townhomes similar to RG1, her current set of townhomes. The property was also shown to have the water and sewer taps already.

The CHF RG1 townhomes were conveniently located near to the main thoroughfare as well as a central bus line. Connie knew from previous grant research, the Colorado Highway Department showed 65,000 cars traveled the Wadsworth Bypass each day and nearby railroad tracks would deter any potential homeowner. She also knew that the area looked blighted from the street view making the property value less than the asking price.

Connie sought out the lien holder and quickly offered $25,000. They countered her offer with $30,000, but Connie countered again with $27,000. This offer was accepted, and the process of purchase began. Faced with the financing dilemma, Connie knew from her earlier experiences that when the Lord tells you to do something, He has already gone before you to pave the way.

Having previously worked with the Arthur H. And Helen K. Johnson Foundation on the RTC purchase, Connie called to inquire about the possibility of a grant proposal for $27,000. The Johnson Foundation informed her that they would approve the grant to buy the property.

Sometimes the Lord moves fast; other times, He moves slowly with one single step at a time, with room to breathe in between and to wait for further instruction. Psalm 27:14 says, "*Wait for the Lord; be strong, and let your heart take courage and wait for the Lord.*" Not knowing how to progress with the newly purchased land, Connie waited for what God would send next.

Because many HUD homes that Colorado Homeless Families leased were located in Jefferson County, and their county Grants & Acquisitions Administrator was familiar with the work of CHF, the administrator contacted Connie about new Community Development Block Grants (CDBG) available from the federal government. There was $500,000 in grant money available for nonprofits, and RB Ranch dba Colorado Homeless Families was on the list as a potential grant recipient because of their help with transitional homeless housing.

The administrator explained to Connie that *"The Community Development Block Grant (CDBG) Program provides annual grants on a formula basis to states, cities, and counties to develop viable urban communities by providing decent housing and a suitable living environment, and by expanding economic opportunities, principally for low- and moderate-income persons. The program is authorized under Title 1 of the Housing and Community Development Act of 1974, Public Law 93-383, as amended 42 U.S.C. 5301 et seq. Part of The Department of Local Affairs enacted in 1974 by President Gerald Ford."*[31]

Connie was thrilled. She knew where to begin her research. Based on the space and the current zoning, the exterior of the 12 townhome units could not be modified. Yet based on the blueprints an additional 4,500 square foot resource center could be designed within three additional townhomes. Connie asked for the interior space to be dedicated to needed offices, a food bank, a case management office, counseling group support rooms and an educational center.

Since the City of Arvada had already approved the exterior of the buildings, a resource center to meet the needs of the community were included within the zoning requirements as long as the buildings' exterior remained the same. Several estimates reflected the cost of approximately $1,000,000 to build the 12 townhomes on the newly acquired property.

Asking God for wisdom, Connie continued to pursue what she believed He had placed in her path. The Colorado State Division of Housing heard about the Colorado Homeless Families program and requested a visit. Connie took the representative on a tour of both the townhomes bought from RTC and the HUD homes spread over two counties. The tour was several hours, and the representative even requested to meet some of the families living in the CHF program.

During the tour, Connie told the representative that Colorado Homeless Families had just received $200,000 from the Jefferson County CDBG Program, but more funding was needed to build on the newly acquired property. From Connie's office, he contacted the Colorado Coalition for the Homeless President and CEO. The Colorado State Division of Housing had just granted Colorado Coalition for the Homeless $5,000,000 for a project called the Lowry Project Fund to build integrated housing for homeless and low-income families located at the former Lowry Air Force Base in Denver. The representative from the Colorado State Division of Housing requested Colorado Coalition for the Homeless to direct $300,000 of their grant money to Colorado Homeless Families.

The Colorado State Division of Housing also authorized a Colorado Housing and Finance Authority (CHFA) loan for the balance at a discounted rate of 4% for the remaining $500,000. The City of Arvada also provided a grant of $50,000 towards building this new project.

Connie saw miracle after miracle as she remained obedient to God. She pursued everything prayerfully, asked for wisdom, and found favor at every turn as God sent people to help and guide the project.

While Denver was seeing the homeless population grow 85%, groundbreaking for RG2 townhomes took place in May 1996. Construction moved forward smoothly and under budget, with the first family moving in 1997.

Set an Example In Conduct

With 22 units in the Colorado Homeless Families campus and at least 20 HUD homes, Connie found standardizing program guidelines was becoming necessary. Additionally, with formerly homeless, and non-nationals, and immigrants living in the complex, many families needed to be taught how to care for and properly utilize their homes. Many non-nationals and immigrants did not know how to use kitchen appliances, toilets, or bathtubs. A walk-through was performed with each family, and each family was also required to sign the Home Maintenance Orientation contract. Each point was thoroughly explained, and all families were expected to perform to standards:

- Vacuum all carpets and mop all non-carpeted floors once per week.
- Clean all toilets, bathtubs, and sinks once per week.
- Take out kitchen trash daily to discourage bugs.
- Empty all wastebaskets when full, at least once per week.
- Change bed sheets once per week.
- Make beds daily, and children must be taught to make their own beds.
- If you are in a HUD home, the lawn must be mowed weekly.
- Shovel the sidewalk after each snowfall.
- Turn heat down to 68 degrees at night, set thermostat to 69-72 degrees during the day, and turn off all lights when not in use.
- Do not allow children to eat or drink outside of the eating area to keep the carpeting sanitary and free from food stains.
- Porches, patios, and balconies are to be kept neat and clean at all times. No clothing, rugs, or other items to be hung, and no clotheslines are permitted.
- Patios are not to be used for storage, and grills, smokers, or hibachis cannot be used on the patio.
- Use of fireplaces is prohibited for safety reasons.
- Noise levels must be kept to a minimum at all hours.
- Cable television is not allowed.

Build Each Other Up

Progress reports were also required from all CHF families every month until documentation showed a habitual responsibility with home maintenance and cleanliness. Then, inspections were done twice per year. Progress reports were used to evaluate if residents were receiving the maximum benefit of the program and to determine if they were following all CHF policies and procedures. Evaluation criteria included:

- Volunteer hours in accordance with capabilities
- Rent paid on time or no later than the 10th of the month
- Mandatory attendance at support group meetings and educational seminars
- Attendance at ESL classes (if required)
- Case management meetings
- Counseling sessions, if needed
- Evidence of initiative to achieve set goals
- Compliance with policies, procedures, rules, and regulations in a positive manner
- Maintaining residence cleanliness
- Responsibility in voicing grievances through the proper process

Encouraging with Counsel

Overseer, a noble task:

When families were first placed with the Colorado Homeless Families program in outlying HUD homes, Executive Director Connie Zimmerman found these families needed very little assistance. Necessities might include some clothing or a few furnishings or household goods. Sometimes a small food donation at the end of the month helped stretch the food budget.

These families, classified as the new poor, knew how to find employment, budget, manage money, and find assistance in needed areas. They were already working hard and determined to get back on their feet as quickly as possible before being accepted into the Colorado Homeless Families program. Most had educations and long work histories in specific areas or industries, and they knew how to set goals and work to achieve those goals. Very little help from CHF was required. Connie found these families had simply been victims of layoffs, the economy's downturn, the collapse of an industry, or experienced a one-time, isolated hardship such as sickness, an accident, or death.

After the purchase of the RTC properties and expanding the desire to help the homeless, Connie found that she was being introduced to more families who could not find gainful employment due to a variety of reasons. Classified as the working poor, their challenges included lack of education and job training, poor money management, and the inability to set goals. There were working poor families who simply didn't know how to make the right choices for pursuing a better life. Sometimes the reasons were difficult to assess, but she knew that whatever the reason, they required more encouragement, greater instruction, and closer guidance. Some family members needed counseling and peer support to overcome the suffering of being homeless or to overcome the trauma of emotional trials.

Oversight by an experienced case manager was critical, especially in identifying specific or complex needs. Turning to those she trusted most and who she knew had the same caring characteristics, she selected her first case manager: Ken Armstrong, her brother. Ken had been volunteering his skills in other areas of RB Ranch, but Connie hired Ken part-time. With his career as a firefighter, his efforts to build an orphanage in Cambodia and his desire to help abandoned children, Connie knew he possessed the attributes she needed to help her begin laying the foundation for case management.

Connie and Ken worked to develop case management requirements and methodology. She relied heavily on Ken's wisdom and was quickly learning that some residents might be unsuccessful in attaining self-sufficiency despite the support and stabilizing factors Colorado Homeless Families offered.

Connie needed case managers for the residents to succeed, and she continued asking the Lord for wisdom to hire the right case managers and to allow them to be God's own workmanship for those who were willing and able to build new lives.

Become all things to all men:

Identifying the role of a case manager was sometimes fluid, as there were different requirements for different families, different personalities, and different levels of needs.

Connie began to slowly add case managers with different skill sets in order to better assist the wide range of resident needs. The case manager would be the individual who worked the closest with families, and it was essential to find the most suitable match to oversee all aspects of the family's life while in transition.

Continuing growth had Colorado Homeless Families adding both full-time and part-time case managers to work with the growing number of families who wanted to change their lives through focus and discipline and having a vision for their future.

The goal was for the family to become self-sufficient in 18 to 24 months, depending on the family's specific educational requirements or health needs. Residents were also required to develop a stable home environment for themselves and their families while at CHF.

CHF used intensive case management to help families establish short and long-term goals and set guidelines that would display initiative to improve both financial and social situations. Each case manager encouraged residents and held them accountable to their established goals while meeting established benchmarks.

Discerning whether a family needed counseling was of utmost concern, as many homeless lives were driven by tragedies in life that would need to be addressed before a person could begin the walk toward self-sufficiency. After that determination, case managers would help the family develop employment strategies, obtain marketable skills, and help residents assess their education requirements for their desired employment goals. Case managers provided guidance to select and enroll in the appropriate trade school, college, or university. Case managers also held regular accountability meetings with all CHF families.

Two are better than one; they have a good reward for their labor:
A system of better accountability, counseling, and task management was evolving with the formation of a new team within CHF. The Resident Service Team (RST) consisted of all case managers, all counselors, and Connie herself. The RST met weekly with collaborative roundtable discussions of each case so all personnel involved in resident management could create the best personalized program as possible. Case managers were able to share ideas and solutions with each other, offer guidance and support in areas of expertise, and counselors could offer insights for how to handle more complex or difficult situations or determine if counseling would be beneficial. These case-by-case review roundtable discussions also helped target needs that may have gone unnoticed or unaddressed, helped track progress, and create an environment for communication, teamwork, and better caseload management.

Connie found that the synergy of the Resident Service Team bringing in a higher level of support to those who needed it most in the community, streamlined the entire case management process.

Work for them as you would for the Lord:
Case managers worked with a wide range of people from all walks of life and in different life stages. As Colorado Homeless Families allotted 35% of their housing for immigrants, there were always refugees from different countries and cultures, as well as single parents, women with children trying to escape bad relationships and families who had lost jobs and livelihoods. Great case managers had their own life experiences, professional training,

and experience working with people in the many capacities required to help overcome adversity.

Connie looked to case managers to be supportive yet firm with the residents. They also needed to be good listeners, non-judgmental, empathetic, and have the ability to work with the family to develop a plan to move them forward within two years.

Residents in the CHF program were assigned the case manager who best fit their specific needs. An arduous task, case managers learned to be part counselor, mother, father, advisor, priest, cheerleader, supervisor, guide, inspector, and advocate.

Run and not grow weary:
Case managers found the most significant challenges were those residents who were unwilling to change their behavior or did not want to make proper choices to improve their lives. The second biggest challenge for case managers was understanding and communicating with families from unfamiliar cultures and diverse backgrounds.

Differing cultures or unwillingness to improve sometimes required difficult conversations, as did those who continually acted in non-compliance with the program's rules.

Unauthorized overnight guests, misuse of facilities, failure to meet goals, accountability issues, and even lack of cleanliness of the CHF home were all necessary conversations faced by case managers. If mishandled, residents would begin to distrust their case manager and would no longer feel supported or comfortable working with the case manager towards their goals.

For we are co-workers in God's service:
The job of the CHF case manager was to ultimately guide the family toward self-sufficiency. Case managers found it an honor to walk alongside these families as they worked to achieve their goals, and every family allowed to enter the program had the potential to move forward and create the life they desired.

The process took time but also required the individuals to work hard, take advantage of the educational and support group meetings, schedule weekly accountability meetings with their case manager, perform their community volunteer service, and attend counseling when required.

Those who did what was needed were the people that successfully left the program and became self-sufficient.

Some families could not thrive in the Colorado Homeless Families program. Some of those were due to mental health issues such as depression, bipolar, PTSD, or social anxieties. Others were not ready to accept assistance or live under the rules and guidelines of the CHF program. Many clients didn't give the program enough time to work and quickly fell back into old habits. Some clients had trust issues and refused to allow others in the CHF community to assist them, which hindered support. And there were others who didn't have the perseverance to strive for a better life, even with all the assistance available through the program.

CHF always celebrated families who graduated from the program, who became self-sufficient, and those who continued to work towards their goals.

There were many families whom the case managers considered success stories even if they left for various reasons before graduating the program. By 2016, 503 residents were successfully housed under the program. 420 families became self-sufficient, and many left early for stable new job opportunities, to get married, or to start their own business. With the transitional support from homelessness to self-sufficiency at CHF, 161 families purchased their own home. 109 individuals graduated from universities, colleges, and trade schools. Case managers became many things to many residents, but through continuous encouragement plus oversight by the Resident Service Team, CHF enjoyed a very high success rate of helping families enjoy victory over homelessness.

Jaclyn Andrews stood at the kitchen sink washing dishes. She saw the headlights bob up and down on the fence in the backyard and knew that Peter was home. She was looking at the clock on the microwave: 8:40 pm. She cringed inside, knowing that he was drunk—again. It wasn't long before she heard cursing and slurred yelling in the garage, and then the door to the kitchen slammed open. There he stood with a black eye, split lip, torn shirt, and the unmistakable smell of alcohol. "Bar fight," thought Jaclyn, "and now he'll take it out on us." One hand fisted at his side; in the other hand, he held — *a gas can*! And her stomach clenched.

Peter was one of "those" guys. Quick-witted, funny, and charming. And beautiful. She met him 20 years ago at the local sports pub. She was with her friends watching the Denver Broncos on Monday Night Football, and he was with his friends doing the same. He sent a round of drinks over, and soon the two parties were joined at one table celebrating the win and the fact that it was…Monday night. As Jaclyn was scraping the snow from her car windows, Peter chivalrously insisted on helping her while she sat in the car with her friends and warmed up. She left the bar, having given him her telephone number, and she knew that her life would be changed forever.

Peter worked hard; and told her that he played hard too. Working for a construction company kept him busy, and he put in long hours. So, when he used the excuse, "I need to unwind a little after a hard day," Jaclyn tried to understand. He was always charming and quick to apologize, he would shower her with a bouquet, little gifts, special notes, or surprise weekend getaways. He would do the same for their two children over the years with surprise gifts, special outings, and small treats. These would always come on the heels of his noisy late nights, drunken outbursts, or some extended rant that he would make them all sit and listen to.

Things had gone from bad to worse last week when their son walked away from a drunken scolding and slammed his bedroom door. Jaclyn tried to run interference, as usual, but Peter grabbed the tools, and soon their son's bedroom door was tossed out into the backyard and set on fire. As was their daughter's door, "just for good measure," Peter yelled. She knew that Peter was struggling with severe depression after losing his job last month, and there wasn't anyone hiring in the construction industry right now. Her part-time job didn't pay the bills other than to buy groceries, so it wasn't long before their home of 15 years went into foreclosure. They had received the notice two days ago.

The gasoline fumes hit her nostrils before the liquid covered her skin. "*Oh my God!*" she shouted as she saw Peter flinging gasoline on the floor and cabinets of their kitchen. "*RUUUUN, kids!*"

Peter flung the gasoline towards their children. The kids were sitting at the kitchen table doing their homework. "*RUUUUN, NOW! GET OUT OF HERE!*" she screamed. The gasoline made the floor slick, and the fumes were thick and sickening.

With eyes watering, mouth sputtering, and heaving coughs, Jaclyn raced after her shrieking children and flew out the front door behind them, running so fast she tripped with such a violent force, it knocked her down the steps and splayed her body on the front lawn. She could hear Peter yelling in the house, and she watched his silhouette continue to hurl gasoline on the walls and curtains of their living room.

Crying and shaking, Jaclyn hurried her sobbing children over to the hose and spigot, where frantically, she tried to rinse off the gasoline that he had furiously flung on them.

Through the sickening fumes, she began to see neighbors coming to their doors, and through blurry eyes, she saw someone running toward her from the street with something in his hand.

She grabbed the blanket from the stranger and quickly threw it over her children. Suddenly, a blanket was over her, and several strong hands and arms grabbed them and ushered them out into the street.

In minutes, sirens filled her ears, and blue and red strobes blinded her fume-filled, watering eyes. Voices kept asking her questions that she had no voice to answer back.

Coughing and gagging, she could only cling to her children as they shook violently. "They're in shock, ma'am. You're in shock." The hands of paramedics worked quickly to remove much of their clothing and to wash their skin and flush their eyes. Jaclyn barely remembered being shoved into the ambulance and transported to the emergency room with her children.

The next day, a long line of suits and badges traipsed through their hospital room: doctors, law enforcement, counselors, and social services all had questions and reports to file.

The police officers who responded to the neighbor's 9-1-1 calls could not find Peter in the home. Later, he was found to have checked himself into a local mental health care facility and was currently under arrest. Since he acted with intent to set fire to their home, including his family, he remained under careful watch.

Doctors and nurses continued to care for the severe burns and blistering on Jaclyn's body from the gasoline. She and her children's bodies were entirely washed and tended, and thankfully, the children did not have any lingering physical effects from the gasoline.

Jaclyn had taken the brunt of it, and her scars would be more permanent. Counselors were helping with the emotional and mental trauma while social services were investigating the welfare of the children, who had clung to Jaclyn throughout the ordeal. Understanding that Jaclyn could not return to their home and had nowhere to go, one social worker gently provided Jaclyn with information about Colorado Homeless Families and made the phone call on her behalf.

Several days later, a caring neighbor drove Jaclyn and her children to their new housing at Colorado Homeless Families. Unable to return to their home because of the crime scene, Jaclyn realized there would not be anything to gather anyway since everything in the house had been damaged by gasoline fumes or fire.

Thankfully, CHF provided Jaclyn with necessities from the food, clothing, and furniture bank. Emotionally traumatized, counseling began at once for both Jaclyn and her children. It took a while before Jaclyn could look in the mirror and not see herself as more than an abused wife with the scars to prove it. She was also having difficulty seeing any positive future for her or her children. And that caused her great fear.

Through counseling, Jaclyn realized that she had lacked positive role models in her life. Her father died when she was young, and her mother, although still alive, was not an emotionally stable or supportive person for Jaclyn's life. Through counseling and support groups and meeting others on the CHF campus, Jaclyn began to find some positives. As her children proved to be resilient, They returned to school and found new friends and playmates within CHF, Jaclyn's case manager helped her identify some goals and create a vision to reach those goals. They also helped her develop a solid plan for furthering her education.

Watching her children play on the CHF playground one afternoon, she began to remember a long-lost dream that she had years before Peter had entered her life: she wanted to manage a childcare facility. She cheerfully conveyed her vision to her case manager, and they mapped out a two-year program for her to become a licensed childcare director.

Over the next two years, Jaclyn worked part-time and attended classes. She worked diligently at her job, studied hard to achieve good grades, and cared deeply for her children, ensuring their emotional, mental, physical, and educational needs always came first. Whenever she or her children earned an "A" on an assignment, they celebrated and set their next goal. Jaclyn's next goal, after one particular assignment was to become fully self-sufficient, no matter what ups and downs occurred.

After receiving her director's license in early childhood education, Jaclyn learned through a colleague about a childcare business that was for sale; it was everything she had dreamed of because it also included a home on the premises where she and her children could live. With a new resolve and a fresh level of confidence, Jaclyn reached out to a friend of her father's. She asked him to help her write a business plan, obtain financing, and prepare all the necessary paperwork to begin her new business. The plan was successful, and Jaclyn now sees that she can live her goal.

As Jaclyn sat at her kitchen table and looked out the window at her children smiling and laughing with the other kids, she quietly pondered her words. Her pen paused above the paper, and with tears in her eyes and a lump in her throat, she began writing:

To Connie Zimmerman and the CHF Staff:

It is bittersweet to write this letter, and I have been putting it off because of this very reason. As I have discussed with you, I will be leaving Colorado Homeless Families soon. I am so blessed to be able to move into a home and take care of my own business and believe that you all have given me the tools to be at that place in my life. I appreciate everything I have received here at CHF. I have had opportunities to spend the last few years growing here discovering who I am while throwing myself back into school. Please know that you all have been a great support system for me. The daily cheers of support when things were good–or bad–have made it much easier for me to know someone cared.

I truly consider each and every one of you my friends. I appreciate the help and support you have given to me and my children as we worked toward the goals you helped us establish. I still have some goals that I will continue to reach for, but I know that you have given me the tools I need to make it. Colorado Homeless Families will always have a special place in our hearts, and I will never forget the help that I received here. I have referred others here and will continue to do so in the future. Now I hope to be able to support CHF in a different way.

Thank you with all my heart,
Jaclyn

Executive Director Connie Zimmerman had always followed the leading of the Lord in all things related to the Colorado Homeless Families organization. The mission was clear: to help the homeless with families and "to elevate families with children from the bonds of homelessness through such causes as personal tragedy..."

One of Connie's strategies for Colorado Homeless Families was to make sure her organization helped those close to home first. She determined that 65% of the transitional housing was reserved for United States citizens. This meant that the remaining 35% of CHF housing for non-nationals and immigrants required heavy scrutiny when selecting families. Background checks, credit checks, references, and criminal history checks were not helpful when vetting non-national applicants, so Connie chose to meet with families personally as part of the selection process to CHF.

The previous day, Connie had received a call from a pastor at a local church, and he asked her to consider accepting a family that he was housing temporarily. So, on this sunny day in May, Connie sat down with Asif Usmani to listen to his story as he provided his verbal application to Colorado Homeless Families:

"I hail from Pakistan, which is 98% Muslim, and I did my study of the Koran in Islam. As a young man, I was taught to kill Christians and Jews, so I was placed in the Pakistan army. However, after a number of years, an encounter with Jesus changed my life. Jesus had spoken to me and told me to leave the army, which would be very difficult and dangerous for me to do. They were planning to promote me in the Pakistan army, so I was brought into an office to take a test first. I suddenly was not able to answer any of the questions on the test, and did such a bad job. The army completely dismissed me from service.

Three months after exiting the army, I followed Jesus. I came to intimately know that Jesus is the way, the truth, and the life. I gave my life to Him when I was 25 years old. Jesus called me to preach His gospel and opened many doors in Pakistan to do so. I was even able to attend and complete a three-year bible college. I started planting churches with the power of the Holy Spirit, and by His power, was successful in planting 24 churches in different areas of the Islamic Republic of Pakistan.

In February 1997, more than 400 Pakistani police and over 70,000 Muslims attacked two villages and burned 13 of the planted churches, damaged 1,500 Christian homes, and destroyed thousands of our bibles. Several hundred Christian girls were kidnapped, savagely raped, and then returned to their villages. This particular incident took place because of a false charge that we Christians had torn up a Koran.

In July 1997, I received an invitation from a church in South Africa, and I departed with actual videotape footage of the day the Pakistan villages were attacked and the churches burned. I showed the videos to the inviting pastor of the South African church, and he in turn made many copies of that video footage and sent them to other pastors in many cities of South Africa.

After seeing this footage of the February 1997 attack, many of the South African pastors assembled to formally protest the Islamic Republic of Pakistan, Muslims, and the Pakistan government. This formal protest took place in front of the High Commission of Pakistan in Pretoria, South Africa—which is the Pakistan Embassy in South Africa. The Embassy Ambassador inquired as to where they had received the information and the videos, and my name was given to them.

Once my name was made known, this prohibited me from ever returning to Pakistan. The local Muslims in South Africa began to persecute me, but at each turn, God intervened and delivered me from harm. Eventually, the South African government insisted that I leave the country so they could work to repair the relationship between the two countries.

My wife and I proceeded to the American Embassy and were told that our family could not be issued visas to the United States.

Later that night, God spoke to my wife, Aqidah (whose name means "faith"), and told her to fast for three days and three nights like Esther did in the Book of Esther in the Bible. After the fast, God told Aqidah to return to the American Embassy.

Having faith that God would provide, we returned. We had no money to pay for anything, including visas, fees, or even airline tickets. We entered the Embassy and both of us fully experienced a third person walking with us. The American Embassy asked no questions when we inquired as to the status of our visas. We were simply told to return in three days to collect our papers.

The church driver who had driven us to the American Embassy asked us how we were going to pay for the airline tickets to the United States. The only thing I could confess was, "We serve a big God. He will pay for our tickets."

During my prayer time, God instructed me to fast for three days and three nights, and to be prepared for spiritual warfare, reminding me of 1 Peter 5:8, "Be sober, be vigilant; because your adversary the devil, as a roaring lion, walketh about, seeking whom he may devour."

After the three days of fasting, I immediately had two visions: 1) I saw an airplane taking off and 2) I saw Jesus sitting at the right hand of God, and He waved His hand and proclaimed, "It is done."

The three of us (Jesus, myself, and Aqidah) went back to the American Embassy after the three days, and 'Hallelujah!' God had completely taken care of the visas, fees, and airline tickets—and we were to depart immediately.

We landed in Colorado Springs and made our way with our two daughters to Denver and have been living in the basement of a local church."

Connie approved this family, and the church where they were staying paid their security deposit. They moved into one of the Colorado Homeless Families' HUD homes and were grateful for the beautiful and spacious accommodations. Not surprisingly, the family was excellent renters and quiet, helpful residents. Asif had spoken English before arriving in the United States. His wife, Aqidah, attended both the beginner and intermediate ESL (English as a Second Language) classes at Colorado Homeless Families to speak the language also.

The family actively participated in all the required classes, and soon Asif found a job in which he excelled. Only after two years, Asif and Aqidah were able to buy their own home. He has written books about his life in Pakistan and travels worldwide, giving his testimony.

Valeria Flores stared at the book in her hands. An acquaintance had suggested she read it and had given her a brand-new copy of "The Art of Happiness." She had read it twice, hoping for answers. The book had some interesting information, but the Dalai Lama claimed that the purpose of life is being happy, and that happiness cannot come from anything except yourself.

Valeria's life was more than just "unhappy." It was in complete upheaval and utter chaos. Her beloved grandfather, who she called Gramps from the time she could talk, had recently passed away. He was her stalwart and biggest supporter, and he was her best friend. Valeria was named after him, Valerio, which is Spanish and Italian for "to flourish" and "to be healthy." Gramps died suddenly, and she could not get to the hospital soon enough to be by his side and hold his hand. She was heartbroken and felt the loss deep in her soul every day.

Five months later, her mom died. When Valeria learned of her death in Mexico, a distant relative said she died from a broken heart after Valerio, Valeria's grandfather passed away. Valeria understood how easily one would want to die of a broken heart. She loved her mom, too. After Valeria's difficult divorce ten years ago, she and her mom had stopped being close. Her mom was vocal about how Valeria had walked away from her marriage too quickly and was upset she did not try harder to make it work rather than become a single mom with a seven- and three-year-old. Valeria's marriage had been doomed from the start, and she could no longer stay married and ignore the serious character flaws and bad decisions her husband made that wreaked havoc on her and their children. So, Valeria and her mom lived and loved in a standoff.

Her ex-husband moved on, and neither she nor her children heard from him, and he never supported his children. This was especially difficult for her son, Santino, when he became a teenager. Gramps was helping to be a guiding figure, but Santino wanted his dad and was resentful he was not around. Teenage resentment was the worst and always resulted in rebellion and troublemaking. He was especially resentful when her daughter, his sister, Angelie, was diagnosed with pulmonary hypertension. Many nights were spent in and out of the hospital, leaving Santino on his own and feeling alone and lacking attention.

Through all this upheaval, Valeria did her best to keep her employment and financial problems from her children. With her daughter Angelie in and out of the hospital, Valeria was absent from work more and more. Her boss counseled her many times, and Valeria asked for grace, but he had a business to run and needed Valeria to work her hours. The hospital bills were beginning to pile up, and insurance did not cover Angelie's medications. For the last set of prescriptions she needed, Valeria had to take out an advance loan on her paycheck, which resulted in her paying 30% interest and got her further behind on bills.

Finally, feeling alone, financially broke, heartbroken from loss, unable to pay her rent or bills, worried about losing Santino to jail, and in fear of losing Angelie to the medical condition, she felt broken, isolated, and with no support. "The Art of Happiness" book was tossed in the trash, and instead, she retrieved her Gramps bible and opened it. The first verse she read was in Lamentations 3:17, "*my soul is bereft of peace; I have forgotten what happiness is...*". The great prophet Jeremiah obviously knew how deeply the soul could grieve.

Looking for options, she stumbled across Colorado Homeless Families transitional housing program. Reading the information, she thought this might be a good choice for her. Valeria needed a place of peace and support, and she needed time. Time to get her life together, time to heal, time to get her finances straightened out, and time to stabilize. This program did not advertise itself as a "free ride" situation but looked to be one of education, guidance, support, and life planning—all the things she so desperately needed.

Valeria was accepted to Colorado Homeless Families and was thrilled when Executive Director Connie Zimmerman showed her the furniture, clothing, and food banks to use. Valeria's first meeting with the support group confirmed her decision that this was the first step to a positive change. Everyone was supportive, helpful, and they all hugged her when she described the profound loss she felt from her only support: Gramps.

She attended every educational seminar and her case manager helped her with many of her questions. Santino adapted to his new school and became steadier with counseling, a strict schedule, volunteer responsibilities, and becoming active in some CHF activities. Angelie also made some new friends, in and out of CHF, and after she was placed on the proper medications, her health began to stabilize quickly. As the family started to settle down and find balance, Valeria began paying off medical bills with a structured payment plan, which helped her re-order her finances.

With encouragement from her case manager and her counselor, Valeria set some goals for herself, and the first one was finding a new job. She felt it was time to leave her current job, so with renewed confidence, she secured a new position within a month with a significant increase in income. This increase allowed Valeria to pay off the medical bills sooner, which helped improve her credit. She learned how crucial good credit was when she attended a CHF home buying class. Sitting in the class, she began to feel something foreign to her: happiness. Feeling happy, and just to assess where she stood, Valeria decided to see if she would qualify for a home loan. She did! She learned that she was more financially stable than she thought, and with the right price, she would be able to purchase a home of her own.

Valeria also learned through CHF counseling to take her time. She wanted to achieve some of the goals she had set, and most importantly, to make sure her children were doing well and were stable in all things. As she excelled at her new job and watched her children begin to thrive, she took her time to find a lovely home, as it was intimidating to purchase her very own home for the first time. Eventually, she found the exact right place for her and her children and found that CHF had provided everything she had needed to prepare her to stand on her own and be successful and happy. The verse she read last night was James 5:13 *Is anyone among you in trouble? Let them pray. Is anyone happy? Let them sing songs of praise.*

Grant

Grant David Emerson was born July 1976 in Bluefield, West Virginia. He was the fourth of eight children living in a three-bedroom house.

Commonly known as one of the worst cities in West Virginia, his hometown boasted a population of a little over 16,000 people. "Wild and Wonderful" was the state slogan, yet, growing up along the Virginia border, Grant knew that Bluefield was neither wild nor wonderful. Like most of West Virginia, Bluefield's history was steeped in the coal industry.

Grant did well in school, received better grades than all his siblings, and had many great friends he could run with through the Appalachian Mountains. With low incomes, high unemployment, and an inferior school system, his plan was simple: graduate high school, get a college scholarship and beat it out of there to the *real* mountains in Colorado.

Jimena

Jimena Okoro was born July 1976 in Niamey, in the Republic of Niger, the landlocked western African country. Niger's neighbors included Algeria to the northwest, Libya to the northeast, Chad to the east, Nigeria and Benin to the south, and Burkina Faso and Mali to the west.

The city of Niamey's population exploded in the 1980s to over 250,000, and the area is located in a millet growing region while manufacturing industries include bricks, ceramic goods, cement, and weaving. French-speaking Jimena enjoyed the Niger River as a young girl, and she would sit on the riverbank for hours and watch the boats. Her favorite was the Niger River Tours, as she would dream of the faraway lands where these visitors would come from.

Grant

Grant excelled in high school and was proud to receive a teaching scholarship. The University of Northern Colorado in Greeley, Colorado, was ranked in the top 100 teaching universities in the United States.

With affordable tuition, his scholarship, financial aid, student loans, and strong work ethic, Grant was on a bus to Colorado two weeks after high school graduation. He was dizzy with excitement as his family bid him farewell at the bus station for the two and a half day, 1,500-mile trip.

Jimena

Jimena's family kept being pressed to offer their daughters to marry surrounding village chiefs. Jimena's husband-to-be already had two wives and nine children.

Jimena knew that Niger had the highest child marriage rate in the world. It was considered sinful for a woman to have sensuous desires, so the doctors often fixed the young girls by mutilating their private parts. Niger girls were further forced into unwanted marriages because they were not allowed, by custom, to make free or informed decisions. In her family, coercion was involved.[32]

Seventy-five percent of girls in Niger were married before the age of 18. Being an intelligent girl, she also knew that less than 5% of these child brides used contraception, so she would likely soon have a child.

Her two older sisters had been given to local village chiefs at ages 15 and 16. At age 17, Jimena herself was given to a nearby 60-year-old village chief in marriage.

Grant

Grant enjoyed his college years in Greeley and graduated with his teaching degree with honors. It was an area he was passionate about and wanted to make a difference in schools where students were considered low-income.

Grant had learned that Title I schools receive federal funds to help ensure that all children have the opportunity to receive a quality education. Grant had a goal: he wanted to teach in a classroom where he could help every child exceed. Growing up in one of the poorest towns in West Virginia, he knew how important it was to help students attain the best education possible. He was offered a teaching position at a Denver County school district considered a Schoolwide Program (SWP). SWP schools used Title I funds to upgrade the school's entire educational program. Grant knew he wanted to make a difference in the overall school system.

Jimena

Within two years of marriage, Jimena had a child. Thankfully, it was a son, as daughters were frowned upon and mistreated.

Jimena had seen her oldest sister once in a local village and learned that Jimena had been given away to her husband for 20,000 Nigerian nairas (about $900), along with two goats, a pig, and some assorted vegetables. Jimena told her sister that once she was married to the village chief, she was turned into his slave and punching bag. He repeatedly told her that he paid so much to marry her that she had to labor by working many hours each day to prove that she was a grateful wife and mother.

The beatings got increasingly brutal, and when the chief's two other wives began beating her, she knew she needed to escape.

Grant

Grant enthusiastically began his teaching career and loved his students and the children's energy.

When a child learned something new, he could see their eyes light up, which would be the high point of his day. He had been living with a college buddy, sharing rent and expenses, however, his friend was now engaged and planning to marry a lovely woman who had two energetic children. Grant knew he would need to move, but his income was at the low end of the teachers' pay scale. He had been looking at shared rentals, but there just was not anyone needing a roommate. Affordable rent on a studio or one-bedroom apartment was not even in his budget.

Jimena

Traumatized from the brutal beatings and sexual violence, Jimena and her son fled under cover of night. She had heard about a religious relief organization while at the local market. A man and his wife were volunteers for this organization, and Jimena had overheard them talking to the market owner.

Jimena followed the couple and told them her story and her need to escape, or she would probably be killed. They provided her with the information and a place to meet after dark, and Jimena was able to flee. Through a series of connections from the relief organization, within ten days, Jimena found herself in Denver, Colorado.

Grant

Unable to find an affordable place to live or a roommate, Grant rented a small studio apartment and worked as a waiter at night and on weekends. The tips were good, but Grant had just received news last week at the school staff meeting that budget cuts were imminent, and there were plans of layoffs. Being a new teacher with less than three years, Grant did not have tenure and was told by the principal and superintendent that he would be the first to be cut. He immediately began looking for a new teaching job. However, Christmas break was not far away, and no schools were hiring at this time. Grant also started looking for other full-time work, but no jobs were available. Looking at his budget over the weekend, he would not be able to keep his apartment.

His first thought was he would need to return to West Virginia, but he knew that things were even worse there. Besides, Grant had worked hard to get his education. He loved Colorado, and he believed there was a bigger reason he was here.

Jimena

The Christmas lights were beautiful, but Jimena did not know what the snow meant. She and her son stayed in shelters but eventually were turned out onto the streets and stayed on park benches and hidden doorways.

Jimena did not speak or understand English, making it even more difficult to ask anyone for help. On one especially frigid morning, a couple on their way to church stopped and asked her if she needed help. Shivering and shaking, and her son crying, she began sobbing. The woman spoke a little French, and they gave her a paper with the words "Colorado Homeless Families" and a phone number. They gave her all the money they had and helped her to a local shelter.

The people told the shelter manager about CHF and provided him with the information. The shelter manager knew Jimena and her son from their previous stay, so he contacted Colorado Homeless Families and helped her find her way there.

Grant

A co-worker at the restaurant who knew Grant was trying to find a new place to live along with a new job told Grant about Colorado Homeless Families. After his shift, he contacted them and arranged a time to meet to complete an application.

They were exactly what he needed to help him get back on his feet. He was a hard worker, but he knew he could overcome this adversity with a little assistance, and this hardship would be short-lived. His father in West Virginia would say, "It's hard cheese for the worker these days." Grant was able to move into

Colorado Homeless Families before the end of the month and began taking advantage of all the programs they offered.

Jimena

After moving into Colorado Homeless Families, Jimena was enrolled in ESL class to learn to speak English. Her case manager helped her identify her work options, and she underwent counseling to overcome the trauma of her life in Niger.

Colorado Homeless Families also provided some contacts for Jimena to obtain pro-bono legal assistance to help her get residency in the United States. One beautiful snowy day, Jimena looked out her window and saw her son helping a tall, good-looking, blond man move snow from the sidewalk. Then the man bent down and began showing her son how to make a snowball.

Grant & Jimena

Grant and Jimena met shortly after both moved into Colorado Homeless Families. They quickly became friends, and soon fell in love and got married. After their marriage, they lived at CHF as a married couple and continued to use all the program's resources.

After a year, Jimena received her permanent resident card and also graduated from a legal transcriptionist training institute. Her fluency in the French language quickly placed her in a managerial position at an international money transfer company. She planned to continue her education to become a paralegal to work in the legal system.

Grant was able to find a new teaching position with a substantial pay increase.

Grant and Jimena had two children together, worked hard to attain their dream, and purchased their own home soon after leaving Colorado Homeless Families. Coming together from opposite nations, differing backgrounds, overcoming obstacles, and progressing with determination for a better life, two worlds eventually collided and came to live in harmony.

169

Susannah Luke nearly tripped on the steps walking to the stage. She was extremely excited and incredibly proud; after four years and a long road, she was delighted to accept her Bachelor of Science degree in Elementary Education. She never thought that she would have the courage to achieve this goal, but she did and earned it with honors. Her brand-new job awaited her after graduation, as did her acceptance to earn a master's degree. She also found herself looking at a home to purchase for her and her sons.

At 17 years old, Susannah had joyfully given birth to her first son, Ethan. It was completely unexpected, and she had not wanted to be a mother that young. She and Justin were in love and had been together for several years with plans for a permanent future.

After high school graduation, Justin found a good-paying and stable job with the U.S. Postal Service. He started in the central processing facility and wanted to work his way up. The other surprise at 19 years old was Oliver. Both of her sons had been short labor and easy babies to care for. She enjoyed staying home with them while Justin worked.

Before she turned 21 years old, Justin and Susannah had bought their first home! In a good school district, it had three bedrooms and two bathrooms, a two-car garage, and a fenced backyard where the boys could play. It was also down the street from a park where other children played, and Susannah had casually met some other Mothers of Pre-schoolers (MOPS). She was shy around these other moms, as most were older than her, but everyone had always said Susannah acted older than her age.

Susannah had to grow up quickly. Her dad left her mom and her after finding "another family." His new wife, her two kids, and the two they had together kept him busy, so he rarely had time for Susannah. Susannah's mom did not make it easy for him to come around, either. She was brutal with her words, always yelling, screaming, and blaming him for everything wrong with their lives. She was selfish and always spent their bill and grocery money on things for herself, and after Susannah's dad left, her mom continued to try to manipulate him and cause problems with his new family.

Eventually, he just stopped communicating and coming around altogether, and last she heard, they had moved to California, or maybe it was Florida.

She didn't even know where he was and never dared to try to find him and reach out. After Susannah got pregnant and had Ethan at 17, her mom sunk into a depression. Susannah realized that sometime during her tweens, she had become the mother in the relationship, and her mother had become the needy child, depending on Susannah for everything.

This dependent relationship had made Susannah shy and introverted, so she never had good friends—and found after she met Justin—she didn't want any other friends anyway. After Susannah had Ethan to take care of, her mom was diagnosed with psychotic depression and checked herself into a mental institution. Her mom's parting words were vile and accusatory towards Susannah; it was a toxic relationship, so Susannah had never gathered the courage to visit her.

After buying their house and being home with her boys, Susannah became more assured of her family's stability. She was still shy, however, and didn't venture out much. While most women her age were finishing college, Susannah engaged her young sons in educational games. She realized one day that she might like to teach in a school. She was nervous when she went to the local college and picked up some information on classes. One night after putting Ethan and Oliver to bed, she nervously told Justin that she was interested in attending classes. Justin was wary but agreed, although he told her she would need to start slow.

Shortly thereafter, when Ethan was four and Oliver was two, Susannah began attending college, taking only two courses.

Sometime during her second semester, Justin announced one night after their sons were asleep that he needed something different for his life. He felt that he had missed out on a lot—becoming a father so young and going to work right away—and that he realized he was not ready to take care of a wife and family. Susannah was stunned.

She cried and begged and told him they should get counseling. She was shamefully willing to do anything and told him so. He remained adamant. The earth began to crumble under her, and she could not gain her footing. Justin slept on the couch that night and for the next week, and early one morning before leaving for work, he told her that he wanted her and the boys to find another place to live.

She was devastated, and for the next week, tried everything she could to talk Justin out of his decision. She even begged him to let her and the boys stay in the house, and he move out instead, but he was insistent and asked her, "*How do you plan to make the house payments if I'm the one that leaves?*" After her fate finally began to sink in, Susannah finally grasped that she had nowhere to go, no income, two boys to care for, and no support system. Her world completely crumbled, and she stood in her pretty living room at a complete loss.

An acquaintance from one of her classes called to check on Susannah since she had inexplicably missed a week of class. Susannah worked up the nerve to tell her, and Gail offered to meet her at the local park to talk. That afternoon, she watched her two beautiful boys play at the park. They were rowdy, full of energy, and boisterous. Usually, Susannah would love the noise, but that day she had a headache, bloodshot eyes, and a broken heart. She sat on the park bench and cried even more. Gail, her school acquaintance, walked towards her with a bag of food for them and two Happy Meals for her sons. After they ate, Gail told her about an organization called CHF and encouraged her to call.

Susannah applied to Colorado Homeless Families and was accepted. The day they moved out of their house, a man approached her as she finished loading her car and handed her divorce papers. She was dumbfounded! She slammed the trunk, loaded her sons, and drove away.

The first week at CHF was the most difficult. She was assigned a case manager and attended support group meetings. They helped her with anything she needed for their home. One of the meetings with her case manager was to identify career goals for herself and guide her on setting up an educational plan. Thankfully, she had not missed a lot of school, so she wouldn't get too off track or delayed. Job hunting was a different story; Susannah had never worked and didn't know how to secure employment. Interviewing for a job made her anxious, and some nights she found herself pacing the floor with nervousness.

Within a short time, and with coaching and guidance from the CHF staff, Susannah was hired as a teacher's assistant in the local school district close to her new home.

The school also worked with her college class schedule to allow her to continue working towards her teaching degree.

The most encouraging thing she found was: her boys adapted to their new environment quickly, and she found them to be resilient, outgoing, and playful. She continued to attend the educational seminars offered by CHF, and she also attended some mental health counseling. She met other people that had a more difficult time than her, and she liked hearing their stories of hope and success.

One of her counselors, however, helped her with something she had needed her entire life: to find the courage to dream her very own dream and have the confidence to become successful in that courage.

"…and Davis passes to Bennett in the slot, he shoots, he scores!"

Billy Bennett lasered the biscuit in the five-hole and jumped for joy at the hat-trick. Billy knew that hat-tricks were rare in hockey, but he had gotten his first one this afternoon. Boy, did he love playing hockey. Last week's game had been a real "barn burner," a game where the crowd is loud, proud, and stomping their feet. Yet, today's game would be burned in his brain. First hat-trick. Ever. It didn't matter that he was only 12, and this was seventh-grade middle school sports. In a few short years, he'd be able to play Junior League Hockey and then try out for the Junior Olympics Hockey Team.

The guys in the locker room whooped and whistled and offered their congratulations. The Wildcats had won the game 4-3, and the coach hugged him and handed him the biscuit—the hockey puck—of the winning goal and the final goal of his hat-trick. Tears stung his eyes as he grabbed his towel and headed for the showers.

Pushing through the locker room doors to the parking lot, Billy's mom, Grace, waited in their car. It was cold, and the snow flurries were beginning. He could see the head of his little brother, Max, in the backseat. Max didn't care much for hockey—or any sport or outdoor activity for that matter; he was quiet and barely said a word. Most nights and weekends, Billy would find him curled up with a book or a drawing pad. It was rare his mom attended a game, and rarer that Max showed up. He was glad they got to see his first-ever hat-trick tonight, even if they may not understand what it was or how proud it made his coach.

Billy piled his gear in the back seat and got in the front. "Congratulations, honey," his mom said and smiled at him. "Thanks, mom." He wanted to ask if they could stop for a burger to celebrate, but he knew that money was tight; Grace worked as a cashier during the day and went to school most nights. It was a big stretch for her to pay for some of the hockey expenses, so he tried not to ask for any more than what was necessary. Grace put the car in gear and headed towards Colorado Homeless Families: their home for the past 18 months.

He watched his mom navigate the snowy streets, and Billy noticed she looked more peaceful than he'd seen in a long time. Three years ago, they had been homeless. Homeless! A word that he still could not speak aloud. He remembered coming home from school to find his mom bruised and weeping in the corner of her bedroom. Hunter, Billy's stepdad, thinking he'd simply return from nine months absence and abandonment of his family, met instead his mom's rancor. He assaulted her.

This time, Billy had to call the police. They arrested Hunter and removed his mom by ambulance for emergency treatment. Billy remembered how frightened he and Max were to be placed in Children's Services for a couple of nights. When they returned to their mom, Billy knew something had changed in Grace even though she tried her best to take care of them. He later learned that she had been severely suffering from the effects of mental, emotional, and physical abuse that left her weary and beaten down. Grace didn't have the energy or the willpower to take care of herself or him and Max.

Billy realized there were days when Grace couldn't get out of bed. It was why he got himself and Max ready for school, made their breakfast and lunch, and got them to the school bus stop. He would get home from school, and Grace would still be in bed, and there would be messages on the answering machine from her work. Billy would make them dinner, help Max with his homework, and make sure they brushed their teeth and got to bed on time. His neighbor and long-time friend, Cody, would drop by on weekends, and they would play street hockey in the driveway, kick the soccer ball around in the backyard, or do some drills and exercises in the garage.

Billy's passion was ice hockey. When his stepdad and mom first moved into this house, Billy dug around in the attic one weekend. He found a pair of ice skates, a wooden hockey stick, and a helmet. They were too big for him, but he tried them on anyway, and he felt something magical wearing them. He asked his mom where they came from, but she didn't know. She said they were probably left there from a previous renter, or maybe an owner.

Billy brought the equipment down from the attic, cleaned it up, and put it in his room. He became mesmerized by the skates and carried the hockey stick wherever he went while he practiced stickhandling. One of the times his stepdad had been nice, he had brought Billy a hockey puck one day, and after that, he and his best friend, Cody, never missed a Colorado Avalanche game on television. Billy would watch how the players glided on the ice, backward skate, passing, handle the puck, and shoot. Billy would even watch the linesmen (referees) who call the players on icing and offside calls. He checked out several books from the library and tried to watch the high school players practice whenever he could.

Walking home from school one day and dreaming of the NHL, Billy noticed a letter taped to the front door. It was addressed to Hunter and Grace, but Billy opened it anyway. The mail basket by the front door had been overflowing to the floor the last two months, so he figured this letter was important. Sobbing, he ran full speed to his friend Cody's house. Mrs. Garcia had always treated Billy as her fourth son; she would know what to do. Crying and shaking, Billy handed the letter to Mrs. Garcia. She read it, gave him a big hug, and told him everything would be okay. She made him a peanut butter and jelly sandwich and told him to stay put as she put on her coat and left with the letter.

On a clear and crisp Saturday morning the following month, Grace pulled their car into Colorado Homeless Families. She explained that this was the last resort for their family. They had nowhere to go, and she had missed a lot of work, so she could not pay the bills. The letter Billy had read from the landlord was an eviction notice, and Mrs. Garcia knew of a place that would take them in and help them. With further encouragement from Mrs. Garcia, Grace had finally been able to get herself out of bed and find a new job, but it would not pay the rent on their house, and she was behind on all their bills.

Grace promised Billy that she would get help—and it was a requirement to live there. Colorado Homeless Families had programs that would help her with mental health counseling to overcome the effects of abuse and another program to help her make goals for the future. She liked her new job, but even though it didn't pay much, she would be attending classes at the college to finish her degree so she could get a better-paying job. Billy had to change schools, but his new school had a hockey team and a better coach. Max took an active interest in the afterschool reading and art program at the new school. Mrs. Garcia would make sure that Billy still got to visit with his best friend Cody by dropping him off for visits on the weekends.

Grace rebuilt her life with help from Colorado Homeless Families and graduated from the program in 2003. She finished her degree, started a career, and bought a home. Billy became more involved in hockey, honing his skills and developing his talents, and played for Team USA in the Junior Olympics.

Webster's Dictionary defines the word "persecution" as 1: the act or practice of persecuting, especially those who differ in origin, religion, or social outlook; 2: the condition of being persecuted, harassed, or annoyed.[33]

The Bible graphically describes the introduction and spread of sin in the world, and it also describes the presence and reality of oppression and persecution in the world. Both the Old and New Testaments provide examples of physical, social, mental, and spiritual persecution. Oppression, harassment, judgment, and punishment are all forms of persecution, and the underlying biblical reason given for persecution consists of an antipathy of evil toward the good[34], and of wicked men opposing God and rejecting his divine precepts.[35] Jesus said that since the world hated Him, it would hate His disciples, and declared that if they persecuted him, they would also persecute His disciples[36]. The Bible's climactic teaching about the believer and persecution says, *"Everyone who wants to live a godly life in Christ Jesus will be persecuted."*[37]

Nepal is a landlocked country in South Asia located between India and China. Mainly situated in the Himalayas, 75% of Nepal is covered by mountains. Due to the desire to keep a delicate balance between its two neighboring countries, Nepal has tried to remain independent, causing the country to become isolated. Due to its years of geographic and self-imposed isolation, Nepal is one of the least developed nations of the world, and more than one-fourth of the population lives below poverty. There are no major cities outside of the capital Kathmandu, and most all Nepalese live in villages or small market centers (municipalities). The population of Nepal in the year 2000 was 23,941,000 in an area slightly larger than the U.S. state of Arkansas.

With such poorly developed countries comes the desire of humanitarians whose mission is to teach the poorer sectors basic skills and bring hope with their help. One such group with a presence in Nepal was Youth with a Mission (YWAM). Founded in 1960 by American missionary Loren Cunningham and his wife Darlene Cunningham, the group's initial focus was to get youth involved in missions. However, YWAM also focused on helping meet the practical and physical needs of the global community through its many relief and development initiatives.[38]

One such family committed to providing relief and hope was the Tamang family. The Tamang family dedicated themselves to teaching those in the poorer communities of Nepal basic skills. They helped to lay pipes so that these communities had fresh water. They also brought much-needed medicine to the sick, helped build roads to remote villages, provided assistance to build schools, aided in constructing houses and community buildings, and assisted people with agricultural needs.

Despite all the Tamang's efforts and accomplishments, the family faced continuous persecution because of the political oppression and division between the Maoist Communist Party and the Nepal government. Often their construction sites were looted and the water pipes were destroyed. Other times, political leaders felt threatened by their aid and would terrorize the family and the local people who worked with them. During the "civil liberties restrictions," use of electricity was limited to only a few hours a day or even every other day, and they were not allowed to leave their home after dark. There were times that it was difficult to send and receive mail as postal workers or government employees would open packages sent to and from other countries. They had no guarantee that mail sent to them would arrive or the mail that the Tamang family sent out would reach its destination. Peace-loving, innocent Nepalese citizens were often the targets of political and economic persecution.

Being born and raised in Nepal brought about many difficulties and challenges. When the Tamang's eldest daughter, Renu was only 12 years old, an insurgency led by Maoist extremists broke out between the insurgents and the government forces. This led to severe restrictions on civil liberties for the Nepalese people, and even the young children were being "drafted" as soldiers. The Communist Party of Nepal (Maoists) used children, usually between 12 and 16 years old, as soldiers, messengers, cooks, porters, and suppliers. The Rama's daughter was just the right age for being forced into becoming a child soldier. For her safety and a better future, the Tamangs knew that they would need to leave Nepal one day soon.

Aside from the dangers of war, the future for women in Nepal was grim. There were few opportunities for women, and two-thirds of female adults were illiterate. Nepalese women have limited access to education, health care, government assistance, and even the markets. Malnutrition and poverty were extreme for women as female children are given less food than male children—especially when the family is experiencing food shortages. Women usually work harder and longer than men, performing the more demanding labor jobs like carrying water, working in the fields, and hauling bricks and mortar.

Day by day, the Tamang family became more concerned about their future, as well as their daughter's. In 2001, they finally decided to leave Nepal for the United States, hoping for a brighter future.

After arriving in the United States, the Tamang family obtained housing at Colorado Homeless Families. They found employment while raising funds for their YWAM work in Nepal. They could enroll their daughter, Renu, in a private school where she could begin to work toward graduation. She completed her first two years of high school classes in just one year, something that her family knew would have never happened had they stayed in Nepal.

Being the oldest Tamang daughter, the family decided to allow Renu to stay in the safety of Colorado Homeless Families while they returned to Nepal to continue their humanitarian work. Upon high school graduation and getting her diploma, Renu had dreams of furthering her education, but she first returned to Nepal to assist her parents in their humanitarian work. She also helped her parents by escorting her younger sisters to and from school, making sure they arrived and returned safely so they could get their education, something she was never afforded.

In 2009, the Tamang family once again were able to return to the United States to raise financial support to fund their humanitarian projects. While visiting this time, the Tamang family discovered with delight that their oldest daughter, Renu, had met a kind and generous young man, named Joe, who had earned his Civil Engineering degree in hopes of helping third world countries.

The couple married in May 2010 and visited the Tamang family in Nepal to assist with their tireless and continuing humanitarian work. Joe and Renu returned to the United States where Renu, because of her skilled artistry, became an international success and a household name to many.

Renu also started a Go Fund Me page and raised over $115,000 for victims in Nepal during the 2015 earthquake.

Nepal continues to evolve as a nation. In 2008, the newly elected Constituent Assembly declared Nepal the Federal Democratic Republic, abolishing the 240-year-old monarchy and electing their first President. A new interim government was formed, and in November 2017, Nepal had its first general election since the civil war ended and the monarchy was abolished.

Humanitarian work continues to help the poor and to assist with the devastating earthquake of 2015 that killed more than 9,000 people and injured nearly 22,000.[39] As the Tamang family understood, Nepal is one of the most disaster-prone countries in the world. Every year during the monsoon season, landslides and floods kill hundreds of people in Nepal. The potential threat of earthquakes, glacial lake outbursts, avalanches, and cold and heat waves always looms large. Climate change and an increasing population further exacerbate the impacts of natural hazards, which each year cause heavy loss of life and damage to property.[40]

The Nepalese remain a conflict-affected people, especially in rural areas, and humanitarian efforts provide healthcare as well as water and sanitation facilities.[41]

Colorado Homeless Families was honored to help this family secure their daughter's safety. Counselors, case managers, and several highly regarded women in the community came together to treat Renu Tamang as part of the family and secure a future for her. From the oppressed and persecuted girl who arrived at CHF, she became a confident, creative, and passionate young woman who is no longer persecuted.

Sasha Petrov arrived in the United States from Russia through the sponsorship of a Christian couple in Arvada, Colorado suburb. She had journeyed with another immigrating family, and at 21 years old, was considered an adult and on her own when arriving.

She was happy to have finally reached this country, and the first thing on her list was finding a Christian church, followed by learning the English language, and getting a job. With the help of her sponsors, who allowed her to live with them, she succeeded in achieving all three in the first six months she was here.

She became active in her new church, worked very hard to learn English, and liked her job at a local manufacturing company. In the first two years, she saved money, made friends, and enjoyed her life in the United States. Her sponsors helped her choose a good car and located a safe and attractive apartment.

Fedir Kovaleva had been in the United States for ten years, living in Nebraska. He had been able to graduate from high school, attended a vocational school, and got a stable job at a motorcycle manufacturer in Lincoln, Nebraska. Fedir liked his apartment, was friends with great neighbors and was active in his church. As he turned 26 years old, he kept feeling something was missing. He had dated but realized that he wanted to settle down and get married. He found himself praying one day, asking God to give him a wife to love. Fedir wanted God to do the choosing, knowing God would pick the perfect wife for him.

Two months later, Fedir traveled to Denver with the youth group from his church to attend a special service focusing on Russian immigrants. While sitting in church service, he looked over and saw the smile and blue eyes. After the service, he asked one of the church leaders to give her a note asking for her telephone number. The leader got her telephone number for him,

Fedir left for Nebraska and prayed during the seven-hour trip back. Fedir called Sasha every day the following week. The following weekend, Fedir drove to meet her sponsor family. They all ate together, had great conversations, and after lunch, they drove to Red Rocks Park and Amphitheatre. They relished being together in the beautiful setting. They talked about their lives in Russia and Ukraine, immigrating to the United States, their families, their jobs, and their hopes and dreams. Fedir boldly told her that he thought God had chosen her for his wife the first moment he saw her in the church.

Sasha said that she knew meeting him was from God, and Fedir asked her to marry him. Sasha gleefully agreed.

They spoke daily by telephone for the next two months, and Fedir visited her every other week in Denver. By spring, wedding plans began, and they were starting to plan their lives.

During one of Fedir's visits, Sasha became ill and had difficulty breathing, and Fedir drove her to the nearest hospital. They took blood and tested for several causes, and after spending most of the day in the emergency room together, the doctor eventually told them that Sasha was in kidney failure.

They started her on dialysis at once, and Fedir stayed by her side for three days. He drove back to Nebraska, only to return that weekend. Fedir and Sasha were together when her doctor informed her that she would need a kidney transplant, and she would die without one.

Without a single doubt that he would be a match, Fedir volunteered to be the donor.

The doctors were astounded that he was, indeed, a perfect match. Her doctor told them it was beyond rare to find a perfect donor on the first try of testing. Yet, Fedir knew that this was God's will and that God prepared him for this moment to be able to help his future wife.

Due to the dialysis and the severity of her kidney failure, Sasha could not keep working. She had savings to pay her rent, but she knew that the recovery period after the transplant would be long, and she did not have enough in her savings to cover rent.

Fedir, by that time, had quit his job in Nebraska and moved to Denver. Sasha was concerned that they would enter their marriage both recovering from transplant surgery, broke, and homeless—and she expressed this situation to the friends who had once been her sponsors.

The sponsors knew they needed to find a solution, so they contacted Colorado Homeless Families about transitional housing. They explained the situation to Executive Director Connie Zimmerman, and they also told her they would make their deposit and pay rent and utilities for them until the couple was on their feet, healthy, and ready to return to work.

Connie agreed, however, one of the guidelines of CHF was the morals clause which prohibited unmarried couples from living together. "Families" was the focus, so Fedir and Sasha needed to get married before living together at CHF.

The requirement moved marriage onto their "to do" list as the first item of priority.

Sasha and Fedir were married in the church where they first saw one another. Fedir wore a black tuxedo and Sasha wore a white dress with a long white veil. Then, they moved into their new home at Colorado Homeless Families and prepared for the transplant surgery scheduled for only ten days later. They would both require hospitalization for at least a week, then significant recovery time at home.

Sasha's transplant was successful, but Fedir became seriously ill after the operation and needed six additional weeks of hospitalization and recovery.

Finally, the doctor offered good news: they both were mending well. Three months after full recovery, they could return to work.

The CHF case manager worked with the young couple to help them achieve a self-sufficient lifestyle. During their two years at CHF, Fedir decided to train to be a mechanic, and Sasha began attending nursing school. Their ultimate dream was to have children, build a new home, and love each other always.

Kaleb Genet entered his senior year of high school with a major goal: graduate at the top of his class and get a scholarship to a university. Two-thirds of the way through the year, he was given the award for student of the month and was praised for receiving higher exam scores than anyone in the school's history. He even beat out his two older siblings, who had gone on to graduate from college: one a lawyer, the other one entering medical school. It was a proud moment for Kaleb, and Connie Zimmerman was there to honor his achievements with a celebration.

Kaleb knew Connie from his community, Colorado Homeless Families, and she was the Executive Director. He didn't tell many people at school where he lived. Other kids already looked at him differently, having immigrated from Ethiopia, but to find out he and his family had nearly been homeless, he didn't want to add to any already-present stigmas. This is why he studied hard and diligently worked to have a better life.

He had heard all the jokes in the school halls about Ethiopia and "the starving kids in Ethiopia." In the real world—and not sitting around the American dinner table—Ethiopia was no joke. Located on the Horn of Africa, it is surrounded by seven countries—and highly tumultuous ones at that. Sudan, Somalia, and Kenya were always making world news. Ethiopia is the second-most populated country in Africa and the third poorest country in the *world*. When he and his family left Ethiopia after getting their Diversity visas, his country's population was over 76 million people in an area a little bigger than Texas. Worse, with the poor economy, the per capita income was a meager 850 in U.S. dollars.[42]

The country his parents grew up in was the same country he lived in where unemployment, and a lack of good-paying jobs, and few educational opportunities existed. It was, at the time, also front and center on the world stage for human rights violations.[43] After Kaleb was in the United States, he learned that the United States government assisted Ethiopia with over $2.3 *billion* in aid between 1991 and 2003. During Ethiopia's severe drought in 2003, the United States provided $553.1 million in assistance, of which $471.7 million was food aid.[44] Even with all this aid pouring into his country, his family's comfort neither improved from year to year, nor did he know anyone who had directly benefited from all this aid.

Kaleb's parents wanted a better life for themselves and their five children. Work, food, and a good education were rare in Ethiopia, but his parents knew something better awaited them in America. Kaleb's father was very encouraging of his children, but it was still difficult to be encouraging if you could not provide them with a place that had opportunities.

After arriving in the United States, the most difficult thing was the new language. His family spoke the Afro-Asiatic languages of Oromo and Amharic.[45] With persistence and help from some fellow Ethiopians who had immigrated to America before them, his parents were able to find jobs. It was a struggle, however, because the job did not pay enough to take care of five highly motivated children. Their family was resourceful and worked hard. Still, due to low incomes, there came a point where they were on the brink of homelessness in their new country.

The Genet's were directed to Colorado Homeless Families and were accepted. The interviewer found that his parents sincerely desired to earn their way into this new life in America and were willing to work hard and do whatever they could to make sure all five of their children could get a good education and have unlimited opportunities for their lives.

After moving into CHF, Kaleb's family worked hard to adapt to living here and took advantage of the CHF classes to learn the English language better. They also worked hard as a family to make sure they gave back to the community that accepted them by helping their neighbors and volunteering to help in any way possible at CHF.

Through case management, his parents quickly found jobs at the Denver airport. No matter what his parents did for a living, the one thing they always taught their children was the value of knowledge and education.

As his celebration wound down, Kaleb's father expressed how proud of him he was and that the medical profession that awaited him would be lucky to have a smart and caring individual. Kaleb also found another reason to celebrate: his parents had been able to overcome so many obstacles with determination and encouragement from one another and the CHF community and staff that they were looking to purchase their own home very soon.

Kaleb came to the understanding that a country could pour millions—or even billions—of dollars into an economy to try to help another country that is suffering. At the same time, most people never see a difference in their lives. Colorado Homeless Families didn't offer that. They provided encouragement, support, and resources that were helpful to people that have a deep desire for a better life.

She was beautiful. Everyone in her hometown thought she would become a beauty queen, international runway model, or marry a billionaire. Or all the above.

With the statuesque height, stunning smile, soft skin, silky blonde hair, Ace Mitchell never seemed to have any problems, and when she looked in the mirror, she really liked what she saw looking back at her. Her looks got her through most things: smiling at her teachers to get extra credit after she failed a test, batting her eyes at the police officers to get out of a speeding ticket, or playing the dumb blonde to get pretty much whatever she wanted—or get out of doing something she didn't want to do.

Born Candace, she became known as "Ace," as she aced her way through life. Until she didn't.

Pregnant at 24 years old, Bella became the best thing that happened to Candace.

Eight years later, Bella was wise beyond her years and knew that her mother used feminine wiles to get everything she wanted.

Ace didn't know where Bella got the smarts, common sense, and intrinsic sensibility as it was not from her. And it was not from the deadbeat father who exited the picture after the first sonogram.

She discovered when Bella was about two years old, that using her looks to get what she wanted wasn't going to last long. A string of bad relationships left her feeling used and useless, and it began to slowly dawn on her that she had only herself to count on. Living a charmed, beauty-queen-like life from an early age, only being superficial, doing the bare minimum to get by, and looking for the next rich and handsome guy to come along, well, that was drying up. No employable skills, no education, no talent, lousy credit, and no way to take care of her daughter, she found herself working fast food minimum wage jobs, waitressing, delivering newspapers, and cleaning houses.

All dead ends. All unfulfilling. All humbling.

Ace had nowhere to turn and could not find a job anywhere. Her rent was past due and batting her lashes at the new apartment manager didn't work. Her car was making noises, and she was desperate. She had exhausted all the employment agencies, and several of them wouldn't even accept her as a potential client because her work references were negative. Lately, when she looked in the mirror, she disliked what she saw looking back at her. And worse, she did not like how her daughter looked at her. She felt humiliated.

The old woman in the apartment next door was always nice to her—actually, she was nice to Bella. She gave Ace the newspaper each day after she was finished. To help her look for the next job, she supposed.

Sitting at the kitchen table, Ace poured over the help wanted ads again as she slurped on Ramen noodles. Nothing.

She looked through the rest of the paper and saw a story about a woman in Arvada who was running a transitional housing nonprofit called Colorado Homeless Families that helped people get on their feet. The woman, Executive Director Connie Zimmerman, was quoted as saying, *"We won't waste any time on people who cannot prove that they want to become self-sufficient. Before we help them find housing, they have to be able to help themselves. They have to be serious. We used to believe everything they said. Some people would say, 'Yeah, I want to further my career.' They have to show they are willing to do it by going out and trying. We only take people that are seriously seeking assistance and not wanting handouts."* At 32 years old, Ace knew it wasn't too late. If someone could help her, she would really like to be given the opportunity to make a sincere effort to get on her feet and make something of her life.

She called Colorado Homeless Families and received the application. It was eight pages long, and it took her several days to complete. She found that she was ashamed. She didn't have a good referral, other than her neighbor, maybe? Character references? She had to dig deep to find those. A good work history for the last five years? Credit check?

She felt defeated. She knew that she was nearing the end of her small arsenal of resources. All her tricks, games, and manipulations amounted to nothing.

Ten days after she returned the application, she met with a case manager at a local restaurant. Nervous, she dressed in her best and walked into the restaurant. The case manager was a woman, business-like yet compassionate and quite easy to talk to.

Ace told the woman her story and, while telling it, felt deeply embarrassed and humiliated. She knew it was time to be honest, or else she would lose this opportunity.

Ace took complete responsibility for the state of her life and held back tears when she told the case manager how much she wanted a better life for herself and her daughter. She told the woman that she had not taken advantage of opportunities presented to her in the past and was disappointed in herself for the current state of her life and horrified at how it affected her daughter. She wanted the opportunity to prove to herself, her daughter, and to others that she could, and would, change her life if given a little help.

The case manager talked about the different groups of the poor, and Ace fell into what Colorado Homeless Families defined as Group 2: the working poor. Ace had never heard of this, but it made sense after it was explained to her. No or little education or training, barely making ends meet, low paying jobs. These individuals were the ones that would be required to sign a contract with CHF to attend a trade school, college, or university. They would need to apply for grants and financial aid. CHF strictly held them to this contract that they had to actively pursue a better life than what they were doing.

Finally, the case manager explained how the CHF program worked, and there were difficult requirements. This was not a "get by" program, nor did it provide handouts. There were requirements to get in, requirements to live there, and requirements to stay. Everyone accepted into the program worked hard to graduate.

For the first time in her life, Ace knew that she needed to do this. Her current life depended on it, her future depended on it, and especially her daughter's life depended on it. She thanked the case manager and told her she would be committed to this program and work hard to turn her life around.

A week later, Ace received a phone call. There was an opening, and she and her daughter had been accepted. She completed the required forms, including the lease, filling out her name: *Candace Mitchell*. She didn't want to be *Ace* anymore. Candace jumped right in from the first day, learning that she was required to:

Pay 30% of her income for rent
Contribute to the CHF community through volunteer service
Meet with case manager weekly to set short- and long-term goals and track progress
Find a steady job
Attend post-secondary school or training
Attend educational classes at Colorado Homeless Families
Attend support groups at Colorado Homeless Families
Take responsibility for yourself

Working with her case manager, Candace found that she did have some undiscovered skills, and her interests were a good fit to attend the largest hospitality program in the region, obtaining her degree in Hospitality Management. Candace was excited to begin and was also thrilled to get a work study job that was flexible with her schedule.

Although it was not a requirement for Candace, she sought counseling. Her eyes were opened to the fact she had poor self-esteem and lacked self-confidence. Her confidence had been in her looks and her manipulations, and she knew that was not a life she wanted to continue. Her counselor helped her understand how to build good friendships and healthy relationships to enhance her life. They also discussed how to be a better parent to Bella, as Candace felt resentment from her daughter.

The educational courses helped Candace learn more about her true self and the lives of others living at Colorado Homeless Families. Many were escaping volatile and violent lives, some with alcohol and abuse. Candace learned that many of them were in the same situation, starting over at some point in their lives. The CHF educational classes and lectures taught her responsible financial management and helped improve her poor credit.

Candace was grateful for the support, learned to help others first, and always encouraged those who needed it. What she really opened her eyes to was she found Colorado Homeless Families wasn't about just bettering your job or your income; the program was helping to lift her out of her own life situation and see so she could reach for a better life.

DO NOT GROW WEARY OF DOING GOOD

<u>Family Education and Resource Center & CHF Offices</u>
Colorado Homeless Families continued to see the fruit of faith in action. With 22 townhomes and 20 HUD homes in which to house families in transition, 1997 saw the completion of the Family Educational and Resource Center.

Centralization was important, and a central space was needed for individual and family counseling, educational courses, seminars, childcare services, ESL classes for non-native or non-English-speaking families, and interviews and reviews for those who committed to successfully graduating from the CHF program. Larger offices were becoming necessary, as was a kitchen area and a larger food bank area. A new Resource Center would better consolidate all CHF resources and activities.

This new building would also be home to the CHF Offices. Having been first located in Connie's house, then stationed in a townhome unit, it was beginning to get crowded. Colorado Homeless Families began to grow as a staff, including Connie Zimmerman, the Executive Director, adding an office manager, administrative assistant, bookkeeper, three case managers, counselors, and a maintenance team. The CHF board was also growing to include eight board members and three advisory board members, so a meeting area was also needed. A new office space enabled the entire staff to work more professionally and efficiently with six upstairs offices and five bathrooms in the new building.

Childcare services were set up on the bottom floor of the new building, as was the food bank. Keeping perishable and nonperishable items close to staff supervision was necessary, as well as the monitoring of food donations from local grocery stores like King Soopers, Safeway, and Great Harvest. Safeway also donated fresh produce, dairy products, and juice weekly.

The original plan was to design a building called CHF Offices. By this time, Connie had learned the Lord was faithful and knew that He would provide the monies needed to build the large facility. She calculated they would need a total of 4,500 sq feet: 1,500 for the top story, 1,500 for the main floor, and 1,500 for the basement. She contacted the Gates Foundation and learned they did not issue grants for offices, however, they would give a grant for education and homeless support services. So, Connie quickly named the building the Family Educational and Resource Center as it became the hub of homeless family resources and education. She applied and received grants from Gates Family Foundation, Jefferson County, Helen K. and Arthur E. Johnson Foundation, Adolph Coors Foundation, and the Boettcher Foundation. These provided the funds to build the center. Rose Construction built the center without a loan against the property.

Resident Community Service

Colorado Homeless Families continued to grow in their unique approach in supporting homeless families. Each family adult was required to contribute at least 5 hours each month of volunteer service to help other families and to assist in the upkeep of the CHF properties and surroundings. Children were encouraged to assist, if possible, but only volunteer hours of those family members 14 years old or older would be counted as part of the resident community service. Studies had shown that volunteering connects people, is good for the mind and body, can aid with career advancement, and can bring a sense of fulfillment to life.[46]

Connie Zimmerman also knew that this would also reduce labor, overhead, and maintenance expenses for Colorado

Homeless Families. Volunteer groundskeeping and clean-up reduced the necessity to hire landscape services to keep the CHF homes looking nice. Volunteer painting and maintenance reduced the need to hire contractors to maintain homes. Volunteer hours working at the CHF food, clothing, and furniture banks and cleaning the CHF offices reduced the overhead that would be required to fully staff and maintain these facilities.

Each CHF individual selected their volunteer opportunity based on their talents and interest. The overall effect was individual residents assisting each other to better the community as a whole. An even greater advantage was that Connie saw CHF residents taking pride in their surroundings and accomplishments. She witnessed a growing spirit of unity and cooperation among the residents, which instilled the value of being a contributing member of society. This unity, cooperation, and feeling like a contributor is something that being homeless can quickly be robbed from a person, as survivor mode becomes the sole purpose of a homeless person.

Volunteers donated more than 4,800 hours each year in a variety of areas: neighborhood security checks and watch program, food/clothing/furniture bank cleaning and organization, painting, and cleaning of properties when families graduated, grounds maintenance, written communication (newsletter, donation letters, etc.), servicing of automobiles, transportation for personal errands, and babysitting and daycare services.

Volunteers followed a schedule and were required to participate on scheduled workdays. Residents were also required to attend HOA meetings to keep well-informed of the neighborhood activities or developments and learn about the projects and upkeep needed in the complex.

<u>Community Volunteers and Partnerships</u>

Working with volunteers outside of the residents was an important part of Colorado Homeless Families, as well as partnering and collaborating with other institutions and nonprofit groups within the seven-county Denver Metro area. Depending on the year or the season, Colorado Homeless Families would receive 10 to 30 phone calls daily from people needing assistance with homelessness. CHF maintained its objective to focus on families who have the initiative to help themselves. More complex issues such as drug or alcohol abuse would be referred to other organizations that could assist with special needs.

Finding itself unable to help every homeless family, partnering with other service organizations was important when CHF did not have housing availability. Referrals were made to and from organizations such as ACCESS Housing, Bridgeway, Sacred Heart House, Samaritan House, Champa House, Lutheran and Ecumenical Refugee Services, Jeffco Action Center, Magdalene Damen House, Pros with a Purpose, and Veterans of American Administration. CHF would collaborate with shelters or other housing and service agencies to try to help any caller who contacted Colorado Homeless Families.

Sometimes requests were made for additional services, and CHF would assist these individuals with referrals to Colorado Coalition for the Homeless, Interfaith Hospitality Network, Family Tree, or local churches. Job training and education were sometimes coordinated with Colorado Works and other local organizations.

All partnerships and collaboration efforts worked for the cause of homelessness and also shared donated resources. When there was an overflow of donations, all agencies shared with one another.

Other partnerships included working with grocery store chains for food bank donations. The organizations of Elks, Kiwanis, and

Shriners provided funds for special needs such as wheelchairs and other health-related requirements.

Local churches and private citizens donated money, personal necessities, furniture, appliances, and clothing. Nearby doctors and dentists offered services at no charge to families living in the Colorado Homeless Families program.

Several large retailers also supplied clothing for the clothing bank (Walmart, Dress Barn), pillows, and bedding (Sleep Number Store), and even Taco Bell and Pizza Hut donated meals each week to families in the CHF Program.

Connie Zimmerman always sought out partnerships and collaborative efforts to make a big difference in the lives of the homeless community. Working together made it easier to bring support, education, and basic necessities to families in need. Whenever possible, Colorado Homeless Families existed on the sustaining volunteer efforts provided by the community. The Colorado Homeless Families' Board of Directors were dedicated community leaders that volunteered to tirelessly work to make CHF a place to help break the bonds of poverty. Sponsors of families were individuals, families, or organizations that would volunteer time, effort, or money to assist CHF residents in becoming self-reliant.

Counseling, Support Groups, and ESL Programs

Professional counselors were contracted to work with many of the families weekly. The stress of homelessness, poverty, and personal tragedies crippled many families before arriving at CHF, which affected personal relationships at home, school, and work. Counselors were available to help families heal from many of the human issues that contributed to their homelessness, trauma from personal tragedies, abuse, and neglect, as well as other barriers they may have faced that created problems in relationships.

Support group meetings were established and required twice per month for all residents at CHF. These meetings were designed to address issues such as credibility and integrity, parenting, marriage and family relationships, boundary issues, and anger management.

Educational seminars focusing on finances and budgeting were also required once each month. The intended goal of Colorado Homeless Families was to attain self-sufficiency and homeownership. Various community leaders and educators volunteered to instruct CHF families on a variety of life skill topics such as banking, money management principles, home buying, improving credit, and also family relationships such as parenting and communication.

Colorado Homeless Families required all non-English speaking residents and immigrants to attend ESL (English as a Second Language) classes. ESL teachers were volunteers, and classes met twice each week at three different levels: beginning, intermediate, and conversational. Communication in English was vital to securing employment, job performance, and job retention.

A Playground

Because children had no alternative than to play in the driveway of the Colorado Homeless Families complex, in 1997, a new playground was constructed, supported by the funding of local donations and the Denver Postal Credit Union. The playground was built by a local Eagle Scout who planned the project for two years and worked for two days with his Boy Scott troop to bring it to completion.

Focusing on families with children, Colorado Homeless Families began to grow with the need of keeping children active and developing social skills, especially where uncertainty and trauma had been widespread. From 1999 to 2002, a small ballpark and a playground were established in the complex, as well as a sitting park with the addition of two new duplexes.

All parks, playgrounds, and children's outdoor facilities were for the use of CHF residents and their guests only. Rules were established for hours, abuse of facilities, acceptable behavior, vandalism, and care/cleanliness of the area. Especially important was the respect to be shown to all neighbors who had fences and yards next to these facilities. Abuse of rules resulted in a fine and loss of privileges.

Returning to her 1986 awareness that homelessness affected children, Connie began to build programs within Colorado Homeless Families that would grow and nurture those young lives who needed it most. The family volunteer program was a requirement for adult family members, but volunteer hours were encouraged for children to help develop a sense of purpose, build social skills, increase self-esteem, and teach them how to work with others toward a common goal. Seasonal programs began to develop and occur, such as the annual Easter egg hunt, summer youth program, summer lunch program, and the annual family summer picnic.

Summer Youth Program
Being thrust into another unknown environment, CHF found that before long, many children were separated into "little gangs" or "loners" within the community. Many children were afraid to interact with others, and fear gave way to some children becoming hostile with other children. Many of the immigrant children at CHF did not speak English, so the CHF staff began to recognize the need to bring the children together as a team so they would be able to work and play together as family, friends, and neighbors.

The summer youth program was designed primarily for children ages 7 to 16. Several times per week throughout the summer months, children gather for fun activities such as swimming, bowling, miniature golf, a variety of outdoor games, and hiking. CHF organized a fundraiser for the program that paid for additional activities like skating, zoo visits, fishing trips, and many other social activities.

The other benefit was that most of the children's parents worked every day, and the Summer Youth Program helped to provide the children living in the CHF program with a safe, fun, and engaging place to interact with caring adults who Connie handpicked. Youth leaders were volunteers, always known and trusted to CHF staff, were high achievers with good character qualities, and demonstrated standards of integrity. The leaders ranged from professional leaders, high school and university students, professional athletes, and church youth leaders. Connie required the youth leaders to be full of energy and compassion and help CHF youth create dreams and goals with healthy boundaries. A popular and successful program, most of the children became great friends with one another.

Grandparent Program

The Grandparent Program began to help young men and boys living in the CHF community who did not have the care and support of a father or a male adult figure in their lives. This vulnerability created personalities that became intimidating and aggressive towards other children. Grandparents adopted these young men ages 8-16 and took them to a wide variety of social activities, helped with homework and tutoring, taught them important life skills, and other activities where the boys needed support and supervision, such as driving lessons or preparation for college or job interviews.

The Grandparent program was found to increase the self-confidence of the youth involved with the program, as well as being a blessing and giving more value to the Grandparents who volunteered their time to help boys in the community grow to be respectful, responsible, and honorable young men.

Christmas Adopt-A-Family Program

Holidays for the homeless, especially Christmas, were an especially stressful time.

Living on tight budgets, busy with jobs and schooling, and focusing on providing basic necessities could be overwhelming. Even with the extra assistance of drawing from Colorado Homeless Families food, furniture, and clothing bank still made affording Christmas gifts a rarity.

Colorado Homeless Families made sure that all families in the program were adopted for Christmas. Members of the community, families, and/or businesses or organizations adopted one or more CHF families and provided them with gifts for Christmas.

Each year on the Saturday before Christmas, more than 300 individuals representing both adopted families and their adoptive families, schools, and businesses gather together to share food and festivities while delivering toys and other gifts to the CHF families participating in the Adopt-A-Family program. CHF families would take their gifts home with much anticipation and joy to unwrap on Christmas Day.

Those adopting the families at CHF helped in extraordinary ways to relieve the stress of the holidays, as well as helping the families continue their journey toward self-sufficiency.

Adopt-A-Family gifts were to be approximately $50-$60 per gift, per individual, at Christmas. Gifts were selected by donors from the family's Christmas list. The lists, made by the parents, represented the needs and wants of the family. Each member of the family could request up to three items. Donation overflow of Christmas gifts, money, clothing, blankets, and toys was given to other homeless programs in the Denver Metro area.

The Basketball Court

Kroenke Sports & Entertainment, the owner of the professional Denver Nuggets basketball team and the Colorado Avalanche hockey team, working in conjunction with Extreme Makeover: Home Edition, built a professional level basketball court on the CHF grounds.

By the time nice weather returned in the spring, players and personnel from the Denver Nuggets volunteered their time to coach and teach CHF children basketball skills.

The newly built ballpark was strictly for the use of CHF residents and their guests. All families were required to sign the rules and liability waiver at orientation. Abuse of rules for using these facilities could result in fines and loss of privileges.

Bicycle Giveaway

Although the Christmas Adopt-A-Family program was successful year after year, one gift Connie Zimmerman always found that CHF children desired was a bicycle. There were times when donors would provide that gift, but it was always dependent upon whether the donor had the funds to donate one.

Pastor Kim Skattum from Crossroads Baptist Church contacted Connie to inform her that he had someone in his church who wanted to donate 100 bicycles to her program. The donor needed to know the children's ages, how many, and what sizes. Connie made a list and provided it to the church, and she was told to organize the children the weekend after Christmas and inform the children to be prepared for the delivery of a "big" gift. With no staff because of the Christmas week, Connie arrived at the CHF complex on a chilly 7°F morning to find two garbage trucks filled with 100 bicycles being handed out to CHF children.

Photo: *2008 Waste Connections 100-bicycle donation to the children living at Colorado Homeless Families*

The bicycle giveaway was a program within the Waste Connections company, which gathered contributions from its employees to purchase brand new bicycles for the children at CHF.

The 2008 nationwide "Christmas Challenge" wanted to do something where you make a difference and are adding something to someone's life. "This is a great way to do it," said Ryan Wurgler, the spokesperson for Waste Connections. The Waste Connections Bicycle donation event provided 1,300 bicycles to underprivileged Denver youth.

Unfortunately, after several days, some of the CHF families reported that the bicycles were being stolen at night. The townhomes were small, and there was no indoor storage or garage. Connie bought chains and locks to secure the bikes.

The following spring, Connie decided to build a six-foot privacy fence for security around the property's perimeter. After several calls for estimates, one man suggested she contact Home Builders Foundation.

She completed the application with the required historical information and the requirements for the project.

The Home Builders Foundation representative surveyed the CHF property and offered to donate $6,000 in supplies to Colorado Homeless Families if the CHF maintenance crew and volunteers could erect the fence themselves with the donation. The donation was also enough to build an enclosure and purchase seven bicycle racks to safely and orderly store more than 70 bicycles. This gave CHF children a location to keep the bicycles and lock them and keep them safe from theft.

Gardens

In 2006, after a house adjacent to the CHF offices was found to be a methamphetamine lab and went into foreclosure, CHF purchased the home and had it demolished for public safety.

After extensive EPA testing and any required remediation, in 2010, a group of 60+ volunteers from the community helped turn this vacant lot into a garden for the families at Colorado Homeless Families. During the growing season, families and their children learned how to grow a variety of fruits and vegetables in their garden plots. The gardens continue today, and volunteers prep the community garden beds each year. Colorado Homeless Families' residents' water, weed, and care for the edible garden—which supplies the families with produce to help feed their families and reduce grocery expenses.

Solar Program

In collaboration with Trees, Water & People and Lakota Solar Enterprises, Colorado Homeless Families had the first of two solar furnaces installed on a CHF residence and the CHF Family Resource Center.

Each solar panel provided a 25% savings in energy costs for a 1,200 square foot home. Installing two panels on a house at CHF allowed for approximately a 50% reduction in energy consumption and heating costs for a family. This provided an affordable heat source for families living below the poverty level.

In winter months in Colorado, it is common for heating and utility bills to exceed $150 per month for families living in transitional housing at CHF. Families pay 30% of their income in rent, and a $150 heating bill can easily exceed their rent payment. Many families cannot afford to pay the heating bill in the winter, so a lot of families keep the heat at 60 degrees or lower. When Denver experienced multiple below zero days, CHF found that many children would become ill.

Reducing energy costs by 25-50% per unit was one of two added benefits of installing and utilizing solar furnaces. Solar furnaces would also reduce dependency on pollution and destructive sources of energy, and the lower costs could help more Colorado Homeless Families in working toward self-sufficiency.

After the initial installation, CHF set a goal to construct and install the solar technology to share with others in the community.

Twelve residents at CHF were invited to South Dakota to receive job training in solar technology from Lakota Solar Enterprises, one of the nation's first 100% Native American-owned and operated renewable energy companies.

The other benefit to the CHF community is it promises to create jobs and skill training for residents who are looking for a career at a time when the economic downturn made it difficult for many residents to find employment.

The solar furnaces constructed at CHF through the skill training plans could be sold to other agencies and people in the community interested in purchasing solar technology at an affordable price. The profit from the sale of each furnace could be reinvested into the program and used to cover operating and program costs for CHF's transitional housing program.

Becoming more self-sufficient was important to CHF as grant funding from state and local pipelines had decreased over time with the changing economy.

The technology and job training program CHF adopted had been used in other poverty-stricken communities, most notably the Pine Ridge Reservation in South Dakota.

Maria Romero sat in the chair across the desk from Connie Zimmerman, the Executive Director of Colorado Homeless Families. Her application was spread out on the desk, and Mrs. Zimmerman had just asked her a question. This was the last step of the application process. Maria smiled, but she could not focus on what Mrs. Zimmerman was saying.

As of last month, Maria and her two pre-teen daughters were homeless. She hated that word: "homeless." Her calls to Access Housing and Sacred Heart House were both unsuccessful. Sacred Heart House suggested she contact Colorado Homeless Families. For now, however, she was living with an acquaintance in a small two-bedroom house. Her friend Sheila was nice enough to take them in after Maria lost her job at one of the now-bankrupt oil companies. Sheila had been a co-worker who had also lost her job but she was able to quickly find another because of her college degree. Sheila's mother needed to move in due to health issues, so Maria and her daughters had to leave. The next stop was either one of the homeless shelters or her car. She had been concerned when she received her pink slip at work and scared when they vacated their apartment. This was a whole new level of fear she didn't know existed. She was getting headaches and her stomach was upset all the time. Her hands shook, and her knees knocked as she walked into the Colorado Homeless Families offices.

As she sat in front of her application, Maria had no idea what she would do if it weren't approved. Her heart began to beat wildly, and her breathing became fast and shallow as the thoughts kept attacking her: "*You have very little money left. You have no place to live.*" Fear and panic finally seized her across her chest as Mrs. Zimmerman asked her if she was okay.

"I think I'm having a heart attack," whispered Maria.

Mrs. Zimmerman quickly left the room and came back with a man Maria had seen sitting in another office down the hall. He knelt in front of her and told her his name, which she couldn't remember.

He told her he was a firefighter but also worked at Colorado Homeless Families. He calmly asked her some questions and directed Mrs. Zimmerman to retrieve a glass of water.

This gentle man with a soothing voice and kind eyes told her to take deep breaths in and out and just focus on deep breathing. Then he told her to close her eyes and relax deep into the chair.

Her trembling began to subside when he softly asked her what made her happy, and she began to cry when she told him the thing she loved most was the giggling of her daughters.

He continued to talk to her, making her breathe, and spent some time walking her through it, relaxing her muscles one at a time.

By the time she opened her eyes, the internal storm was over, and he made her drink a glass of water. She was so embarrassed, and more tears rolled down her cheeks.

This had never happened to her before, and here she was trying hard to make a good impression so she could get some housing to keep her daughters safe. The man told her she did not have a heart attack but had experienced an anxiety attack, and Maria thought, *"How much worse could things get?"*

Maria's application to Colorado Homeless Families had been successful up until today. The telephone screening went well as the nice lady on the phone asked many questions.

Maria had to explain how she had become homeless. She had not completed college when her husband left her and their two young daughters. She had to go to work and had been working at the office of an oil company as a file clerk and also did receptionist work. It did not pay great, but she could make ends meet if she carefully budgeted, and she did get medical insurance for her family. She had been trying to return to school, but there was no one to help her with her children, and they had been too young to be left alone at night.

She received some severance pay when she lost her job, which only paid for three months of living expenses. She was sure she would have been able to find a permanent job during that time, but no one seemed to be hiring, and she did not have her college degree.

She was working for several temporary agencies, and they were keeping her employed, but she told the screener, she was determined to make things better for her family.

Maria was told that the second step of the application process was the criminal background check. Colorado Homeless Families placed extremely high importance on the safety and well-being of their families. They screened out felons or serious offenders of any kind. Drug and alcohol violators were referred to other fully equipped organizations to watch for continuing offenses. Misdemeanors of any kind were investigated in-depth.

Colorado Homeless Families performed reference checks of current and previous employers and landlords. Maria learned her previous landlord told CHF that she had been a great tenant but just could not pay the rent anymore and left the apartment clean and in move-in ready condition for the next family.

CHF also required four character references. Her friend had given Maria a great recommendation, having known her work ethic. Maria and her daughters helped Sheila with all the household chores and cleaning, were quiet, and the children were very smart and well-behaved. Maria was told the vetting process was thorough and included a credit check. This was a big concern for her as her ex-husband had left her with a mountain of debt and poor credit. She had been slowly working to repair it and build her good credit. And of course, she knew the loss of her job and the long difficult task of trying to find a new one would affect her credit.

A case manager from Colorado Homeless Families reviewed all her information with her at a local restaurant. The case manager was a genuinely nice lady. In fact, she even bought Maria a coffee and donut when they met. Because Colorado Homeless Families did not allow applicants going through the first step to know where the complex was located, case managers met with applicants off-site. The case manager reviewed all the requirements of the lease agreement, as well as the policies and procedures for residents. After the meeting, the case manager told Maria that her application and the complete investigation would be reviewed with the Executive Director, who would perform a final interview at the CHF offices.

Which is why Maria was sitting here today feeling terrified and worse, having an anxiety attack. She was afraid of what Mrs. Zimmerman must think of her, but she seemed genuinely concerned about Maria and asked if she wanted to take some extra time to relax or if she wanted to re-schedule.

Thinking of her daughters having to sleep in their car soon, Maria needed to keep moving through this day. She finally remembered Mrs. Zimmerman's question: *"Do you have any dreams or goals, Maria?"*

Maria told her that she had two job interviews scheduled this coming week for permanent placement, and she had also picked up the college course schedule for the next semester as the case manager recommended. Maria explained, it's difficult to have dreams and goals when you don't know where your next meal is coming from.

She said, "My most important goal is that my children be safe."

She had liked college and had always wanted to go back and earn her accounting degree, and she was also extremely interested in the computer classes she saw in the course schedule. Her dream was to finish college and find a good-paying job with a stable company. She wanted to own her own home and hopefully find a house where she could have an office, and her daughters could each have their own room and a backyard to play with friends. Maria hoped that she could eventually become involved in her daughters' school by volunteering or even to help tutor students who needed extra help.

Her schedule with her temporary jobs kept her from attending church regularly, and she was looking forward to settling into a home church for her and her daughters' benefit.

Mrs. Zimmerman stood up from her desk, arranged the application and paperwork in the file, and placed it in her desk drawer. Her hand came out holding a key, and she asked, "Maria, would you be interested in seeing one of the townhome units that might be available for you right away?"

Andrew Rusev would lay in bed as a young teenager in the Vidin Providence of Bulgaria and dream about the United States of America. It seemed that everyone Andrew knew lived in fear, and their providence lay between the borders of Romania and Serbia, where there was always some kind of political, economic, and even geological and environmental unrest.

After meeting Eileen, he learned they had a dream in common: a deep desire to live in America. They both loved the mountains and visited the alpine ranges in southeast Bulgaria on their short honeymoon. Returning to their low-paying jobs in Vidin, they continued to dream of a great future and prayed that America held that future for them.

The Revolutions of 1989 in Central and Eastern Europe created even more uncertainty in the country of Bulgaria. Emerging from communism, Bulgarians were encouraged by the new political climate, however, the slow process and overall instability of the country[47] was what made Andrew and Eileen finally decided to leave. They still believed that better opportunities for employment and education lay on the horizon for them in the United States.

Andrew and Eileen Rusev and their four small children came to Colorado with its beautiful mountains with unshakable hopes for a new and improved life of better employment and homeownership—something that was never a dream in Bulgaria.

Their first challenge was the language. Neither spoke English very well, and they arrived in the United States at a time when unemployment was high, and the economy was in a steep downturn. After weeks of searching, Andrew found a low-paying, labor-intensive job. They had found a small, shabby apartment when they arrived, but his job barely covered rent and utilities. Necessities such as food and clothing were stretched, and Andrew had begun to let fear creep into his thoughts. They found a local church and turned to its food bank, which helped cover their food needs. Month after month, their new life in the United States was a struggle. The fear grew in Andrew, knowing that if they had any small emergency or even an unexpected bill, their family would not be able to make it, and their dream would be over.

Andrew and Eileen felt their world crumble beneath them when Andrew was notified that he would be laid off from his job in 30 days. Two weeks later, Andrew and Eileen received a notice that the rent on their apartment was being raised at the beginning of the month.

Andrew immediately began a new job search, but there was nothing available. After many sleepless nights and pacing the apartment with worry, Andrew finally realized that they were at the end of the line. He knew that if something did not change in the next two weeks, they could not pay the rent, nor would they be able to eat. Then, he asked himself, where would they go? There was no one to turn to, and they had no family that could help or even any friends to live with. He did not know anyone that he could borrow money to pay their rent. The panic set in when he passed a park the next day on his way to work and saw homeless families living there. The anguish was almost unbearable, imagining he and Eileen and their four young children living under blankets, begging for food and money.

On the next trip to the church food bank, he was able to converse with a nice man about their situation, asking him if he knew of any work. The man told them to apply for Colorado Homeless Families transitional housing program and provided their information. Andrew and Eileen were thrilled when they were accepted. It was such a relief knowing their children would be warm and they would have something to eat. After the move into their CHF home, their case manager took them to the resource banks and explained that they could use the furniture, clothing, and food banks when they needed it. Andrew and Eileen were comforted knowing that whatever their family needed, Colorado Homeless Families could provide for them or help them.

The Rusev's case manager began to help them with a job search, and Andrew finally returned to work. Even though the new job paid slightly over minimum wage, their housing, food, and clothing situation had drastically improved. They took advantage of all the English language courses, the educational classes, and the support groups. They gleaned valuable information about how to live in their new country and embraced their new community quickly. The family also exceeded with volunteer activities and helped with whatever was needed. Andrew, especially, was appreciative to have another job, happy to have his family secure, and grateful to receive the support he needed when they were at their lowest point. Out of gratitude, he worked hard at his new job and always went above and beyond anything asked of him. He was a cheerful worker and volunteer and continually did what he was told without hesitation.

Executive Director Connie Zimmerman took notice of Andrew and saw in his file that he was a solid, hardworking individual. When Colorado Homeless Families needed to hire a maintenance worker, Andrew was the first person that Connie thought of and offered him the job. His work ethic never wavered, and he worked especially hard to take care of the staff and family's needs in his community.

After two years in the program, Andrew and Eileen were able to leave the program, having become entirely self-sufficient. They were able to purchase their own home and learned how to be fiscally responsible. Their case manager encouraged Eileen to set her own educational and professional goals, and as the children get older, Eileen will begin working toward her college education. Andrew and Eileen enjoy their new home in their new country and continue to live with deep gratitude. The dream that Andrew had in Bulgaria did, indeed, come true.

Five-year-old Lewis Hall slept like an angel thought his mother, Dani, watching him lay on the sofa in their apartment at Colorado Homeless Families.

Dani sat across the room in tears. Lewis had just finished a tantrum of epic proportions due to attention deficit hyperactivity disorder (ADHD). Her son had been diagnosed a couple of years ago when what she thought was the "terrible twos" became the "terrible threes—and fours." Dani had learned that this chronic condition included attention difficulty, hyperactivity, and impulsiveness. Many children carry this disorder into adulthood, and their emotions become like volcanos ready to erupt without warning. Doctors also warned Dani that ADHD contributes to low self-esteem, troubled relationships, and difficulty at school or work. She was heartbroken at hearing these words and didn't want that for her son. Lewis, named after her father, means "renowned warrior," and she had hoped that Lewis would be a warrior in life.

Adding to the intensity of Lewis' ADHD was her ex-husband. His long family history of mental problems and alcoholism had passed down to her ex-husband—in spades. He had never exhibited these behaviors when they were dating. She should have seen that his constant "life of the party" character was always followed by several days of moodiness.

Like a lot of people, hindsight is 20/20. She thought that their love would be enough, and worse, she thought she could fix him. After years of watching his spiraling depression and increased drinking, his violent behavior began, and she no longer felt safe. She didn't think he would ever hurt Lewis, but she wasn't willing to risk that. As it turned out, his behavior *was* hurting her son, learning that her husband's violent behavior, temper, and drinking made Lewis' ADHD worse.

Dani did the brave thing after one particularly terrible night of drinking: she fled with Lewis.

On the advice of a well-meaning neighbor, they went to a shelter in Denver that had been renowned for helping homeless mothers with children who wanted to become self-sufficient. They offered her and Lewis their In-House Stabilization Program, which provided temporary housing, food, clothing, transportation, and case management. They helped her with job placement, but Dani knew this was *only* temporary, and what she was earning would never cover rent, car payment, bills, and the extra care, special schooling, and pediatric ADHD medication needed for Lewis.

Dani continued to search for better alternatives to her situation and stumbled on a program called Colorado Homeless Families. She was hesitant to make yet another move, as every small change in routine or environment would worsen Lewis' ADHD, and he would act out more frequently with increased intensity. *"Lord, I need stability,"* Dani would pray day after day. She eventually applied to Colorado Homeless Families and was eventually accepted.

At first, Lewis continued to act out as he had a difficult time adjusting to yet another change. Dani prayed that this would be the stabilization they needed to get on track. The grounds of CHF were beautiful, and all the children who lived there seemed so happy playing together on their wonderful new playground. Lewis always had difficulties fitting in, both at their house with the neighborhood children and then again at the first shelter. At CHF, she saw that Lewis stayed to himself most of the time and was very reluctant to make friends. Dani would read to Lewis during their quiet time, and he would fall asleep. She would look out the window and see the children playing together and would wonder if these beautiful children knew how blessed they were to have homes and feel safe and secure. She even gave the CHF playground children a name: "little warriors."

All Dani knew was to keep moving forward. Her case manager encouraged her to do all she could to keep taking steps forward, setting goals, creating a stabilizing environment, and continuing with counseling. With counseling, medication, and attending his specialized school, Dani saw Lewis begin to improve.

As he felt safer and more stable, Dani saw him start to play with another child, then another, and then a group. He also began to call the other children his friends.

On one summer evening, Dani looked out her window and saw Lewis playing among all the other CHF children. She was so overwhelmed that tears came to her eyes. She saw that Lewis had come entirely out of his shell as he ran around playing excitedly with the other children. "My son *is* a warrior," she cried to herself.

Stabilizing Lewis helped stabilize Dani. Counseling for abuse victims was mandatory, as were support groups. Through the CHF program, she was able to get both good counseling and support, and her case manager continued to monitor her progress towards her goals. She had left the part-time job she had found while at the first shelter and found a barista job closer to CHF that offered her better hours and better pay. However, her case manager pushed her to set higher goals. One evening, she wrote down her goal: what she wanted was to put her bachelor's degree to work in the science field. She had completed her degree before leaving her husband, but jobs were rare with this specialized degree, and she was afraid that too much time may have elapsed between earning her degree and finding a job in that field. She knew resume gaps were not good, but Dani was encouraged that if she continued her pursuit of stabilizing her life with help and persistence, the job situation would stabilize also.

She and her case manager continued to look for a position in the science field. With great tenacity, Dani found herself hired by one of the Denver Metro municipalities in the laboratory testing units. Dani was challenged by her new job and it was the career she had dreamed of with unlimited growth and advancement opportunities.

The tears that came as she looked at her son asleep on the sofa were not so much about the tantrum he had just thrown. This had been his only tantrum in six months, and Dani was incredibly thankful for that. Dani also knew that the tantrum Lewis had thrown was because she had just told him that they had graduated from the CHF program and would be moving to their own home soon.

Lewis, understandably, did not want to leave his friends, which caused some distress at another change. Dani knew that this new change would be an exciting move and the last one they would have for a long, long time, further stabilizing their lives, thanks to Colorado Homeless Families.

The thunder rolled, and the lighting hit close. The gusty wind and driving rain rattled the windows forcing Dwight to go to the front of his house to watch the front yard light up with lightning.

Within seconds, his power went out; then, he saw the culprit: toppled trees and broken branches had knocked down the power line to his house. Branches and debris scattered his yard, and he could see part of a neighbor's roof tumbling down the street, wreaking havoc in the nearby park and destroying more trees in the process. "Great, all we need now is hail," grumbled Dwight of these ongoing Colorado summer storms.

Dwight Davis just wanted to be left alone. By everyone. Neighbors, kids, door-to-door salesmen, the storms, the Jehovah's Witnesses, and even his family. He had been through enough in his 50 years. The demise of two marriages, the loss of a career, and a brutal fight with cancer several years ago, which he won, left him feeling angry and resentful. Then these people—these "homeless" people—began moving into the townhomes across the street about a decade ago. And they built even *more* housing! And then even *more*!

He did not want homeless or low-income people living in his neighborhood. "Not in my backyard," was what he shouted each time he called the City of Arvada to complain about this housing.

The City staff tried to reason with him, explaining that the Colorado Homeless Families complex was well-maintained, had no code violations, nor had there been any noise, trash, or neighbor complaints. There had not even been a crime reported in the complex since it became Colorado Homeless Families. In fact, Colorado Homeless Families had been pivotal in the removal of the sex offenders living in his very neighborhood. Dwight never got anywhere with the City and always hung up the phone frustrated because they wouldn't do anything.

Because he worked from home, his daughter thought he was a built-in babysitter, so she would drop off his six-year-old grandson, Noah, so that she could get to her appointments easier. Noah was a good enough kid, just a little rambunctious for him. *He liked it quiet!*

Dwight didn't bother anyone, and he didn't want to be bothered. Noah quickly became attached to some kids his age playing in the nearby lot. Those kids belonged to the homeless and low-income families, and they were always out playing on the monkey bars and running around the playground, laughing, and shrieking. Earlier this year, however, Noah came home for lunch with his eyeglasses broken. Dwight immediately picked up the phone. He knew the Colorado Homeless Families' phone number by heart. He was always calling them to complain about those kids playing outside, that he didn't like the immigrant presence in the community, or that all the homeless do is bring unsavory characters and trouble to his neighborhood.

Whenever he called the CHF office, they always explained that Colorado Homeless Families was a transitional housing program with high standards for all residents.

If there was a specific complaint he had, they would talk with the resident in question and thoroughly investigate. If the resident did not take corrective action and immediately follow CHF guidelines, the resident would be required to leave.

Dwight had been told numerous times that the maintenance crew and resident volunteers kept the common grounds neat, and the outdoors and landscapes were well-maintained, so if he saw anything out of order, please let the CHF Office know. They claimed to be "helping those in need, but those in need could also be a blessing to their community and city." On this day, Noah's broken glasses were the final straw, and they were going to hear about it. He was going to make them pay.

The people who answered the phone were always nice. Dwight did not trust "nice."

He demanded to talk to the manager at once. "Those kids broke my grandson's glasses this morning!" he roared.

Unaffected, Connie Zimmerman explained that sometimes things happen when kids have fun and play together. "I'm NOT paying for broken glasses that your kids caused!" he bellowed.

"Of course, Mr. Davis, we'll pay for Noah's glasses. Get me the price to replace them, and we will be happy to do so. The kids here really enjoy playing with Noah; he is a joy to be around, and he has such good manners. He's a good boy, Mr. Davis." Dwight hung up the phone, hoping that every time he called, he made them a little bit more miserable to where they would move their people somewhere else. *"Not in my backyard,"* he thought again.

As he had been standing at the window on this stormy summer day, he had seen a part of old lady Backstrom's roof peel off in the wind and first land on the trees between Colorado Homeless Families and his house before it tumbled on down the street to the park. He was *not* going to be responsible for the damage from old lady Backstrom's roof or the damage to the trees and power lines. Looking across at Colorado Homeless Families, there didn't appear to be any damage to—anything.

Madder than a hornet, Dwight was able to contact Colorado Homeless Families. After the storm, Connie and one of her case managers, a retired police officer named Samuel, showed up on his doorstep.

Dwight insisted their crew, "clean up the mess in my front yard as the trees were partially your responsibility and should have been maintained years ago."

"We'll have Colorado Homeless Families maintenance people come over and clean up any damage right away, Mr. Davis," Connie told him.

Dwight demanded they also repair the electrical lines that went into his house.

Wanting to place the responsibility with the appropriate party, Samuel explained, "Mr. Davis, this storm damage would be covered by insurance, and you should contact your insurance company to pay for the repairs."

"I don't even have the money for any deductible to repair this damage!" declared Dwight. "You people need to take care of this!"

Dwight watched Connie and Samuel walk towards their car when Connie slowed, she gently nodded her head, and turned and spoke, "Mr. Davis, I would like to help you. I know someone who could repair the wires to your home if that would be okay with you." God had spoken to Connie: *"If it is in your capacity to bless your neighbor, then do it."*

Dwight was dumbfounded, "Could you? Would you? I need it done right away; I have no power!"

Connie replied, "Yes, let me see what I can do. I'll have our maintenance guys clean up the trees and damage. And I'll get someone out here to fix your power line."

Dwight went inside and slammed the front door. When he saw Mrs. Zimmerman gently nod her head, he knew that she had heard from God. The next day, Mrs. Zimmerman's electrician coordinated with the power company and quickly attended to the power line and repairs.

Over the next week, Dwight picked up the phone on two separate occasions to call Colorado Homeless Families and complain about the noisy children, but he quickly replaced the receiver, never having completed those calls. Connie knew their neighbor would never call again because Proverbs 16:7 says, *"When a man's ways please the Lord, he maketh even his enemies to be at peace with him."*

The world before 9/11 looked much different than the world after 9/11, which split the world into an "us" vs. "them" arena, with many believing that religion was the biggest divider.

In southeast Asia, the Islamic Republic of Pakistan became an independent nation in 1947 and was formed as a multi-racial and multi-religious nation. Its 1973 Constitution guarantees religious freedom to all, with Muslims being the 97% majority and the religious minorities including Christians, Hindus, Buddhists, and Sikhs at 3%. The Islam religion itself ensures religious freedom to the whole of humanity. Against Islamic principles, some Muslims are adamant about denying religious freedom to other faiths in Pakistan.[48]

Christians were especially targeted, particularly in the aftermath of 9/11, primarily due to Pakistan's decision to join those fighting *against* Al Qaeda and the Taliban. Sixteen-year-old Sajir Deen and his parents knew, however, the Christian community in Pakistan had been under threat for several decades. The "blasphemy laws," passed in 1984 by General Muhammad Zia-ul-Haq, the four-star general who became the sixth President of Pakistan, had been used with great effectiveness to coerce land and other businesses from Christians.

The blasphemy laws carried a mandatory death penalty for any action or comment that could be construed as disrespect for Islam or the Prophet Muhammad. This law had been used to terrorize the Christian community and other religious minorities for years.

The largest employment sector in Pakistan was the small and medium-sized businesses, which employed more than 78% of Pakistan's non-agriculture labor force.[49] After 9/11, Sajir and his family, who were all Christians, began experiencing the common practice of either refusing to hire or the firing of Christian workers. Pakistan's labor code imposed rigid hiring conditions and burdensome firing procedures. Even though the employer had to pay the equivalent of 90 weeks of salary in severance and penalties for a dismissal[50], the firing of his Christian family members and close friends began to escalate.

Knowing they would need to flee the country, Sajir's family chose to immigrate to the United States. Immediately following 9/11, when confronted by the United States with a choice, Pakistan made a strategic decision. Its government stood aside and allowed the U.S.-led coalition to destroy the Taliban regime. The country actively helped in arresting more than 500 Al Qaeda operatives and Taliban members. Pakistani forces played a leading part in tracking down Khalid Sheikh Mohammed, Abu Zubaydah, and other key Al Qaeda figures. [51]

Because Pakistan decided to stand with the United States government on the "war on terror," it was easier for Sajir's family to enter the United States than if they were from enemy nations. Seeking refuge, they put in their applications for permanent legal residence in the United States. Sajir's family went through a rigorous and interrogative-like interview process. They were not detained, however, they still felt there was a shadow of suspicion. They wanted to believe that it was because of their Christian values and belief system that allowed them to progress quickly through the process.

With no way to support themselves, Colorado Homeless Families was contacted on behalf of Sajir's family and was asked to help them in any way possible. CHF had housed 6 Pakistani families in the past, and all had successfully graduated from the program, became self-sufficient, and were enjoying their life and careers in the United States as American citizens. Connie Zimmerman, Executive Director of Colorado Homeless Families, had an opening and accepted Sajir's family into the program.

The Deen family was appreciative from the moment they arrived at their townhome. Even though Sajir's parents spoke a little English, they still wanted to attend ESL courses and educational seminars to help them assimilate to their new country. They worked closely with their case manager who was well-qualified to mentor newly-arrived refugee families in Colorado. They asked to spend extra time with the case manager who showed a special interest in helping them adjust and acclimate to their new culture, helped them find a Christian church, and helped them find proper jobs that would give them the best start to their new life.

Sixteen-year-old Sajir, who did speak English, took well to his new school. He excelled in his classes and graduated from high school with excellent grades. He began planning to attend a local university with his sights set on becoming a doctor.

Sajir and his family realized their dream when they graduated from Colorado Homeless Families, moved into their own home, and celebrate daily their opportunity to live the Christian life freely in the United States.

Dean felt the tears at the back of his eyes. He and his wife, Margaret, faithfully attended church services at Denver Presbyterian.

Today, they were listening to a woman speak about the many homeless families she was helping through her nonprofit, Colorado Homeless Families. She spoke of these families called the "working poor" who were families that worked hard but earned low wages and could not keep up with the rising living costs, including housing. These families lacked financial resources, professional training, and education. Even more than those, one of their biggest challenges was that these families also lacked community and a support network of family and friends that could help them obtain affordable housing and many of the other things that many hardworking people can achieve.

As Connie Zimmerman extolled the benefits of a program such as Colorado Homeless Families that would help people become more self-sufficient, Dean reflected on his own life and was overcome and touched by these stories. A profoundly empathic person, he committed in his heart to help in any way he could.

Concern for others cultivated a deep connection to the Colorado Homeless Families organization and the struggling families they were dedicated to helping, and Dean began to send regular large monetary donations. After the passing of his dear wife of seven decades, Dean made an appointment with Connie Zimmerman. He knew in his heart that his giving was not nearly enough, and he wanted to find out how he could help these families even more.

On a beautiful summer morning, Dean took a guided tour of the Colorado Homeless Families complex and the outlying HUD transitional homes. After seeing all 42 homes, he enjoyed watching the children on their designated playground and walking through the bountiful community garden. Dean visited the office building and resource center where education seminars, job training, counseling, and support meetings were held. Dean happily explored the food, clothing, and furniture bank and was able to see how these services helped provide the support so desperately needed by families working to become self-sufficient.

Deeply touched by all the assistance provided but knowing more was needed, he sat at Connie Zimmerman's desk at the end of the tour. "What do you need?" he asked, ready and willing to give whatever was needed most. Connie had mentioned needing to replace a balcony on one of the buildings several items on the guided tour, and Dean handed Connie a check to replace it. It was in desperate need of repair, but Colorado Homeless Families could never find the extra funds for the repairs.

Month after month, Dean would call Connie and ask, "What do you need?" Holidays were always made brighter at Colorado Homeless Families through the generosity of Dean. At Thanksgiving, he purchased 50 turkeys for all the CHF families. On one visit, he remembered meeting a Pakistani family who had come to the United States to escape religious persecution. His heart went out to them, and he gifted them a large donation to help with their new life in America.

Dean, lovingly known as the "generous angel," continued to donate money for repairs to the facilities. One of his donations was able to replace many older furnaces because he did not want the families to be cold during the frigid, Colorado winters.

Gena, a woman who had successfully graduated from the Colorado Homeless Families program several years earlier, had called CHF. She asked for assistance as she had been diagnosed with a brain tumor and had missed three months of work after the surgery for recovery. Gena desperately needed help with her rent and food expenses to avoid becoming homeless again. One of

Dean's "What do you need" phone calls led him to donate all the money necessary to cover Gena's expenses during recovery.

Connie's last visit with Dean was at his home, where she sat with him, and they prayed together. Although he was very ill, it was always his deep pleasure to support CHF. He presented Connie with a final check before slipping into a coma and passing away later that day.

Dean's children continue their father's legacy of generous giving to Colorado Homeless Families with food, clothing, and even Margaret's artwork that had been on display at a local gallery. Dean wanted to make sure that something happy hung in each Colorado Homeless Families' homes.

Casper Janssen sat in his well-worn recliner and stared at The Price Is Right game show. This is where he sat every morning while Bob Barker smiled at the contestants who won prizes and money. If Casper watched another commercial for Ultra Downey, Dial soap, or Rice-a-Roni, he would lose his mind.

His attention turned to the large picture window. The view of the red, octagon STOP sign and the run-down house catty-corner from theirs never changed.

"Face it," Casper thought to himself, "you're bored." Having been a Certified Public Accountant for his entire career, he was already listless after only nine months of retirement.

Casper had tackled a lengthy list of "honey-dos" to take care of when he retired; he finished them all in less than 60 days.

Norma, his wife, worked part-time and had clubs, societies, friends, volunteer work, and bible study that kept her life engaged and fulfilled. He and Norma took the first of many planned trips to the Netherlands three months ago and had a wonderful time. They had also taken a trip to Virginia to visit their daughter and her family and to Seattle to visit their son. Now here he sat on a Tuesday morning, him, Bob Barker, and the forty-something housewife named "Julie" who had just won a refrigerator and was bouncing up and down with excitement.

Casper shut off the television and listened to the grandfather clock tick-tick-tick in the hallway. It kept ticking every hour, keeping daily records of his lack of purpose. He thought back to their trip to the Netherlands, specifically some locals they had met while taking a break from touring the tulip gardens in spectacular bloom. The couple they met during lunch inquired his name: Casper. His new friend told him his name had a Dutch origin—Gaspar—and meant "bringer of treasure".

He knew his family had Scandinavian roots somewhere, but he never paid much attention to stuff like that. His new friends mentioned that Gasper was one of the Three Magi who brought gifts to the infant Jesus along with Melchior and Balthasar. His wife, Norma, loved hearing that story from their new friends, but Casper joked that the meaning of his name, "bringer of treasure," meant he was good at getting his clients' tax refunds.

Something stuck with Casper about that conversation. He found in the quiet moments that he wanted to continue to fulfill his name and be able to bring treasure to others in whatever way he could. He rose from the chair and decided to take a stroll. Fresh air might shake the theme song playing from The Price Is Right out of his mind. Crossing the street, he stared at the dilapidated house catty-corner from theirs. He'd seen several families in and out of it over the years. He figured they were homeless or squatters.

The Colorado economy had taken a terrible downturn in recent years, and he felt awful for those who were so disastrously affected by it. His neighbors tried to chase out those who stayed in the house, but Casper could see their pain, so he and Norma sometimes tried to help them with food and household goods. Most moved on after only a short stay.

As he looked at the run-down house, he wondered about buying it, but he really wasn't that handy, and he wouldn't be able to complete most of the renovations needed without having to hire professionals. More than that, he knew from working with clients at his office that he primarily liked interacting with people. Interacting with young people especially energized him and gave him purpose.

He knew from raising his two kids that he enjoyed nurturing. Hadn't his kids grown to be loving, energetic, and confident mature adults with integrity? He was proud of both of them. He was good at supporting and teaching them as they were growing up.

Casper wandered around the neighborhood, waving at some of the other retirees and stopping to help a little boy fix the training wheels on his new bike. He petted the neighbor's dogs and chatted with Dave, their mailman of 25 years.

Entering the house, he flipped through the stack of mail and stopped on a flyer addressed to Norma from Colorado Homeless Families. Intrigued, he sat down at his desk and opened it.

Something nudged him. He re-read the flyer from front to back. The flyer praised the benefits of one of their youth programs and the strong sense of community it had fostered within the youth.

He called the telephone number on the flyer and asked to speak with whoever was in charge about the possibility of volunteering in some way with the youth. He was transferred to a woman who introduced herself as Connie Zimmerman, Executive Director.

Connie described the CHF program and explained how most of the children's parents worked long hours, so there was a need of interaction with caring adults.

The staff at Colorado Homeless Families had noticed that some of the children were isolating themselves into small groups based upon their family background, Connie explained.

There were reports that many of the young boys in the community who did not have the counsel of a father or male adult figure in their lives were starting to become intimidating and aggressive towards the other kids. Connie explained that CHF was beginning a "Grandparent Program," where "grandparents" could "adopt" these young men, especially guys between the ages of 8 and 16 years old, because during this time many influences affect them and can change their future in meaningful ways. Quality men and women could now spend quality time with them.

The Grandparent Program was flexible and might include driving to sporting activities, helping young people with homework, tutoring, teaching those of age to drive, and many other things to support the CHF youth. The goal of The Grandparent Program was to significantly increase the self-confidence of the youth who are involved with the program, as well as blessing and giving more value to the grandparents who volunteer their time to make a lasting and positive difference in a child's life.

"*Where do I sign up, and when can I start?*" declared Casper.

Giddy with excitement, six-year-old Jayda leaped from her bed and ran, full speed, down the hall. "Mommy, Mommy, Mommy," she yelled, "I'm six today. Six, six, six, six!" Jumping up and down, Jayda's mom tried to contain the explosion of delight coming from her little girl. "Go get dressed, and I'll have your pancakes ready," Tamara told her.

Jayda sprinted to the bathroom, put her hair into a ponytail, washed her face, brushed her teeth, then ran to her room and put on the birthday outfit her daddy had given her. Mommy and daddy had just gotten a divorce, but daddy came by last night and gave her a hug and a gift before he went to work. He let her open the fancy wrapped box, and in it, she found a glittery pink shirt with rainbows and matching pants. She was s-o-o excited, but still a little disappointed that daddy would not be able to make her party.

Tamara finished making pancakes in time for her little, pink Tasmanian devil to whirl into the kitchen. She was glad to see Jayda coming out of her blue mood. The divorce had taken a toll on them all, but Jayda especially because she had a special bond with her dad. Jayda cried for days when Darnell had moved out.

Their marriage had been bad for a while, but like many married couples, they tried to work it out for the sake of their daughter.

They were trying to keep things civil, but it was difficult. Especially now that he had taken on a night job and was living in a house with four rowdy, single guys, she did not like Jayda spending any time there. Added to her blue mood was that Jayda would not get to spend much time with her stepsister anymore. The two would see much less of each other now that Darnell was gone, and Jayda adored her stepsister.

Tamara wanted Jayda to have wonderful memories and solid relationships, so she reached out and invited Jayda's stepsister to the birthday party, which would be a great surprise for her. Tamara had scrimped and saved, cut coupons, and searched for sales for Jayda to have a good birthday party.

"A great memory," she thought as she bought the streamers and the balloons. Living on a shoestring budget was difficult, but her job at the mall did not pay very well, and it made her angry that these companies kept you scheduled at less than 40 hours, so there were no benefits.

She tried to talk to her boss about it several times and explained that she was having a difficult time making her rent without full-time hours. Those conversations were ignored by her boss, and she knew that working a second job was not an option as she needed to be home at night with Jayda. She knew she had to figure something out quickly.

She did not want to leave her house because there were great memories, and it was the only home Jayda had known. The landlord would come knocking soon, she knew.

Jayda settled into Saturday morning cartoons with her large company of stuffed animals. Tamara got busy cleaning the house, decorating, and baking Jayda's party cake. She hoped that Jayda and her friends would see past the sparseness of the decorations. She had saved most of the money set aside for the party for all the kids to go to Chuck E. Cheese for dinner.

Soon guests began arriving, and Jayda's delight was infectious. The party was so fun, and Tamara was glad to see everyone invited attended, including her stepdaughter bringing several of her friends. Some of the moms stayed to help and enjoy the afternoon.

Everyone had a fun time, and they laughed and laughed that the candles on Jayda's cake would not blow out. Tamara had found the trick candles on a clearance sale, and she read on the package that they would re-light. Jayda and her friends roared with laughter while trying to keep them blown out, and Tamara was mindful of taking as many pictures as possible for a sixth birthday memory book. By mid-afternoon, having let the girls have cake and ice cream *first*, it was time to leave for Chuck E. Cheese for dinner.

"Look at the firetrucks, mommy," said Jayda with wide eyes as they made their way home from Chuck E. Cheese, where everyone had a crazy great time. Tamara heard the sirens and saw several firetrucks on her block, but as she got closer to her house, she saw they were next door.

"I hope the Jackson's are okay," she thought to herself. Mr. and Mrs. Jackson were retired, and they were terrific neighbors. Mrs. Jackson had even baked cookies for Jayda's party, and Mr. Jackson had kindly mowed her lawn earlier in the week.

As she eased her car closer to her house, Tamara's heart dropped into her stomach, and she gasped. "Oh, *NOOO!*" she cried and slammed on the brakes behind a firetruck. She yelled at Jayda to stay put in the back seat, and she jumped out of the car and ran towards the firefighter standing in the street.

Then she saw the horror that her house was nothing but burned-out walls and smoldering ash.

In the days following, the fire investigator deemed the fire to be accidental, likely caused by the trick candles Tamara had bought. "One must have re-ignited and lit a nearby napkin," he told her.

With nowhere to go, Tamara and Jayda stayed with a family of one of the friends that attended Jayda's birthday party. They had a small, spare bedroom and offered it to them for as long as they needed it. Jayda's crying every night broke Tamara's heart; all their memories were gone, Jayda's precious stuffed animals and books, her birthday gifts, their clothes, and furniture. Everything was gone. Memories were ash.

Jayda's school counselor heard about the devastating fire and told Tamara about Colorado Homeless Families. "They can even help with clothing and furniture," she said. Tamara dialed 4-1-1 and asked for their number.

Within a short time, Tamara and Jayda were headed to their new place. Jayda had gone back into her blue mood and was especially upset about leaving her school and friends. Both were nervous and had no idea what to expect in these new circumstances. CHF helped Tamara select furniture and clothing from the bank, and some of the neighbors helped them move in and get set up. Darnell had been able to earn a little extra money and helped buy some housewares, some stuffed animals and a few books for Jayda.

By the beginning of summer, Jayda began to emerge from her blue mood and made some friends at CHF. She understood that these kids were just like her as they played together.

Jayda began to build new memories during her first summer. The CHF summer program had youth leaders who engaged them in a wide variety of activities. Jayda learned to swim, learned to fish, and enjoyed her trip to the Denver Zoo and Museum of Natural History.

Tamara, through counseling, support groups, educational seminars, and working with a case manager, was able to re-enter the workforce that worked with her new schedule. She also set some personal, professional, and educational goals for herself. She began attending a local university full-time, with plans to graduate with a Bachelor of Arts in Communication Studies. Having her degree, Tamara set her goal to work in Human Resources and help guide others through the maze of problems that she experienced and work to change hiring and scheduling policies.

Tamara and Jayda sat at their dining room table, enjoying one of their new favorite hobbies: working on a jigsaw puzzle. When

Jayda put the final piece in the puzzle, Tamara reflected that they had lost so much in the fire but have been able to rebuild, renew, and restart, making new memories.

Lily Bennett woke with a start. The first thing that came to her thoughts was, *"I came that they may have and enjoy life, and have it in abundance to the full, till it overflows."* She remembered that as being the last half of John 10:10. She had not been to church in *years*. Why did she remember that now?

This verse certainly gave her pause; she didn't have a life, much less enjoy it. "Abundance" and "overflowing" were words that made her cry because she knew they were a promise but did not see those words anywhere in her life.

As she began to stir, her hip bumped the steering wheel. Trying to stretch and move was impossible when you sleep in a car, and she had been doing that for a month.

She quietly opened the car door, careful not to disturb her two daughters sleeping in the back. The girls, 14-year-old Daisy and 12-year-old Poppy, lay side by side in the cargo area of her old, beat-up SUV. She crossed her fingers that it would start each time she turned the key.

Her daughters were buried under blankets she bought at Goodwill last week when the weather became chilly at night. They would park wherever they could, usually in a park with a public bathroom nearby. Sometimes the police would drive by at night, see them, and make them move on. Last night, either no police officer had seen them, or if they did, they didn't care and just drove on.

Lily walked with her backpack across the park to the bathrooms, and the grass crunched under her feet from the freeze that came last night. Looking back at her car, the windows had frosted over, and she knew it would not be long until it would be too cold to stay in the car. She washed up as best she could, brushed her teeth, put her hair in a ponytail, and changed into clean clothes.

As she stared at her reflection in the mirror, the verse came again: *"I came that they may have and enjoy life, and have it in abundance to the full, till it overflows."* *"Lord,"* she prayed, *"please help us. We are desperate, and I'll do anything to have and enjoy life."*

Daisy and Poppy were stirring when Lily returned to the car. They knew the drill: take their backpacks and head to the bathroom. The one thing that Lily instilled into both of her daughters was that education is crucial. So, even when they were evicted from their apartment and forced to live in the car, Lily would see to it that they would never miss school.

After dropping her daughters off at school, she drove to her job at the fast-food restaurant. She had been part of the "significant layoffs" announced by the telecommunications firms: Qwest, AT&T, WorldCom, Sprint, and many others who were experiencing the downsizing in the industry.[52] She had been there for nearly ten years, where she had started in the mailroom and had worked in several different departments. Her two-year Associate of Arts degree in Liberal Arts seemed worthless in applying for new jobs.

She finally applied at several temporary agencies, and they kept her working, but nothing ever materialized for permanent placement.

The temp jobs were barely able to keep her afloat. Her ex had defaulted on child support more than ten years ago, so she needed an income sizable enough to care for all three of them.

Although she was glad when she was hired at the fast-food restaurant full time, the starting pay for a fast-food worker was just barely $5.50 an hour. Within two months, she borrowed money because she was short on the rent. The month before they were evicted, she began going to a local food bank so they would be able to eat something other than just fast food from where she worked.

Their apartment superintendent was understanding, but he could no longer grant her rent extensions, forcing her and her daughters to their car for survival. "It's only temporary," she told them, but ever the optimists, they saw it as an adventure.

Lily was worried, concerned for their safety, and terrified that it would become permanent. Cleaning up tables one day at work, she found a newspaper and saved it to read on her break—still scouring the help wanted ads. On page three, there was an article about the "working poor," which was defined as persons who spent at least 27 weeks in the labor force but whose incomes still fell below the official poverty level.

In 2004, there were nearly 7.6 million individuals classified as "working poor," and the working poor rate was higher for women, but this classification diminishes as workers attain higher levels of education.[53] She tore out the article and folded it in her pocket.

"I am a working poor person," she thought as she returned from her break.

Lily picked her daughters up from school, and they usually went to a local library. Or if she had to work, she would park the car under the brightest light in the parking lot so they could do their homework. She would bring them food on her break, make them use the bathrooms and then go back to the car until she was finished with her shift. One night at the library, as her daughters did their homework, Lily pulled the newspaper article on the working poor from her pocket and began to do some research. She discovered an organization in the Denver area called Colorado Homeless Families. They were a transitional housing organization dedicated to helping the homeless get back on their feet. The Executive Director, Connie Zimmerman, talked about the plight of the working poor, so Lily wrote down the contact information and applied the next day.

One week later, Lily and her daughters were moving with excitement into their townhome at Colorado Homeless Families.

They required items from the CHF furniture bank and food bank to get started, but Lily was extremely relieved for her daughters to be out of their car, eating nutritious food, and having a safe and comfortable place to sleep at night.

Lily knew this program was a godsend, and God had answered her prayer of *"help me."* She decided to fully immerse her and her daughters in the CHF program, and immediately made some good friends that felt like the family she'd never had.

Through case management and goal setting, Lily became determined to advance her education from a general Liberal Arts degree into something usable. She had been interested in kinesiology and specializing in sports rehabilitation but decided to make that a long-term goal. She kept her fast-food job because they offered her flexible hours for her classes to become a certified medical assistant.

Lily, Daisy, and Poppy celebrated Christmas at Colorado Homeless Families and were happily adopted by a wonderfully warm family who participated in the Adopt-A-Family Christmas Program. Lily excelled at her coursework and was on track to finish with honors. Daisy was called to the principal's office one day the following spring. Thinking she was in trouble, and her mom would have to be notified, she was surprised when she found out she had made the Principal's Honor Roll. Lily threw her a party attended by many CHF families and their new friends. Lily decided to return to church and looked forward to graduating from the program and becoming independent and successful.

Daisy wrote a letter to the CHF staff: *Just a few years ago, I was too worried about my family to do well in school. My mom never believed she would do so well, and I never thought I would do so well in school. CHF has given us a new life. Now we are on our way to becoming self-sufficient like regular families! Soon, I know we will have our own home and now my mom does not have to cry at night. I am so thankful that CHF is here to help families like us.*

Emily Carter sat in sixth period U.S. History II class as Mrs. Felterman droned on about progressivism in history. "Progressives" wanted a more accountable government that would improve society in the United States.

Emily had a tough time keeping her eyes open and watched as the clock ticked from 1:43 to 1:44 to 1:45. *"Thirty minutes left"*—as she stifled a yawn.

Thankfully, she was assigned a seat by the window and watched a squirrel with its flicking tail bounce from one flowering tree to another. April was a difficult month to endure. Spring break was long over, but the last day of school in May seemed too far away to get excited. The days were nice in April, and she longed to get outside and be active.

That morning, she attended one of the career meetings offered by her high school. Counselors offered her information meant to help students prepare for college, explore careers, and develop a future in the workforce.

Being a junior, she knew good grades were important for college, and that had never been a problem. The checklist they supplied her with this morning emphasized the importance of volunteer work, especially in an area of interest for her. The thing is, she didn't even *know* what that interest was, and her mom and dad were urging her to look into career aptitude testing to find some possibilities.

She knew what she liked: people, young to old. She liked helping. She was good at inspiring others to action, which made her a good cheerleader, a good student council member, and a good mentor to underclassmen.

A j-o-b? Not sure yet.

Emily's school always promoted itself as a community-driven and achievement-oriented high school, so each school club and organization were required to pick a community charity to help each semester. One of her friends knew a couple of students at their high school that had lost their homes and were staying at a place that helped the family get back on their feet.

Last semester, she and all the school's Honor Society members held a food drive. They collected two pallets of food for this organization. Emily learned that some people living there had lost their jobs, others worked at such low paying jobs they could not even afford food. So, Colorado Homeless Families had a food bank where their residents could get food and a warehouse where they could get furniture, clothes, or other things they needed.

The food drive at the school lasted a week, and on Saturday, the Honor Society members loaded their cars with all the food and took it to the Colorado Homeless Families food bank.

Emily was surprised. When she heard the word "homeless," she thought of the dirty people pushing shopping carts and living in tents or under blankets along the roads. She never understood how things could ever get so bad for someone to have to live like that, but what shocked her the most was to find there were all ages of people that lived in the very nice homes at Colorado Homeless Families.

She watched as several older people cleaned, swept, and tidied the grounds, but then there was a playground too, and she could see children playing and hear them laughing. Kids! She had no idea that homelessness affected kids.

After unloading the cars, Mrs. Zimmerman, the Executive Director of CHF, thanked the Honor Society members and gave them all a big hug. Emily decided to ask her about the children she saw playing and wanted to know if they were homeless at one time. Mrs. Zimmerman told her, "Yes, they were." She explained to Emily how important it was for the children to play together and engage with other children to help them overcome some of the challenges they may have had while watching their family succumb to homelessness. She explained that it is within everyone's ability to improve conditions of life, ours and others, and we should intervene and help whenever possible.

The children at CHF had recently taken part in an Easter egg hunt, and they all received free lunches during the summer along with tutoring services for those who may have been struggling in school. Mrs. Zimmerman explained that while these children live here, their parent—or both parents—are working and going to school to get back on their feet to make better lives for the entire family, so the children take part in the Summer Youth Program. Children 7 to 16 participate twice each week, and volunteer Youth Leaders keep them active and connected with fun activities such as swimming, bowling, miniature golf, various outside games, hiking, and fishing.

They also visit the Zoo and other activities appropriate for the youth. Mrs. Zimmerman explained that the Summer Youth Program provides these vulnerable children with fun and safe activities when they are out of school for the summer.

Emily looked at the classroom clock: 2:10. Just enough time for Mrs. Felterman to write out the assignment on the board that was due next week: *Progressivism in society today. What policies do you believe need to be reformed? Civil service? Food safety? Rights for workers? Economic and resulting homelessness? And who is a person that you would consider to be a modern-day progressive?*

Emily smiled and wrote: *Mrs. Connie Zimmerman.* Closing her notebook just as the class was released, Emily looked forward to the last day of school, for she would be volunteering at the Colorado Homeless Families' Summer Youth Program.

She was excited. She had found her interest.

ALL THINGS WORK TOGETHER FOR GOOD

New Duplexes

While surveying the Colorado Homeless Families property to build a perimeter fence, Home Builders Foundation offered to build three duplex homes for Colorado Homeless Families. Executive Director Connie Zimmerman replied that there was not a property available to her at that time. Still, the representative asked her to think about it and get back to them. They liked what she was doing with the Colorado Homeless Families program, and they were willing to help with whatever was needed.

Connie began to pray, *"God, You are out ahead and moving, so You must want us to build these."* One morning as she walked around the property, she remembered an empty half-acre lot next to the CHF complex where the children would play. One day, she noticed a man placing a sign announcing he was going to build something. The next time Connie saw the man in the empty lot, she approached him.

He told Connie that he had purchased the property and was going to build some townhomes. She said to him that the children who lived at the Colorado Homeless Families complex had been playing on the property and needed a place to continue to play. He told her he had already obtained permits to build townhomes. Connie offered to buy the land for what he paid for it telling him, *"Remember, God blesses those who help the homeless."* She asked him to seriously consider it and let her know because she needed his property for the homeless transitional housing community.

The very next day, Connie received his call offering to sell her the property, but she needed to pay for the cost of the building permits. Quickly obtaining a one-year bridge loan with a long-term banking partner, Connie sent out three grant requests to help pay the $104,000 for the land and permits.

Within six months, all the grants were issued to pay off the bridge loan. Connie had developed a stable and trusting relationship with the local bank, and they frequently contacted her to inquire about any needs they could help her with to expand the good work in the community that she was doing at CHF. On this particular day, the bank was offering a nice loan at an excellent rate. Not having any current needs, Connie wondered if something was on the horizon. She knew not to get ahead of God, praying, *"God, is this You going before me? Is this moving forward what You want for CHF?"*

Meanwhile, on the other side of the half-acre lot for which Connie had just received grant money, was one and a half acres owned by a couple that had several unused and unoccupied buildings. Connie contacted the owners, and within days, they came over to discuss selling the property. While they walked around, Connie was praying, *"Lord, how much should I offer to buy this property for? I don't know what the true value is, so what do I offer?"*

Listening to the Lord, the seller pointed to properties around the neighborhood, telling Connie that one is $200,000, that one is $150,000. *"$100,000"* is what the Lord spoke to Connie, and that is what she offered them.

The man's wife spoke up and said, "That's what he said he wanted to get for it!"

Connie notified the CHF board members, and they agreed to proceed. She also contacted Home Builders Foundation, and she accepted their offer to build three duplexes as she had finally acquired the land needed. When they arrived to survey the land, the representative invited Connie to also contact HomeAid Colorado, a nonprofit that would like to help in the building process.

HomeAid was founded in 1989 by the Orange County chapter of the Building Industry Association of Southern California. Headquartered in Irvine, California, HomeAid is a nonprofit organization that provides housing for the homeless. It builds multi-unit developments for homeless families and individuals.

After a project is built, HomeAid donates it to a charity or nonprofit to continue operations. HomeAid's ultimate vision to end homelessness starts at the core by asking the question, "Where does someone go when they find themselves without a home?"

The strength of HomeAid is that it leverages the resources of the home building community and its corporate partners. HomeAid has been the leading nonprofit developer of housing and programmatic facilities for people experiencing or at risk of homelessness. They operated through a network of 19 affiliates in 13 states[54], one of which is HomeAid Colorado, which had generously agreed to build the new duplexes for Colorado Homeless Families.

With all the pieces in place, First Bank offered to oversee the building finances and pay the builders from the additional loan, the grant money, and HomeAid Colorado's donations. With loans, grants, and donations, Colorado Homeless Families only paid 30% of the new duplexes.

January 2004 saw the new and much-needed addition to the Colorado Homeless Families complex with the dedication of two duplexes. HomeAid Colorado organized the contractors, labor, materials, and consulting services. All subcontractors donated their work and most of the materials. Each duplex included a 1,200 square foot three-bedroom unit and a 1,000 square foot two-bedroom unit. These new units would allow Colorado Homeless Families to offer transitional housing to six more families.

Hollywood's Extreme Makeover: Home Edition

November 2004 was the target date for the third duplex completion. However, HomeAid had exciting news for Colorado Homeless Families: ABC Television Network's show Extreme Makeover: Home Edition wanted to build the third duplex. 15.75 million viewers watched this Emmy-winning program each week during the 2004-2005 TV season, making it the 15th most popular series on television.[55]

The plan began in November 2004, when Extreme Makeover: Home Edition partnered with the volunteers of HomeAid Colorado and Standard Pacific Homes to build the third duplex.

Although Connie had never seen the program, HomeAid was excited about the prospect of this partnership, and the CHF board voted to allow the project to move forward. Extreme Makeover: Home Edition was ready to film almost immediately over a 10-day timeframe.

Connie and the CHF staff were enthusiastic. National exposure for the homeless problem was a good thing. Not knowing what this television program was all about, Connie, her staff, and the board of directors watched the program the following Sunday. The board decided that they would ask for everything allowable during the first sit-down meeting with ABC.

Extreme Makeover: Home Edition expressed their desire to help select the two families that were going to move into the home, as these families would be profiled on the program and receive a vacation while the project was under construction. The television show producers turned to two individuals: Connie Zimmerman, founder and executive director of Colorado Homeless Families, and the director of a local homeless shelter in Jefferson County, Colorado, to help select which two families would receive the new duplex units.

Twenty families living in shelters throughout the metro area were interviewed, ensuring that all of them fit the first two requirements: to be homeless and have children. Connie knew there was a third requirement that was more important: they had to be someone with the initiative to help themselves, and to want to make their goals and dreams come true. Colorado Homeless Families had interviewed a lot of people over time and found many of those interviewed lived with the attitude of, "I'm a victim. Everything has gone wrong. I will never be able to work again. Just give me money so I can survive." Connie told the producers that the ones that Colorado Homeless Families were focused on helping were the people that just kept getting up one more time, over and over if necessary, and wanted to improve their life at any cost.

After the vetting process, Extreme Makeover: Home Edition and Colorado Homeless Families selected the two families: One family with four children that were currently living in a shelter and a single mother with two children living on a friend's couch. Extreme Makeover: Home Edition sent the families, all expenses paid to Disneyland for a week.

With the recipient families on vacation, the process began. Before groundbreaking, Extreme Home Makeover: Home Edition held an opening ceremony. All the neighbors were invited to join in the carnival, kids activities, a live gospel choir, and a local high school marching band. Neighbors had their street blocked off all week, and a line of trucks and trailers parked up and down the street, night and day. Extreme Makeover: Home Edition offered all neighbors a paid hotel room for a week because of the 24-hours-a-day disturbance. Nobody took their offer because everyone was excited to see this event, and they wanted to watch the progress.

More than 600 construction, design, and carpentry volunteers worked around the clock to build a duplex for two local homeless families. The show's executive producer said this project was, "like no other he had filmed, as the show normally would take a family's pre-existing home and renovate it in one week. Since the families are homeless, they do not have homes to renovate."

Everyone from project managers to volunteers to neighbors noticed that a project that would have taken at least 90 days to complete had to be finished in just under a week, which is the "Extreme Makeover" miraculous trademark feat, and all work is donated or volunteered. With the media coverage, the division president of Standard Pacific Homes noted, "We all learned a lot about homelessness this week. These people had jobs. It is not always about drugs and alcohol. It impacts the working poor and children."

Outsiders wondered how, in less than six days, would volunteer workers build the 2,200-square-foot duplex? One would be a three-bedroom, two-bath unit, while the other included two bedrooms and two baths. Volunteers worked around-the-clock shifts of roughly 125 people, building the duplex from the ground up, working 24 hours a day as four massive light towers lit up the site.

The duplex project was expected to be completed in about 72 hours. It turned out that the complete duplex, from the foundation to the landscaping, was built in about 79 hours by workers of HomeAid Colorado and Standard Pacific Homes.

Standard Pacific Homes was incorporated in 1961 by Arthur Svendsen and Ronald Foell and began the construction of its first subdivision in 1965. Operations expanded to include San Diego in 1969, Texas in 1978, Arizona in 1998, Colorado in 2000, and Florida in 2002. It reached one billion in annual revenues for the first time in 1999. In June 2015, Standard Pacific Homes and Ryland Homes announced a merger, making the combined company the nation's fourth-largest homebuilder. Following the merger, the name was changed to CalAtlantic Group, Inc, traded on the New York Stock Exchange (NYSE) under the ticker symbol

CAA. In February 2018, the company was acquired by Lennar Corporation (LEN), creating the largest homebuilder in the U.S. with combined revenues of $17 billion and a presence in 21 states.

Crowds of neighborhood people visited the site, noting that because of the time constraint of building from bare dirt, this home was constructed with fast-drying concrete, steel girders, and I-beams. This was a better choice for the wear and tear of numerous families living in it over the years. As the interior was being finished with the installation of cherry wood cabinets, granite countertops, and light fixtures, the Extreme Makeover: Home Edition team completed the interior, furnishing the home with donations from Sears, decorating the girl's room with butterflies and the boys' rooms with math and extreme-sports themes, the delivering of sofas and other furniture, down to the details of putting pots and pans in the kitchen, toothbrushes in the bathrooms, and socks in the drawers.

Returning from the Disneyland vacation, the two Colorado Homeless Families experienced the "reveal" and moved into their new homes. The Extreme Makeover: Home Edition duplex, park, and community center were formally dedicated on February 11, 2005 with a ceremony, builder captain, and trade partners, and a special salute with tours of the project. Extreme Makeover: Home Edition premiered the Colorado Homeless Families Episode 214 on February 13, 2005. Extreme Makeover: Home Edition was also named the winner of a Primetime Emmy Award in 2005.

Above and Beyond

As with all Extreme Makeover: Home Edition episodes, the ABC Network always went above and beyond the scope of their build. Wanting to do something special for Colorado Homeless Families and all they were doing to help the homeless families, Extreme Makeover: Home Edition donated new cameras, a new television for the Educational Center, new furniture, and also decorated the conference room, kitchen, and eating area with new appliances and modern colors.

Working in conjunction with Kroenke Sports & Entertainment, the owner of the professional Denver Nuggets basketball team and the Colorado Avalanche hockey team, Extreme Makeover: Home Edition constructed a professional level basketball court for the CHF children.

Extreme Makeover: Home Edition also built a new toddler play area including a nearby park with picnic tables for the parents' named Renaissance Park, (Renaissance meaning "re-birth").

And finally, for every family living in the Colorado Homeless Families' program, Extreme Makeover: Home Edition gifted 50 vacuums, 50 toolsets, 50 sets of dishes, pans, and linens, all donated by Sears.

The Impact of Seven Days

Considerable planning and coordination went into this project with the following day-by-day breakdown:

Day 1: Extreme Makeover: Home Edition producers met with the families to obtain their personal stories. The selected families were sent to Disneyland while the duplex was built.

Day 2: This day is usually considered the demolition day, but since the building lot was already empty, Extreme Makeover: Home Edition held a neighborhood carnival party complete with clowns, food, marching bands, and a choir. At the end of Day 2, the foundation of the duplex was poured.

Day 3: As the foundation cured, framing took place, the panelized flooring system set in, interior drywall hung, and windows and doors were installed.

Day 4: All the painting, both exterior and interior, was completed, and Extreme Makeover: Home Edition also finished room designs. The duplex units were made handicap accessible for any future needs, front yard landscaping installed, and the basketball court, playground, and park were built.

Day 5: Extreme Makeover: Home Edition took all the families located at the homeless shelters where interviews took place to Sears for the American Dream Campaign donations. Personal shoppers helped families pick out whatever they needed. Most families picked clothing, socks, shoes, and coats.

Day 6: The revitalization of the Colorado Homeless Families' Education and Resource Center was completed with assistance from volunteers from Sears American Dream Campaign. The required inspections were performed for the duplex, and the Extreme Makeover: Home Edition team made final adjustments and readied for family move-in.

Day 7: The selected families returned from Disneyland, and the new homes were revealed live. The new basketball court for the neighborhood, playground, and the Renaissance Park were also unveiled. The CHF Family Education and Resource Center was shown off with new electronics, entertainment center, desks, tables, computers, and furniture. The final gifting on the donated household goods to CHF families was also televised.

Photo: Extreme Makeover: Home Edition host Ty Pennington with CHF Executive Director Connie Zimmerman.

Mom and Dad had been selling everything they owned in garage sales lately. Eight-year-old Zachary didn't understand why they sold the leather recliner Mom bought Dad for Christmas two years ago or the fancy dishes Grammy left to Mom when she died.

His tears dripped on his pillow as he listened to the thumping and bumping in the next room where his parents were packing.

"*This is real*," Zachary thought. His parents had been talking to him and his little brother, Dylan, for the past few months. "Daddy can't find a job," and, "Mom's part-time job can't pay for our house," and the worst one, "We will probably have to move soon." He didn't understand what those words meant, but he could read the sadness drawn on their faces. He heard whispers in the kitchen late at night. He saw his dad pacing the backyard in the afternoon when he and Dylan got off the bus after school.

Zachary peeked through the door opening at night and could see men loading Dad's tools into their pickup trucks, then shaking Dad's hand. Dad would drop his head as the men drove away.

One day, he and Dylan came home from school and found some of their games and old clothes gone. He never really played with the games anymore, and the clothes were even too small for Dylan, but still...

Zach listened as Dylan cried himself to sleep. Early one Saturday morning, Dad woke them. "C'mon Dylan, c'mon Zach! Time to get up. We need to get going." Zachary's heart thudded, and he didn't know what the funny feeling was in his stomach.

He wanted to cry, but Dad smiled and said, "Let's go, champ." Dad always made things feel like an adventure, like when Dad's company gave him basketball tickets two years ago, and he carried Zachary on his shoulders down to the floor after the game so he could see some of the Denver Nuggets players celebrate their win. One of the players even high-fived him! All his friends liked

Carmelo Anthony, but Zachary's favorite Nugget was Nenê, the center, and power forward. From that high-five moment, Zachary was a basketball fan forever, and that summer, Dad hung a basketball hoop over their garage door. He and Dylan would shoot the basketball for hours until Dad got home from work. Dad would put Dylan on his shoulders to make a basket, and they would all make loud cheering noises. That Christmas, Zachary got a Denver Nuggets sweatshirt and a brand-new red, white, and blue basketball.

"Let's go, champ," Dad said louder. It was cold and dark outside. And a *Saturday*. He wanted to watch cartoons; then he remembered someone had bought the television yesterday.

Zachary dressed and put on his Denver Nuggets sweatshirt, and he and Dad left the house. Mom and Dylan were already in the car loaded with the boxes Zachary had heard them packing.

As they left the driveway, Zachary looked back to see the basketball hoop hanging above the garage door. "*WAIT, WAIT,*" cried Zachary. "You forgot my hoop!"

Dad pulled the car over and said, "We can't take it, champ. I'm sorry."

Zachary cried all the way to Aunt Beverly's. She lived in a house with a basement, and Mom and Dad said they would live with her for just a little while. Aunt Beverly was nice, but the basement was small, and she did not like Zachary and Dylan to come upstairs.

Zachary started a new school near Aunt Beverly's house, which he didn't like. Mostly, he missed his friends and his neighborhood and "Barkley," his neighbor's dog who could catch a frisbee. Zachary knew that if his parents ever let him get a dog, he would call him Exel, after Nick Van Exel, the Denver Nuggets player who high-fived him a couple of years ago.

After school one day, Mom and Dad had the car loaded and told them that they would be moving again. They seemed happier and said that the place was nice, they would not be living in a basement, and there would be other kids to play with. Zachary was glad to be leaving Aunt Beverly's.

After a short drive, a nice lady named Connie came outside to meet the family, and she walked with them to a new house. Mom said it was a duplex, it was nicer than Aunt Beverly's basement and, Zachary and Dylan they could have their own rooms. Dad said to go play while the grown-ups talked, and Miss Connie pointed them to the playground...*where there was a basketball hoop!* Zachary and Dylan played until it was almost dark when Mom came to get them for dinner.

Zachary's new school near the Colorado Homeless Families ranch was okay, and Dylan liked his teacher. They met some other boys in the CHF neighborhood who liked basketball, too. Mom started working all day. Dad helped in the neighborhood and started going to school for a degree. They also started going to church and made some new friends there.

After their family lived at Colorado Homeless Families for a while, a television show started filming the building of another house next door, a townhouse like theirs. Zachary wanted to stay home from school and watch the workers, but Dad said, "If I have to go to school, so do you, champ." After school, though, Zachary saw some men working on a different project. They were measuring and doing something to the ground. The next day, he saw them painting the Denver Nuggets logo!

The Denver Nuggets team came and played with all the kids in the neighborhood. Zachary and Dylan both got a new basketball, and now Zachary had two basketballs and a Denver Nuggets court to play on! Miss Connie called it Denver Nuggets Day, and it was the best day ever because they got to meet some of the players and shoot baskets with them. Zachary got lots of autographs, and the players and coaches said they would be back again to visit soon.

Matthew Walker sat on the front steps of his home, or rather, his soon-to-be ex-home. Matthew had always believed that if a man had a decent job, worked hard, and took care of his family, everything would be golden.

It was a beautiful, albeit chilly night, and he inhaled the crisp air thick with the smell of a neighbor's fireplace. He always loved that smokey smell found outdoors during cool autumn nights. Blustery breezes blew crisp leaves across the sidewalk, and he stared up at the golden harvest moon suspended in the sky. It was so close, it looked like he could reach out and touch it.

Tears ran down his cheeks. Why couldn't he scoop up some of that gold and put it in his pocket? A little piece of gold would solve their financial problems. His wife Ashley was upstairs putting their twin boys to bed. It was her turn to read to them. Since they had been quarreling lately, he thought it would be better just to sit outside and create a little quiet space between them.

They had never quarreled like they had lately. Quarreling wasn't even the right word: fighting. Arguing. Several weeks ago, their raised voices woke up their sons and frightened them so that it took thirty minutes to calm them down and get them back to sleep. Matthew and Ashley had gone to bed furious at each other.

He hated that. Worse, he hated that they had never learned to deal with addressing conflicts. Ashley hated that too. They loved each other, but they'd never learned how to stand *together* and face their problems with a unified goal in mind. They always turned on each other. The cracks in their seven-year relationship were showing. Even the boys were exhibiting behavioral issues because of their parents' constant conflicts.

The boys were sensitive and knew something was seriously wrong when Matthew and Ashley began to pack all their belongings in boxes last week. Matthew remembered being that young and vulnerable. When he was young, he lived with his Grandma. He remembered she would take him to church. He liked flipping through the hymnal, trying to find the song they would sing. One of Grandma's favorites was an old hymn:

> *"I have no silver or no gold, no earthly mansion do*
> *I own.*
> *But I have peace, wonderful peace in my soul.*
> *I have no fear what man can do, the Lord I serve*
> *will take me through.*
> *Some day, wonderful day, I'm going home—"*

Matthew couldn't remember the rest of the song, but he remembered the longing for, "peace, wonderful peace in my soul." Grandma would drive them home after church and serve Sunday dinner after she let him say grace. Now, that was a good memory, and on this night, he longed for that homespun peace in his ten o'clock soul.

Grandma began needing help with the bills when Matthew was 14 years old, so he'd gone to work after school, on weekends, and then full-time in the summers from there on. She knew how to stretch the dollars and could do a lot with his paychecks. He never wanted to spend anything on himself, but only to help her. Matthew loved working. He worked hard—and studied harder. Grandma was proud of his grades and his work ethic, both. She had such an infectiously positive outlook. Sadly, Matthew had never known either his mom or his dad. It bothered Matthew to see Grandma's health declining knowing he would soon be all alone. That time came four years later when Matthew was eighteen years old.

Cut loose from his one real parent, he'd thankfully met Ashley at one of his part-time jobs, and they'd been dating for about six months when Grandma died. He knew they were just kids, probably too young to get married, but he loved Ashley and didn't want to see his life without her. Grandma had loved her, too. With her blessing, they decided to get married. Their goal was to buy a home before they started a family.

They rented a house close to their jobs. Ashley continued to work at a home improvement store, while Matthew worked two jobs in the construction and electrical business.

Three years later, Ashley became pregnant. Although they were over the moon, it was sooner than planned. When they found out it was twins, Matthew knew that working two jobs wouldn't be ideal if he wanted to be a good father. He needed to spend more time at home. It was their intent that Ashley stay home with their children rather than hand them over to daycare. Their family goals meant they would soon lose Ashley's income. Matthew needed a better wage. After the twins were born, he began searching for a new job.

After a year, he found that he was a top applicant for a Colorado Department of Transportation (CDOT) position. A good-paying state government job would help Matthew and Ashley attain their dream of owning a home sooner than later. By the end of that year, Matthew was selected from several hundred applicants. With elation, he began his new job.

Six months into his job, however, Matthew woke up one morning with a slight fever and a little nausea. Not feeling too terrible, he went to work. He fought the nausea and upset stomach for about a week before Ashley begged him to see a doctor. He made an appointment for early the next week and went on his lunch hour. The doctor's examination noted that the symptoms suggested Matthew had an intestinal tract infection; they prescribed Matthew an antibiotic and recommended staying home with rest and hydration. Matthew hated to miss work, but the doctor issued a work release form, so Matthew went home.

Five days later, Ashley rushed Matthew to the hospital. He had awakened with a high fever, was vomiting, and was writhing with abdominal pain. The emergency room doctor told Ashley that Matthew had appendicitis. The inflamed appendix had burst. Although Matthew's pain level had declined, the burst appendix was spilling bacteria and debris into his abdominal cavity, and Matthew was facing a life-threatening infection.

He was rushed into surgery. The severity of the inflammation and bacteria kept Matthew in intensive care for two weeks. Still concerned about the life-threatening infection, Matthew spent another month in the hospital so they could monitor him closely.

Matthew's health insurance covered some of the expenses, but the bills were rapidly increasing between deductibles, ICU expenses, and non-covered hospital costs. Having only six months of employment, Matthew didn't have much in his sick leave bank. With no income, regular household bills were also climbing.

Ashley soon used all their savings to pay rent and utility bills. They had to use their credit cards to pay for food and other household necessities. CDOT qualified him for the Family and Medical Leave Act, but the 12 weeks of leave was still unpaid, so there was no income to pay any bills. The Act also protected an employee's job for 12 weeks, however, it was unknown how long Matthew would need to recover.

Out of the hospital and back at home, Matthew recovered among stacks of unpaid hospital bills, past due credit card statements, and overdue rent and utilities. Feeling the stress and strain, both Matthew and Ashley began to argue. Released to resume work, Matthew could return to his job, but the amount of debt was so burdensome he could not meet even his minimum financial obligations. They were facing eviction. Would they be living on the street with their sons?

Ashley had found some information about Colorado Homeless Families at the local library several days ago when she took their sons for reading hour. Matthew had glanced at it but found his pride would never allow that kind of help. He reminded himself that he was a hard worker, and he put nothing above taking care of his family. Speaking this aloud led to yet another argument with Ashley. She wanted to complete the application while Matthew didn't. That is, until one night, after a physically grueling day at work. Matthew sat alone at their kitchen table peering at bill after bill after bill. There was no place for pride in this decision. His family was facing homelessness—and soon.

Breathing in the crisp autumn air, Matthew finally made peace with moving to the Colorado Homeless Families community in a few days. When they were approved, Executive Director Connie Zimmerman gave them a tour of the resources and grounds. She explained that counseling was available to them that would be able to help them through this rough patch. She talked about working with a case manager and the educational seminars that could help them with many of the life skills they'd never learned as young married people. Connie explained the food bank, clothing shop, and the furniture warehouse, which they could utilize so they could use their paycheck to repay their debts and rebuild their credit. She gave them a tour of the playground and showed them that their twins would have other children to play with. This would be an opportunity for them to learn good behavior. Connie told them about several of the successes of CHF: people who had been precisely where Matthew and Ashley were today.

Ashley also realized this was an opportunity for her to attend college classes and find a career path so that when their children began school, she could go back to a good job.

Matthew had to swallow his pride, but he knew they were making the right decision after the CHF tour.

It was still unfathomable to consider his family was "near homeless," but one of Grandma's favorite hymns took hold in his heart. As he watched the golden harvest moon rise in the sky, Matthew realized that making this move to Colorado Homeless Families was giving him peace, wonderful peace in his soul.

Sandra Matthews rarely jumped. She was over forty, a white woman, and over-forty white women don't jump. When Sandra left her job for the day, she literally jumped for joy thinking about her new promotion at the assisted living community.

She was going to be the new Life Enrichment Coordinator. Her first position there had been a QMAP, a Qualified Medication Administration Person. It was not an overly exciting position, but she enjoyed visiting the residents when administering the patients' medications. Her position did not require a degree or even a license, but she did have to take a training class and successfully complete the course.

Based on the physician's authorization in her job, she was not allowed to make any medical or psychological judgments, assessments, or evaluate the resident in any way. However, her new job would put her in charge of developing and coordinating resident activities, volunteer programs, managing several in-house events, and what they called "managing resources." She would be recruiting and training all the volunteers in the community. It was exciting. Sandra's new job was considered a management position.

This was a substantial increase in her income, but she was also eligible for health and dental benefits for her family and paid vacation and sick time.

The last time Sandra jumped for joy was when she left the church after she married her sweetheart, Darren. She was still in college when they married, but she had been over the moon for him since he sat behind her in math class during their high school sophomore year. Darren had never planned to go to college, and neither of them wanted to wait until after she graduated from college to get married, so they made it work and planned the church wedding for the summer of her junior year.

They wrote their own vows, invited their family and friends, and celebrated their new life. Working hard and being diligent in her studies, Sandra graduated from college at 22 years old, receiving her bachelor's degree in social work. Unlike Darren, who was anxious to get out in the world and start working after high school, Sandra was not in a hurry to get a job after college.

She really wanted to be a mom, stay home to raise her children, and home school them.

Within three years, Darren and Sandra had their first two children, and she was glad they were only a year apart in age. Darren's job supported the family, and they could move into a larger apartment. Sandra enjoyed this bigger apartment and got to know some of the other young moms on the playground and swimming pool. Sandra was completely happy raising her family, and when the children were of school age, they decided to home school them. This kept Sandra busy and focused day after day, and she saw her kids thrive.

Darren's paycheck paid their rent and expenses, but there was never any additional for nice things, a new car, or even dinners out at restaurants. Vacations were an extravagance that they could never afford, so Sandra was creative and found enjoyable, no-cost activities for their family. They economized and saved for birthdays and Christmas. One day, when her children were studying, Sandra read the newspaper and saw an article that talked about the economic downturns. What she saw surprised her, although it should not have. The poverty level for a family of four in Colorado was $14,800 per year[56]. At Darren's income of $18,000, she realized they were living remarkably close to poverty level!

As her two older children turned into teenagers, they became more involved in activities with friends and neighbors and became more independent. Sandra now considered they could help babysit the youngest and she could go to work. However, she learned that she was pregnant again.

Although she was happy for the news, she would have to put off working. Her five-year-old would benefit from continued home schooling, and she would also have to care for a newborn.

While in the hospital with the new baby, she quietly reflected on the last decade. Things between her and Darren had become increasingly tense over the years, and now with two teens, a pre-school age child, and a toddler, their family of six was ready to burst the seams of the apartment. Unfortunately, she and Darren had not planned on four children, especially not with the youngest being born when she was nearing 40 years old.

Darren's income was less than $25,000 per year, only $600 per month above the newest poverty level guidelines—and with few benefits *and* four children. They lived in an apartment fit for four, not six, and things were getting tight. Their income was stretched beyond its limit, as was Darren's patience. Sandra could feel the taut thread of their life pulling with the stress of a low income, unpaid bills, the threatening layoffs, two unplanned children, and an increase in Darren's unexplained time spent away from home.

She suspected that Darren had been spending money at bars, and she also knew that he had broken their marriage vows several times. He would fail to come home for consecutive days at a time. His temper was quick, and he had little interest in her or the children anymore. The last time they argued, he pushed her before he called her a vile name and left for the night.

Sandra took her vows seriously though and refused to quit her marriage. She and the children tried hard not to aggravate Darren, but be supportive of him, rather, and always be on their best behavior for him.

When their son joined the military at age 18, and her daughter moved to Seattle the following year with friends, Sandra was left to raise her 6- and 11-year-old without any help.

Sandra finally decided to leave after twenty years of marriage. She felt her happy union had deteriorated beyond repair as she kept walking on eggshells with Darren. This was neither good for her nor her children, but he didn't take the news lightly. When she told her husband she was leaving, he slapped her, yelling, and grabbed her by the hair, forcing her to her knees. The neighbors called the authorities when they heard him screaming. Sandra, aching and bruised, along with her frightened children, were taken to a local shelter where they were provided with necessities, a social worker, and counselor to develop a family plan.

Sandra knew that self-sufficiency needed to be her personal goal, but having no work resume and with two children, she felt a dark cloud overtaking her. With no idea of where to begin, no idea where to go, and worse, no idea where hope could be found, she realized she had no confidence, no life partner, and no skills. Most mornings when she woke up, she could already feel the dark cloud hovering above her.

The shelter recommended Colorado Homeless Families as the best way for Sandra to find real hope by getting on her feet.

Within two weeks of contacting them, she and her two children moved into the transitional housing community. Knowing she would need work, Sandra placed her children in the public school system, and to her amazement, they loved it. They blossomed with new friends and school activities. Her case manager began helping Sandra identify her strengths and talents. It helped that Sandra had her bachelor's degree, but she also wanted to make sure that the job she took would be personally rewarding.

Until she found perfect job, Sandra decided to follow several of her interests and try out the differences. She had always loved music, so she worked part-time as a piano teacher. She also worked as a part-time teacher for a local county home school program. Having homeschooled her children, the program was glad to accept her and put her skills to use. With her love of children, she also worked part-time as a childcare provider.

She knew that part-time jobs were not going to be her permanent path, and her case manager, although encouraging, continued to urge her, and hold her accountable, to find permanent, full-time employment and to find something that would allow her to use her college degree paid accordingly.

She was reminded of her earlier experiences. During one of her summers in college, she'd volunteered at an assisted living facility where she planned and implemented resident activities

She remembered it to be a wonderful experience, and she added it to her resume for social work.

At the Colorado Homeless Families community, with strong urging, encouragement, and counseling, Sandra begin to move forward. Sandra was finally able to resolve her feelings of failure in her marriage.

She also found peace and performed well at her workplace resulting in more confidence to find a full-time position. Within a short time, Sandra was hired full-time at a well-respected, contemporary assisted living community in the QMAP position.

She loved mingling with the residents and staff.

As Sandra jumped for joy at her promotion. With her new salary, she would be making more than twice the poverty level income, and she knew that soon she would be able to find a home to purchase and live on her own and support her and her children. The thought of owning her *first* home, and her *own* home, made her once again jump for joy.

She had said her goodbyes at the Colorado Homeless Families office that morning, accompanied by lots of hugging, clapping, and tears. Stepping into her now empty townhome, memories flooded her, and tears of closure began to fall. It was a little over two years ago when she and her children walked into this home, All she felt that first night was a sense of hope as she closed her eyes.

She had become attached to it from the moment she stepped foot in their home at Colorado Homeless Families. That security blanket did exactly what it was intended to do: it granted her the much-needed feeling of security for the past two years.

The check-out list was long, but her clan had helped. They cleaned the stove and refrigerator: in, under, and behind—check. Washed all surfaces: walls, cabinets, baseboards, and windows—check. Swept and mopped floors and steam cleaned carpets—check. Cleaned all bathrooms thoroughly and inside all cabinets and closets–check. Tidied yard, patio, and all trash tossed—check.

Jennifer Carter loaded the last box of their belongings into the U-Haul trailer and went back inside for a final check of anything she may have left behind or something she and her family missed on the final check-out list.

Everyone offered congratulations, and even though she was excited and happy, she felt a little nervous as though someone was removing the security blanket from around her shoulders.

Jennifer remembered a quote by Mary Shelley, the English novelist, that said, "Nothing is so painful to the human mind as a great and sudden change."

Jennifer had come to Colorado from the east coast. She and her husband had a beautiful, stable, loving home filled with children. Although she had earned her college degree, she chose to stay home to raise her children while her husband worked at his successful medical practice. Yet, life began to crumble quickly when her husband was accused of molestation.

Lawyers, accusations, the trial, the stress, and worse, the gossips that eventually caused the closure of her husband's medical practice took its toll on their family and relationships, both personal and professional.

In the end, it didn't matter that her husband was acquitted; the stress had sent them all to rock bottom. This experience eventually led her husband to be diagnosed with a form of post-traumatic stress disorder (PTSD), and her large family was suddenly forced to try to live on his disability insurance.

Their comfortable, happy, solid life was gone.

Jennifer moved her depressed husband and their children to Colorado. They all perked up with the sunlit outdoors. She believed their fresh air and clean start would begin to heal them. She was sincerely interested in getting her master's degree in counseling, hoping to get a great job that could support the entire family.

The move to Colorado did not do quite what she had hoped. Her husband's depression worsened when a violent temper appeared, and he became abusive. Combining these symptoms with her husband's several suicide attempts; Jennifer began to fear the worst. That darkness filled the corners one night as he threatened their children's lives with a handgun. Jennifer convinced him to calm down and give her the gun, and then she called the police.

Her husband, charged with the felony he committed, was sent to prison.

Jennifer was devastated at this turn of events and tried to do everything to support herself and her family. Even moving to a small, inexpensive apartment, with seven children to care for, classes to attend, and only being able to work 20 hours a week, she saw this would not be enough to save them.

Surveying the money she had tried to set aside, she realized that she was teetering on the edge of desperation, seeing as they would soon be homeless. In all probability, they would be living on the streets of Denver.

Fearing the worst, she confided in a co-worker, and he told her to inquire about a program called Colorado Homeless Families. Within a short time, Jennifer and her children moved into this townhome—the same home she was now vacating two years later.

She remembered the day they moved in, not knowing what to expect. She felt cared for, and she especially felt safe now that her ex-husband would not be able to find her or their children.

She had never thought that she would be a single mom, but the first night in their new place gave her the realization that they finally had a secure home and were going to be offered the exact help they needed. When she met with Connie Zimmerman, the Executive Director of Colorado Homeless Families, this supportive and loving woman told her that it is quite easy to fall into poverty and homelessness. Jennifer's story shows how it can happen to anyone. All these things had given Jennifer a glimmer of hope as she closed her eyes that first night.

Jennifer loved that her children quickly adapted to the CHF program. She was able to pay reduced rent while she worked part-time, received financial aid to finish her degree, and was grateful they were all attending family therapy sessions to help them deal with the changes and the trauma of the last few years. Jennifer enjoyed the support group and attended all the seminars and educational opportunities offered, including financial counseling.

It was not long, Jennifer reflected, before her children's grades began to improve, as stability anchored the family. The children had other kids to play with and they enjoyed all the wonderful activities and youth programs CHF offered.

The security blanket that Jennifer felt around her shoulders helped her come home excited at the prospect of a new and self-sufficient life.

One day as she watched her children play, she felt the sun on her face and realized she felt confidence to live life on life's terms. She had accepted her circumstances, but they were improving as she took small steps each day to do the next thing, do the right things, and do loving things. Building a good life, she no longer battled continuously overwhelming thoughts.

It took them a little time to settle in, and Jennifer was not oblivious to the fact that there would still be some rough times before they could move forward. Her children were laughing and enjoying everyday pleasures as they began to rebuild their lives. What CHF had done for her family felt incredible coming just when she needed it the most. Jennifer had even made some good friends, something she had not had since her much-loved community turned their backs on her after her husband's ordeal.

"Mom! M-o-m! MO-O-O-OM!! Her kids yelling to get her attention brought her from her daydream. "Let's go, Mom. Our new house is waiting!"

Jennifer smiled, knowing that at Thanksgiving next week, she could return thanks for a list of blessings. Thankful for her children, for their health and safety, thankful that Colorado Homeless Families gave her a way to begin a new life, thankful for her master's degree and her new job, and thankful for their new house, Jennifer would indeed celebrate Thanksgiving.

The president of HomeAid Colorado spoke to reporters, "Imagine electricians, painters, plumbers, and drywallers all stumbling over each other with another twenty guys on the roof. You have people putting in cabinets and fixtures and running into the air conditioning guys. Nobody minds it because we all know that when we are finished with this wonderful home, two families will begin to heal."

For the first time in the history of ABC Television Network show Extreme Makeover, everyone working on the new duplex at Colorado Homeless Families knew that the impact of what they were building would go far beyond just one house and one family.

One duplex unit would become home to Frankie Correa and his wife and four children, while Dusty Medeiros and her two children would live in the adjacent unit. When they graduate from the Colorado Homeless Families program and are self-sufficient, back on their feet, two other families will move into the duplex built by HomeAid Colorado, Standard Pacific Homes, and Extreme Makeover: Home Edition. After those two new families graduate from transitional housing, two more families will move in, and so on.

Said Paul DeMeo, Extreme Makeover's building and planning designer, "We don't even know how many families this one project ultimately will touch. We've never been able to be that kind of force for change before."

The Correa family with four children were living in a night shelter. Frank was one of 30 employees laid off from their jobs at a box and packaging company after 9/11. He only had enough money saved to pay two months of rent and, like most people during this economic downturn, could not find stable, permanent employment after that.

Frank continued to work temporary jobs for years, but nothing ever became permanent. Sadly, he moved his family into a local Jeffco Action Center homeless shelter founded in 1968 that provided essential human services on a temporary basis and helped people stabilize their family environment.

Serving only as a temporary homeless shelter, residents would eat breakfast, then they were required to vacate the building between the hours of 7:00 am – 5:30 pm. The Correa family shared a 10' x 12' room at the shelter, and Frank would go to work after breakfast, and three of his children would go to school. His wife and youngest child would have nowhere to go and would ride the city buses during the day if there was no other place to stay warm.

Extreme Makeover: Home Edition changed their lives. After the screening process and multiple interviews, they were selected as one of two families to move into the new duplex being constructed at the Colorado Homeless Families complex. The weeklong Disneyland vacation bestowed upon them while the duplex was being built and the television show was filmed as beyond their wildest dreams.

Upon returning from Disneyland, the "reveal" of their new home was an incredible, once-in-a-lifetime experience. What came after arriving home was something Frank never expected: he was offered a job working for a lumber company that subcontracts to Standard Pacific Homes who helped build the duplex. With a new job, a new place to live, and the counseling and case management services from Colorado Homeless Families, Mrs. Correa set her sights on returning to school to become a defense attorney.

The Medeiros family was the other recipient of the Extreme Makeover duplex.

Dusty, a single mother with two children, was employed at a local computer store for nine years. After the divorce, she found that with the loss of the second income, she did not earn enough to support her family. Losing their home, the family was forced to live with neighbors and friends, sleeping on their sofas.

Picked from the many applications to Colorado Homeless Families, this program would help get her on the right path to self-sufficiency. She looked forward to working with her case manager to begin to map out a plan for the future. That dream and goal motivated her to become self-sufficient.

Dusty and her two children were also sent to Disneyland for a weeklong adventure vacation and were able to come back to the unveiling of the newly built duplex which they could move into immediately.

For both families selected by Colorado Homeless Families and Extreme Makeover: Home Edition, moving into the new duplex showed them it cost only the determination to start over on the road to self-sufficiency.

Casey Blackwell hated Pennsylvania. Even with the beautiful Appalachian Mountains hobnobbing with redbuds and quilted dogwoods from end to end, even with the Pocono folklore and Allegheny hills, she nevertheless despised her Pennsylvania home.

Casey was now a Colorado gal through-and-through. She'd been eager to join the Colorado Mountain Club's "completer list" of those mountain climbers who climbed all 58 of Colorado's 14,000-foot peaks. Now, those were true mountains. She had only completed half but had a goal to finish the other half before she was 35 years old.

When she arrived fresh-faced in Colorado, she soon married Nash Henley, also from Pennsylvania. With much in common, Nash was the best-looking and most charming guy working at a grand, multi-storied sporting goods store in downtown Denver. They'd met when he helped her buy a new pair of hiking boots. They began dating, and soon thereafter, he asked her to marry him when they reached the peak of Mount Sherman. They moved into Nash's apartment because it was the bigger of their two places, and Casey had two roommates.

Within a year, Nash began making remarks about moving back to Pennsylvania. It was disappointing, but when his father fell ill the following year, they made the move back anyway, moving into his dad's house to take care of him for the next four years until he passed away. The full-time caretaker role fell to Casey, as Nash hopped from job to job and joined his old high school buddies for the evening and weekend sports leagues.

She loved Nash's father and took his well-being and care very seriously. During their shared lunches, they would have great conversations, and he always gave her wise words of advice such as "Your life is your responsibility," or "The way someone treats you is a reflection of how they feel about themselves." Casey's two favorites were "Just keep going. No matter what," and "Do what you're afraid to do." She knew that to be true from her days hiking the mountains.

After Mr. Henley died and his debts were settled, Casey found out she was pregnant. She told Nash she wanted to return to Colorado after the baby was born. She had tried to find work in Pennsylvania, but temporary jobs were the best she could manage, and Nash was still hopping from blue-collar job to blue-collar job. After the baby was born, they packed baby Grace in her car seat and all they could fit in a rented cargo trailer and headed back to the Rockies in Colorado.

As excited as Casey was to return to Colorado, the economy seemed even worse than in Pennsylvania. After sleeping on a cousin's sofa bed for six weeks, they were getting desperate. Part-time and temporary work would not pay their bills, especially since Casey learned she was pregnant again. Her cousin gave her the phone number for Colorado Homeless Families, but Nash insisted they would get through this and refused to contact them.

He began to drink heavily and feeling trapped, he became angry at their situation. He told her *this* was her fault for making them leave Pennsylvania.

After baby Emma was born, Casey's cousin told them she would be moving. They would need to find another place to live.

Officially homeless, Casey felt abominable with two small children and an angry, violent husband, Casey retrieved the phone number from her purse and called Colorado Homeless Families. She told the case manager that she just knew she should hold onto that slip of paper with their phone number, and she pleaded her case for help.

It was not easy to leave Nash behind, but his lack of hope and faith caused a depression with an explosive and violent temper leaving her little choice. She cringed at the thought of not only staying with him but exposing her daughters to his behavior. She had seen this same drinking problem and temper before in her father and two of her boyfriends. When she realized it, she was always strong enough to walk away. Casey knew she would feel stronger once she removed herself, but she had never had to take children away from their father before. At that moment, Mr. Henley's wise words came back to her:

> *"Your life is your responsibility."*
> *"The way someone treats you is a reflection of how they feel about themselves."*
> *"Just keep going. No matter what."*
> *"Do what you're afraid to do."*

Casey and her daughters moved into Colorado Homeless Families. She felt an immediate sense of refuge and community.

The daycare volunteers at CHF took care of her daughters while she underwent counseling and met with her case manager. Being emotionally strong physically active, and always caring about the safety and well-being of others, she told her case manager she would be interested in pursuing a career in law enforcement. Together they found her the best alternatives.

She enrolled in the Law Enforcement Academy located only ten miles from Colorado Homeless Families, and she was able to obtain a variety of scholarships and grants to help her with the tuition, books, and required equipment. Being a full-time college program, some of the grant money paid for living expenses, too.

This was a difficult decision as she had two small girls to care for and desperately needed to spend time with them. She was home every night and found a part-time job on the weekends to help with some expenses.

The staff and volunteers at CHF provided excellent daycare for her daughters, and the environment was always encouraging and supportive. What Casey found most helpful was having volunteers to help keep her car running while attending school. She did her own volunteer time providing babysitting services or her favorite activity: the neighborhood watch and security check programs. She was able to practice the tactical skills that she was learning every day to help watch over the safety and well-being of her new home and refuge.

Shortly after she completed the Law Enforcement Academy Program, she was excited to learn she had the highest scores in her class. She focused on obtaining the Colorado Peace Officer Standards and Training Board (POST) certification. She got her first job working for the State of Colorado for the Department of Public Safety.

With Nash getting help for his drinking and anger management, he began to pay child support, and they worked out a suitable custody arrangement. This allowed Casey the extra time to continue to pursue her bachelor's degree in criminology. Exactly two years from the day she moved in, Casey graduated from the Colorado Homeless Families program.

Thankful, Casey fully embraced her new self-sufficient life in taking care of her daughters and being able to teach them what their grandfather had told her: *"Just keep going. No matter what,"* and *"Do what you're afraid to do."*

When Marta met Steven in her hometown in Russia, it was love at first sight. She had never believed in that fairy tale, not even with her first husband, Alexei. This handsome American engineer frequently came into the restaurant where she worked. She came to learn that his favorite meal was pelmeni, and his favorite dinner drink was sbiten. He was friendly to everyone but seemed to be especially attentive with Marta.

Their conversations eventually turned personal, and he revealed that he was from the United States working in Russia. His blue eyes twinkled when he asked about her. She told him that her husband had died leaving just her and her young daughter, Annika. She worked long hours at the restaurant during the day and early evening, but she tried to be home each night so that she could spend time with her daughter before bedtime.

As they began to date, she quickly fell in love with Steven. He splurged on her and spoiled Annika with all the things that girls adored. Although Marta found herself in love, she knew it would probably not last as his return to the United States was inevitable.

Steven asked her to marry him and return to the United States as his wife and family. She was thrilled and excited as he showed her pictures of the beautiful city of Denver, Colorado. They would move there when Steven's contract in Russia finished.

The move to the United States happened quickly after all the legal paperwork was complete. Marta believed in her husband and her new country. She was delighted that Annika adapted quickly to her new surroundings and school friends. Marta found that she missed her few family members, her co-workers, and the mothers of Annika's friends with whom she had enjoyed spending time back home, but she loved her new life.

It was a little challenging to make friends in her new city, and Steven didn't have friends or relatives in the area to introduce her to. Since Marta was friendly and outgoing, she knew she would soon make a couple of friends. She also looked forward to becoming involved in Annika's school activities.

Steven's generous engineering income and benefits package allowed them to settle into a beautiful sprawling home with mountain views, and Steven encouraged her to decorate it as she wished. She let Annika pick the colors for her very own room, and Marta enjoyed shopping, decorating, and taking care of her family. They began to thrive, also enjoying skiing and winter weekends in the mountains. Marta herself enjoyed this new sport, so much so she began working at the largest sporting goods store in Colorado in the ski shop. There, she made friends with great customers, had terrific co-workers, and thoroughly enjoyed her well-paying job.

Several years after settling in, Marta began to notice slight changes in Steven. He had become emotionally erratic. He seemed angry and irritable. His work hours were fewer and fewer, and one day, she noticed that some groceries she had just bought the week before were mysteriously missing.

Try as she might to talk to him, Steven would become irrational and explosive. He even pushed her to the floor one night, which left her enormously shaken. She had never seen that side of him. Several months later, when she tried to use her credit card at the grocery store, it was declined.

Arriving back home, Marta quietly went into Steven's office. She found past due notices for all the credit cards, automobile payments, utilities, and even the mortgage payments were not being made. Marta stood frozen, unsure what to do. So far, she had been able to shield Annika from all of this, but she was a bright and perceptive young girl and had asked Marta one evening "What is wrong with Papa?" when she saw him blankly staring out the dining room window.

Eventually, Steven did not recognize Marta or Annika. He would get angry and force his family to the basement, most times without dinner. He yelled at them *"chort!"* and *"враг!"* which Marta knew to mean "demon" and "enemy."

Frightened by his crazy behavior, the fear of him hurting Annika, Marta would do as her husband demanded.

Marta would sneak up the stairs in the morning, drive Annika to school, and go to her job. As if the loss of Stevan's affection and his income were not enough, sadly, her own work hours were being reduced. Last week, she had only worked 10 hours. She snuck a glance at her schedule for next week, and it showed only six hours. Marta couldn't support her family on those hours. She would cash her checks and purchase food for herself and Annika, but the walls were closing in, and she didn't know why or how to fight it. Desperation and fear filled her every hour like drops of poison in a cup. She had no close friends or relatives to run to.

Despite Steven's volatile behavior, she still dearly loved her husband and begged him to see a doctor. He would just scream at her and chase her to the basement.

What little food Marta was able to buy, she gave to Annika first. One day Marta was so famished at work, she fainted. A friend and co-worker shared her lunch with Marta asking, "What's wrong? Is everything okay?"

Marta finally broke down. She confided in her friend. Her friend told her about a woman she'd heard speak at their church describing a place called Colorado Homeless Families.

On her next shift, Marta found a flyer in her locker from her friend and called during her break. After the telephone screening, Marta was told she would need to meet a case manager for an interview.

Since their automobiles had been repossessed, Marta and Annika took the bus to the interview. A case manager and Connie Zimmerman, the CHF Director, attended the interview noticing how thin they were, both trembling from fear and hunger. Connie immediately ordered them something to eat, and Marta remembered being embarrassed at how ravenous she was. Marta hoped this nonprofit could help them because she had nowhere else to turn.

Marta sobbed when she and Annika were approved to move into Colorado Homeless Families. She and her case manager picked a day the following week to move in, but first, they were sent to the CHF food bank to get food and other provisions to hold them until they could move in.

The day they moved into CHF was a cold, desolate day, both rainy, and windy. A gray sky fit Marta's frazzled mood. Thankfully, maintenance workers from Colorado Homeless Families came to their home with a truck to take some of their furniture to CHF.

As Marta closed the door to her once beautiful, sprawling home, she saw her husband sitting in a chair and staring at the walls. She wanted to hold him, to tell him she loved him, to ask him if he understood what was happening. Nothing seemed to register to him, so she quietly closed the door and left.

Marta and Annika moved into a two-bedroom, two-bath apartment located next to the CHF offices. Since her job at the sporting goods store had dwindled to nothing, she took the first job she could get as a custodian cleaning office. Marta missed her once flourishing life, but not the fear and uncertainty that near-starvation had brought. She was thankful for the continued support services offered through the CHF Resource Center and continued to improve her English language skills. She learned and sought counseling through the Resource Center.

As Marta lovingly looked at Annika, she saw a strong young woman who weathered this storm and overcame great obstacles.

Although Annika's home life had been uncertain and on the brink of homelessness, she continued to be an excellent student and received outstanding grades in school. The following spring, Annika proudly received four different scholarships, one of which was so prestigious, it is only offered to 40 students in the entire state of Colorado based on high grades, leadership ability, hard work, and the potential to make a significant contribution to the community of Colorado.

Marta was especially excited about the Boettcher Foundation Scholarship because it represented five years of college in which Annika could receive her bachelor's degree as well as a masters.

Marta was proud that Annika could study abroad for a year in Spain through the prestigious scholarships she received. While Marta worked hard at her full-time custodial job, she was thankful for CHF. Now, Annika was able to complete her education, return home, and secure an important career to take care of herself and her mother. Marta and Annika expressed their gratefulness for the opportunity to start over at Colorado Homeless Families, and Marta developed her own goals for her future.

Twenty-eight-year-old Ivy Reynolds was raised in the Cumberland Mountains of Kentucky by her maternal grandparents. She'd never known her father and little of her mother who had dumped her as an infant with her grandparents forcing them to take the responsibility of raising her.

A quiet and introverted girl, Ivy fell behind in school. Always afraid the teacher might call on her, she would hide behind the kid who sat in front of her when the teacher looked in her direction. Ivy attended church with Grandma every Sunday. It gave her great comfort to trace her fingers on the pages of Grandma's Bible. She would always look for words or phrases she understood and liked:

"Give thanks to the Lord for He is good and His love endures forever," and *"Trust in the Lord with all your heart."*

There were a lot of words she didn't understand, like *endures*, but she understood the gist of most of the words.

When she was ten years old, she got her own bible; the cover was white with gold lettering. Each member of her Sunday school class had to recite the books of the bible in chronological order.

Memorizing things was something she was no good at. When her Sunday School teacher raised a white Bible as the reward for students who memorized all the books of the Bible, she worked hard for weeks to earn it. "Genesis, Exodus, Leviticus," she repeated aloud. With a nervous stomach and knocking knees, she stood in front of the congregation on Palm Sunday and recited the books in perfect order. Her voice shook, and she mispronounced Habakkuk, but she did it and received her very own Bible.

Her grandmother died when Ivy was 17 years old, and her grandfather six months later. Ivy was only 18 and only one month out of high school. Her grandparents' death left her devastated with nowhere to go. That is when she discovered the book of Lamentations, and the verse, "Peace has left my soul. I have forgotten what it is like to be happy. So I say, 'My strength is gone, and so has my hope from the Lord.'"[57]

The boy she was dating at the time, Lonnie Dean, asked her to get married. Alone, afraid, and insecure, she and Lonnie Dean married at the Pulaski County courthouse. He was several years older than she, but other than drinking on the weekends with his friends, he seemed like a good prospect because he owned his own home and had a stable job with a local ironworks manufacturing company. She liked him.

Not knowing what else to do, Ivy went to work at a local discount store. She had learned from Grandma to set aside a little money from each check for an emergency. Grandma never explained to Ivy what an "emergency" would be, but Ivy never wanted to understand it anyway.

Lonnie Dean continued to party with his friends on the weekends and even brought them into their home. She would get up on Saturday mornings to get ready for work or Sundays to go to church and find she needed to tiptoe her way around sleeping drunks, alcohol containers, and a filthy, dirty house that she would spend the rest of the weekend cleaning. She tried to talk to Lonnie Dean about his partying friends and not bringing them into their home, but that resulted with him not coming home for three days. She would also receive the silent treatment for a week beyond that.

Two years to the day they were married, she found out she was pregnant. Being an only child and having no other family, Ivy was happy at the news. She cooked a special meal and lit a candle at dinner to celebrate the news with Lonnie Dean. His happiness, however, did not mirror her own. He wasn't angry, but he wasn't as pleased about the news as she was.

He became upset when she told him that she would like to quit her job when the baby came. Ivy was optimistic and looked forward to being a mother. Connor James was born a healthy baby. Her husband picked the first name; Ivy picked James after her grandfather. Ivy was "over the moon" with joy.

Connor was an angel baby, but when the terrible two's hit and he began to get crabby, Lonnie Dean started staying away from home. By then, Ivy had become miserable with her marriage. Connor was the joy of her life, and she wanted to give him a stable home and a loving environment more than she had ever wanted anything. She went to church every Sunday with her white Bible, and Connor toddled into Sunday School.

At a doctor's check-up when Connor was four, the kind and caring nurse asked her how *she* felt. Ivy mentioned that she had felt feverish, had a headache and sore throat, and felt fatigued. The nurse scheduled Ivy for a visit of her own, and after several tests, Ivy found out she had gotten a sexually transmitted disease (STD).

Furious, she confronted Lonnie Dean that night, only to earn a backhand across her face and his absence for a solid week.

When Connor started school, Ivy returned to work at the discount store, ensuring her work hours stayed within Connor's school hours.

Lonnie Dean came and went as he pleased, but Ivy always felt nervous and apprehensive when he was home, waiting for the next push or a slap. Knowing she would not be able to sustain this lifestyle forever, Ivy again began to save, setting aside a small and unnoticeable amount of her paycheck each week per Grandma's advice "in case of an emergency."

By the time Connor was seven, Lonnie Dean was a full-blown alcoholic who barely lived with them, unable to sustain the long-haul of raising a child. The final time he came home, he shoved Ivy so hard she fell into the counter and broke her wrist, and when Connor tried to help her, Lonnie Dean knocked him over.

"Stay put, and stay down, boy!" he screamed, stomping out the door.

Ivy and Connor went to the hospital, and handed a form the next day, Ivy filed a police report for a restraining order. She filed for divorce by week's end using some of the "in case of an emergency" money. She realized they could stay in the house until the divorce was final, but never having been given ownership, eventually she would have to leave their home. She didn't want to live in Lonnie Dean's house anyway.

Ivy had nowhere to go and, longing for comfort, pulled out Grandma's bible one night. In the very back was a brief note written from her mother to her grandparents when Ivy was four years old. There was no return address, but it was postmarked from Colorado.

Alone, afraid, and insecure, Ivy realized this was the "emergency" that Grandma was talking about. She loaded as many things as she could get in their car, and left for Colorado with Conner, hoping for something much better than her last decade in Kentucky with Lonnie Dean.

Thankfully, she had enough to live in a cheap motel in Denver with her small emergency savings. They also attended a local church and befriended a family with a son Connor's age. Ivy was glad for the quality friendships. She determined to get her life on track. Through a temporary agency, she found a small paying, full-time job. She and Connor were sleeping on the floor of their new friends' home until, after looking all over the city for apartments, she found that she would never be able to pay rent with what she earned from her job. She withdrew from her friends, hiding the truth, and things became awkwardly silent.

The next afternoon visiting a nearby park, Ivy met a woman who knew the Executive Director of Colorado Homeless Families. The woman said that Ivy and Connor were the perfect candidates. Her very situation was apparently "exactly why CHF existed."

Ivy applied and was accepted at Colorado Homeless Families. They set her up in the various programs and support systems. At CHF, Ivy was told she would receive guidance, counseling, encouragement, as well as any help she needed to get herself and Connor's life turned around. Ivy's biggest concern was that she had no family or friends in Colorado, but she told Connie that she believed she was hardworking, honest, responsible, and had strong convictions.

Colorado Homeless Families let Ivy and Connor pick their furniture from the furniture bank and any other provisions they required after their move-in. Even after moving into their new townhome, Ivy still felt very alone, not very smart, and fearful. Doubts that plagued her as a young girl and a teenager continued to wrap their tentacles like vines tightening around her ankles. She knew she needed specific kinds of help to cut and pull away the binding twines of her predicament. She hoped that CHF could work miracles.

After a short time, Connie Zimmerman saw that Ivy was thriving with educational seminars, counseling for past trauma, and case management oversight. Ivy had gained a confidence she never had before, and CHF staff recognized that she became an inspiration to others in the community with her eagerness to get back on track. One of the most noticeable things about Ivy was her persistently great attitude. She was increasingly gracious and thankful for everything and everyone around her.

Under the tutelage of her case manager, Ivy progressed dramatically. She secured a new job with a renowned and reputable construction company. Her salary tripled, and Ivy discovered a new level of self-respect. She and Connor were blossoming as Ivy furthered her education, and Connor was popular and active in his school. They both found a sense of community in Colorado Homeless Families and were the first to meet and greet new families.

As Ivy retrieved her white Bible with gold letters, she no longer identified with Lamentations. Her reading for the day was from 2 Corinthians.

"This all-surpassing power is from God and not from us. We are hard-pressed on every side, but not crushed; perplexed, but not in despair; persecuted, but not abandoned; struck down, but not destroyed."[58]

Ivy smiled at such deep truths. She looked forward, now, to graduating from the CHF program, buying her own home, and finding love. In her journal, she wrote: *"With a home comes peace and security. One of the greatest rewards of security is that our children sense that they can sleep peacefully and not live in fear of not knowing where they will sleep. Colorado Homeless Families changes lives and changes people for the better for our community."*

As of 2004, more than 142,000 refugees from Myanmar lived in nine camps along the Thai-Myanmar border, and some refugees had lived in these refugee camps for decades.[59]

The flight of refugees from ethnic conflict in Myanmar began in 1988. With human rights abuses, and economic deprivation, refugees formed long lines to cross into Thailand believing anything was better than home. The Tham Hin refugee camp hosted over 9,000 people, and the head of the United Nations refugee agency and the U.S. State Department's Bureau of Population, Refugees, and Migration, visited the overcrowded refugee camps on a four-day mission in 2004.

Soon, they hoped, there would be an easing of the congested camps as the nations of the United States, Canada, Australia, Britain, Finland, the Netherlands, New Zealand, Sweden, and Norway began new settlement programs to provide Thailand relief for their number of refugees begging for resettlement. By the end of 2006, the United States planned to accept at least 2,700 refugees.[60] With no legal right to work in Thailand or even to leave the camps, refugees lived in limbo completely dependent on services provided by relief organizations.

Visits to overcrowded refugee camps revealed atrocious living conditions. One refugee was heard claiming:

"The Bible talks about hell. I am stuck in a 55-foot room, 40-feet wide, with 80 people in the room, sometimes 150 people, three toilets. Always there are problems. We can't get hot water. We use a naked [electrical] wire to heat the water. This is hell."[61]

Most of the camps were isolated in mountainous areas difficult to access. Many camps had no electricity. Camps had no phone service. In the rainy season, flash floods damaged the infrastructure and caused casualties. Other camps, such as Mae La Camp, the largest refugee camp with more than 40,000 refugees, were at least a one-hour drive from the nearest town so health care and education opportunities are extremely limited.

Due to overcrowding, there was a lack of room between the temporary houses, built from bamboo and teak leaves, and had caused many fires in the camp; they also decay quickly.[62]

These refugees' lives were restricted because they could not legally or practically leave the camps. An attempt to leave resulted in the Thailand police arresting them. If adults want to earn money, they had to do it secretly outside the camps, so most refugees didn't take the risk. Relying so heavily on relief aid made refugees feel dependent and bored. After years in horrendous living conditions, lack of hope made suicide an increasing problem in the refugee camps.

"It is so strict to live here. There is nothing to do. I am not allowed to go outside the camp. There is no job, no work. So much stress and depression. I feel that I am going to go crazy here."
    –Burmese refugee | Nu Po camp | Tak province[63]

Domestic violence was routine and child abuse was widespread, as was depression and addictions. Approximately half of the adults suffered from mental illness and depression, which contributed to the neglect and abuse of children.[64]

Chronic malnutrition made refugees fragile and more susceptible to various diseases and illnesses. Most refugee camps did not have sufficient food to provide to their populations; they relied heavily on the weekly food distributions and humanitarian assistance provided by non-governmental organizations and community-based organizations. The United Nations High Commissioner for Refugees (UNHCR) recommends that each refugee receive more than 2,100 calories per day, but camps fall short of this standard. Drinking water was collected from wells and streams, creating cases of cholera and malaria. Thirty percent of refugee camps did not have adequate waste disposal services or latrines.[65]

Children were not only at substantial risk of abuse and neglect, but also exploitation. Many girls married young, sometimes to spouses who abused them. Children suffered from chronic malnutrition and respiratory infections. Almost half of the camp population was under 18 years of age, and many children were born in the refugee camps, a problem because they could not have birth certificates and were stateless, which jeopardized their future.[66]

Sud and Dao Liang and their three children were just one family uprooted from Myanmar, also known as Burma. Life in their particular refugee camp at the Thai-Myanmar border was a daily struggle to survive. They were supplied with a little shack with dirt floors, and their daily food was far below the required 2,100 calories per day with one bowl of rice with chili to share among their entire family. Each day when they awoke, they were persistent in their hope they would be able to leave the camp.

One day, their wish came true; they were granted permission to be transferred to the United States—Denver, Colorado, to be exact.

Upon arriving in Denver, the Liangs discovered they were eligible for the Refugee Cash Assistance (RCA) program, which provided funds for living assistance to immigrants.[67] The Liangs received four months of assistance and a small apartment. Unfortunately, no-one realized that getting immigrants to their new location with a small stipend is not all that is required for refugee resettlement.

The Liangs were left on their own with no further resources. Their small apartment was thoroughly infested with bedbugs. The transition to America was vastly more complicated than they expected.

Within the allotted four months, they were out of relief money, with no employment to be found. They spoke very little of the English language, and they were soon homeless. They had, however, found a local church to attend and were faithful in their attendance. A church leader learned of their circumstances and referred them to Colorado Homeless Families.

Sud and Dao Liang applied to the CHF program and were accepted. They were thrilled to move into their new home, and for the first time in their life, they felt the beautiful breath of relief. They were in a safe, clean, and supportive environment. Yet, the Liangs had never experienced living accommodations such as this.

Because of this family's particular background and challenges, two case managers were assigned to help them. The Liangs had to learn how to do everyday tasks such as turning on and off the lights, using a bathtub and toilet correctly, storing food in a refrigerator, cooking on a stove, and using an oven, and utilizing all the appliances like a washer/dryer, dishwasher, and microwave, but they were quick to learn and were excited to experience something new each day.

They immersed themselves into the English as a Second Language (ESL) classes and were able to communicate proficiently within a short time. They were happy to be living a new life in America, and they were quick to offer to help others in the Colorado Homeless Families' community. They commonly offered to run errands, shop for groceries, help with childcare, and give rides to appointments to other CHF families.

They also volunteered to help maintain the CHF grounds, yards, and especially the playground. In refugee camps, children do not have anywhere to play and enjoy being children in the fresh air and sunshine, free from danger. They would spend hours with their children outside playing. Very few families at CHF did not come to know them because the Liangs were outgoing, friendly, and always willing to help anyone.

Finding a job that would be suitable for Sud was important. Living as a refugee causes a person to feel unusable, nonfunctional, and lacking purpose. Sud worked with his case managers to find employment. Eventually, he was hired for a position at a textile company whose focus was specialty knitted apparel.

The company was in its infancy, but they soon learned that Sud was their hardest worker and most loyal employee. Sud went above and beyond his job description and worked as though this company was his own.

The owner of the company informed Connie Zimmerman, Executive Director of Colorado Homeless Families that Sud's hard work and diligence had increased sales by at least 20% since he had been hired.

Management trusted Sud's work ethic and honesty so that when there was a job opening at the company, they would hire whoever Sud recommended without question, which was usually a CHF community resident whom Sud wanted to help.

The Liang family persisted, even through the dark times that would—and did—break other people.

They continue to live their "American dream" by working hard, being thankful for every opportunity offered, and continually helping others in any way possible. They wish to be reflectors of the assistance and support they received at Colorado Homeless Families.

Colorado Homeless Families offers transitional housing for those who need to get their life on track. Some families stay for a year or 18 months, others for two years, and sometimes even longer if they are dedicated to a long-term plan such as seeking a college degree.

Most families stay in touch with the staff of CHF and often write letters of thanks while updating the hard-working, encouraging staff on their status and how much their lives have changed.

Nelson, a young doctor, fled with his wife, Goëlle, from the Republic of the Congo amid civil war, violence, massive human rights violations, and extreme poverty. Many who leave their countries do so with only the clothes on their back to pursue their dream of living in America in a life free of turmoil and war.

This is one such letter:

My name is Nelson Sunga, and my wife Goëlle and I have four children. I grew up in the Democratic Republic of Congo, formerly Zaire, where I went to school and became a medical doctor. I worked in rural areas of the Congo for several years, but the working conditions were difficult.

I also managed a refugee program for a couple of years, but at the time, there was a lot of armed conflicts in the Congo and in the neighboring countries. My wife and I felt for our safety and that of our family, we needed to leave our home country. Many people we knew wanted to leave the Congo for America where they could be safe and raise their families in a non-violent place.

God answered our prayers and opened the doors for us to come to America. Coming to a new country with only our clothes and a few things in a suitcase was a new adventure for us. We did not know what to expect or where we were going to live.

We lived in Maryland for one year, and then moved to Colorado and was introduced to the Colorado Homeless Families Program. I had an idea that I could find a position as a doctor which would give us a good income, then we could have a nice place to live. I was not prepared for what can happen to a foreign-trained physician in the United States. I could not work as a physician and would need to go back to school to become a medical doctor in the U.S. Because I could not work as a physician, but still had to support my family, I took a job as a pharmacy technician. It was sometimes humbling and sometimes humiliating as people did not understand how a medical doctor could end up working as a pharmacy technician. However, I knew that was not the end of my story.

To get through disappointments, you must have a plan. During the two years at Colorado Homeless Families, we were always encouraged to figure out a way to become self-sufficient in the United States. With the help from the CHF staff, my wife learned English, and she went to school to be trained as a nurse's aide. This enabled her to find a stable job at a nursing home which allowed me to begin a master's program in Public Health at the University of Colorado. I was able to finish that program. Due to economic circumstances, however, many public health organizations could not hire new graduates.

One of my professors found an internship program for me. I trained there for two years. This professor also supported my willingness to start a Ph.D. program in Epidemiology knowing this would increase my chances to find a better job. I started the Ph.D. program and plan to graduate soon. The Lord has also blessed me with the possibility of working for the Federal Government after my graduation.

I wanted to tell my story as it can give hope to someone else who may have left a good career in their country of origin and cannot do the same thing professionally in the United States. Do not be discouraged. Trust in God. Use the resources at Colorado Homeless Families to figure out how to overcome roadblocks. Work hard to learn the language, culture, and be open-minded to any new opportunities that may come from God.

Nelson and Goëlle lived at Colorado Homeless Families for two and a half years, eventually purchasing the house they lived in. Due to continuing challenges, they were allowed to receive CHF food bank privileges. CHF Executive Director Connie Zimmerman, along with many CHF friends, was invited to attend Nelson's graduation ceremony at Anschutz Medical Center at the University of Colorado.

After many years of hard work and study, Nelson received his Ph.D. in Medicines and visited Colorado Homeless Families. He showed everyone a letter from the Centers for Disease Control and Prevention (CDC). The letter informed him that out of 500 applicants, Nelson was one of 80 new hires. A real estate friend of Colorado Homeless Families sold Nelson and Goëlle's home quickly so they could get to Atlanta for his new job.

Colorado Homeless Families helped Nelson and his family so much through the years, and he has pledged to give back to the program with donations, becoming an active member on the board of directors, being a mentor to families in need, and looking forward to adopting families for Christmas.

WHAT COUNTS IS A NEW CREATION

Many Are Gathered Together

At the creation of Colorado Homeless Families, the first families Connie selected to help and placed into the $1-a-year-lease-program HUD homes didn't need a lot of support and resources. They were self-starting, knew how to manage money and budget expenses, were educated, had been in careers, already had goals, but simply needed a little help and a little time to get back on their feet.

As the Colorado Homeless Families housing program grew throughout three different cities, logistics became a significant issue. Accepting applications from individuals who were less self-starting and goal-oriented required providing more support, as did the homeless immigrants who were experiencing culture shock and communication issues. Housing these individuals in outlying HUD homes made it more difficult for them to travel the CHF Education and Resource Center for support, meetings, education, counseling, case management, and events.

Connie began to assess safety, consolidation, and long-term planning efforts. This assessment led her to do three things.

1) For safety reasons, Connie decided it was best for single parent mothers and other vulnerable families to live in the CHF townhome community with daytime security for their children and nighttime security to attend the required meetings.

CHF employees and families closely supervised the children's play areas, the food bank and other CHF assistance programs that were within a secure walking distance from the CHF townhomes.

2) To relieve CHF of too many HUD homes scattered over a large area, Connie decided to limit the HUD properties to a maximum of 20. She selected the nicer ones that required less maintenance, as well as HUD properties closest to the CHF Complex. She would use the Federal Affordable Housing grants that were offered to nonprofits to purchase those of the 20 that Colorado Homeless Families didn't already own. The remainder of the outlying HUD properties that were rented through the $1-a-year-lease-program would be released back to HUD, who would then offer a pass-through sale to the CHF family living in the home. Working directly with the family, HUD required a $500 down payment after mortgage lender approval.

3) HUD regulations limited the length of time a family could stay in the $1-a-year-lease-program home to 24 months. However, Colorado Homeless Families had a maximum of five years to purchase the HUD home if they desired. Colorado Homeless Families had been slowly acquiring ownership of these homes through the Federal Affordable Housing grants and to date, 15 of the 20 HUD homes Connie selected to keep had already been purchased. Connie's plan for these 20 homes was for continued use as transitional housing with the possibility of a future sale with the equity transferred toward construction of expanding or centralizing the CHF transitional housing community.

The remaining five of the 20 HUD properties she selected to keep were in the city of Westminster, and the purchase expiration date was coming soon. Connie needed to either purchase those homes from HUD or return the homes to HUD, which would require the families to vacate. Her decision was to move forward with the purchase and utilization of those HUD homes.

The clock was ticking, and there were no CHF funds available to purchase the houses. Affordable housing grants were the only means CHF had to be able to purchase prior homes, but grants were slowly drying up in the current economy.

The City of Westminster maintained a Community Development Block Grant (CDBG) Program which provided annual grants on a formula basis to states, cities, and counties to develop viable urban communities by providing safe housing and a suitable living environment, and by expanding economic opportunities, principally for low- and moderate-income persons.

Connie was thoroughly familiar with this program, and a new CDBG Program Director had just been named. Unfortunately, the new CDBG Director verbally denied Colorado Homeless Families any additional grant funding to purchase the remaining five HUD homes.

Undeterred, Connie stated that she needed to apply anyway because she needed the grants to keep the homes. As a nonprofit, she could not afford mortgages. The CDBG Director sternly replied that the City of Westminster had helped Colorado Homeless Families enough over the years, and even if she applied, she would be denied further grant money.

Speaking in faith, Connie said that she needed these grants, and she would not bother the city with additional requests. She applied and sent in the grant request for $80,000 to purchase the remaining five homes.

Connie received a phone call from the Colorado Division of Housing and the representative said she saw that Connie had applied to purchase the five properties. She told Connie everyone thought it was wonderful what Colorado Homeless Families was doing and the county and state portions would be approved. However, the City of Westminster was still denying the grant request.

Wanting to help Connie, the woman offered to contact CHFA on her behalf and would even take care of completing the paperwork and loan applications for her. This way, Colorado Homeless Families could still get the money to purchase the five remaining homes.

Disturbed at this turn of events, Connie prayed, *"Lord, did you send this woman to help me? I don't want a loan or a mortgage; I wanted the grant money. Lord, every animal of the forest is yours, and the cattle on a thousand hills says Psalm 50:10. Lord, I'm trying to help the homeless people, so why do I need to get a loan when You own the cattle on a thousand hills? Lord, You need to turn around that Director's heart, and I need to get the approval from the city. You can do anything, Lord."*

Having mortgages on the ten properties at RG1 and the 12 properties at RG2, Connie knew taking on additional mortgages was not wise. She called the new CDBG Director and told him she had submitted the application and was expecting to get the grants she needed. His response was a very curt, "You are not going to get it." Connie replied that Colorado Homeless Families would be represented at the next city council meeting, but he strongly advised her not to attend.

Connie searched her heart and inquired of God. She ultimately found that she should not attend the city council meeting.

The day after the city council meeting, the CDBG Director called and told her that she was approved for the grant and he would send the papers for signature. Connie asked what changed.

He said the city council members inquired about the missing attendance of Colorado Homeless Families, as the city had been a longtime supporter of helping this nonprofit. They strongly desired to continue. He told her the city council insisted CHF get their grant request. The CDBG Director had no choice but to approve the grant money.

Connie's friend Steve, a real estate broker and representative for the initial RTC townhome purchase, helped Colorado Homeless Families by verifying the closing documents prior to the HUD property purchases. Volunteering his time and at no cost to CHF, the purchase of the final five HUD properties closed without incident.

301

Eventually selling three outlying HUD homes, the funds were used to pay off loans on the transitional housing community and begin transitional housing expansion projects along with children's play areas, a basketball court, a sitting park, and a large garden area for CHF family use.

Resist The Devil and He Will Flee From You

In 2005, Connie Zimmerman discovered that the property next to the Family Education & Resource Center had been rented, and the new renter set up a methamphetamine lab. It was becoming a danger to the families at CHF and the surrounding neighborhood. Meth labs were also known to negatively affect property values in the surrounding neighborhoods.

Between 1994 and 2004, methamphetamine use rose from just under two percent of the U.S. adult population to approximately five percent. In 2006, the United Nations World Drug Report called meth the most abused hard drug on Earth.[68] This is why, in large part, meth labs were popping up in neighborhoods all over the United States. Connie witnessed firsthand, however, that where there is meth, there is crime, drug traffic, violent behavior, and all forms of abuse. Additionally, the byproducts of meth labs contaminate the surroundings with harmful fumes and highly explosive chemical compounds.

In the hands of the untrained chemists simultaneously using meth and working with the flammable chemical components, a working meth lab is just as unsafe as a ticking time bomb.

The presence of the drug traffic forced Colorado Homeless Families to temporarily suspend nighttime support group meetings and educational seminars. By 2006, local police regularly arrested tenants and their guests at their home.

In June 2006, the drug house property eventually went into foreclosure, and all remaining tenants were forced to leave. Upon foreclosure, Colorado Homeless Families purchased the home. Connie found that getting rid of a meth lab was dangerous and expensive. Meth cookers dump battery acid, solvents, and other toxic materials into rivers or the ground. Much of the waste is highly flammable and explosive.

One pound of meth produces six pounds of toxic waste. No one knows where this toxic waste was dumped – possibly into the ground, sewers, or septic systems contaminating surface water, groundwater, and nearby wells. Even months after meth labs have been closed, the chemical residue remained and can be corrosive, explosive, flammable, toxic, and possibly radioactive. Inside a home, traces of chemicals can permeate the walls, drapes, carpets, and furniture of a laboratory site.[69]

Methamphetamine-affected properties require extensive environmental testing and cleanup by the Colorado Department of Health and Environment and certified ecological consultants. All site areas undergo rigorous toxicology, radiation, and hazard waste tests to determine the remediation options for the owner of the property.

Colorado Homeless Families followed all protocols and found the best course of action was to demolish the home. This purchase, the CHF Board decided, protected all the families living at CHF and the surrounding neighbors, thereby rehabilitating the neighborhood from drug traffic.

Hoping to use the property for a much-needed parking expansion for the CHF program, they found the zoning would not allow for a parking lot. Instead, after the rigorous testing, the ground was deemed safe, so gardens were installed for the families living at CHF. The detached garage on the property was also cleared by thorough testing and was put into use by CHF maintenance to store tools and equipment.

Colorado Home Families was praised by surrounding neighbors, with expressed gratitude and appreciation for beautifying the area and protecting the neighborhood from the hazards of the meth lab and increasing crime. Studies had been released showing that having a meth lab within one-tenth of a mile decreased a home's value by 6.5 percent, a decline that is not always completely offset when meth labs are decontaminated.[70]

Farm House Extension Project – An Award Winner

In 2005, Colorado Homeless Families Executive Director Connie Zimmerman was looking at the south side of their office building property towards the beautiful duplex built by Extreme Home Makeover. Always listening for God to speak to her, Connie looked beyond the CHF property.

Knowing God has no property boundaries, she saw a farmhouse that sat on about one acre, and it was set amidst a grove of beautiful, large trees. Connie decided to walk over to the property and knock on the door. She asked the owners if they would consider selling the property. The woman said that it had previously been for sale, but they hadn't received any offers for their asking price of $160,000. Connie told them CHF would be interested and to please let her know. They called Connie the next day and told her they would agree to sell the property to Colorado Homeless Families.

Placing a call to the Arthur H. and Helen K. Johnson Foundation, she investigated the possibility of a grant for $150,000 to purchase the farmhouse. The Johnson Foundation provided the funds, and the .77-acre lot with the three-bedroom farmhouse became the property of Colorado Homeless Families.

After purchasing the land with the $150,000 grant, the cash portion of the construction project was still over $900,000. Colorado Homeless Families worked with a diverse group of supporters that made it possible for seven new townhomes to be built on the farmhouse property.

To reach the construction goal, funds were obtained through a variety of channels: City of Arvada ($143,000), Gates Foundation ($140,000), Adolph Coors Foundation ($50,000), Daniels Fund ($50,000), and the Boettcher Foundation ($15,000). Colorado Homeless Families raised an additional $510,000 from the sale of four older transitional HUD homes at scattered sites around the City of Arvada.

With the land already purchased, KB Homes, a community homebuilder, was contracted to build the seven new units under the direction of HomeAid Colorado, and HomeAid Colorado raised an additional $328,734 in in-kind contributions.

Photo: Four of the seven Farmhouse Extension Project townhomes in 2010.

After three years of planning, fundraising, and numerous time extensions, Colorado Homeless Families was able to break ground for seven new transitional homes in May 2010. Referred to as "The Farm House Extension," the groundbreaking was held at the CHF Park, with the CHF Board of Directors, staff, and local dignitaries invited. HomeAid Colorado kicked off the groundbreaking ceremony with words of encouragement for CHF and their commitment to helping the homeless. Ed Talbot, Executive Director of Arvada Housing Authority was present and was acknowledged for all his help.

The groundbreaking also included the testimony of three former CHF residents and how living at Colorado Homeless Families had changed their lives.

Scheduled completion was October 2010, with an actual completion date of December 2010. CHF held an open house for the "Farm House Extension Project," and the first family was able to move in by the end of that week. During 2011, seven families were living in the farmhouse extension housing.

In 2011, Ed Talbot, Executive Director of Arvada Housing Authority, nominated Connie Zimmerman and CHF's Farm House Extension as the Project of Excellence, and Colorado Homeless Families won the National Association of Housing Redevelopment Officials (NAHRO) Affordable Housing Project Award. CHF was chosen from among housing and community development advocates to provide adequate and affordable housing to all Americans, especially those with low to moderate income.

Photo: Larry Zimmerman (left) and Connie Zimmerman, Executive Director of Colorado Homeless Families, accept the 2011 Colorado Chapter of the National Association of Housing and Redevelopment Officials (CoNAHRO) State Award of Excellence from Ed Talbot, Executive Director of the Arvada Housing Authority. The Award of Excellence recognizes outstanding innovation and achievement in housing and community development programs throughout the United States on a state, regional, and national level. Colorado Homeless Families also won the Regional Award of Excellence, presented June 2011 in Utah.

Handsome Jacob Dawson lay on his bed in the cell of Denver County Jail and Detention Center.

This solitude and boredom of being locked behind bars allowed him more time than he wanted to reflect on his life. Today, especially, he remembered standing in the doorway of his party house gazing across the non-existent lawn that was scattered with the remnants of one of his famous parties. His friends used the lawn as a parking lot, which he always thought was hysterical because he knew it made the neighbors angry. Some of his friends thought crawling through the windows instead of using the door was funny. Ah, life had been good.

He used to walk over and sway in the breeze of the big shade tree, loving the feeling of pure pleasure that meth brought. *There's no feeling like it in the world, and nothing but meth can make you feel it*, Jacob thought. He and his friends would have quite the soirees most nights: sitting around with music (the louder, the better), drinking, and getting high.

One night they sat around creating new nicknames for themselves. J-Dawg was his. He liked his new moniker. He even had it tattooed on his neck compliments of one of his new prison buddies. He was trying to remember all the new names of his friends who used to spread out, and pass out, all over his house. Lil Wills, K-Cap, GrungeMan, Morri$, PeeGee, T-Crane, DJ-Jethro, Joe-M, Big Bertie, Mad-Max, and even Peaches and Domino would stay over. Always. A. Party. There was at least a dozen or more people that came and went during parties. He forgot their names. One night he remembered two of the girls screaming and fist fighting about who was gonna pay for the crystal. It got loud around 3:00 am and the cops showed up, arrested a few of the loud ones, then left. He and his geeker friends always had a good time getting jacked up, getting boisterous, and running around the playground next door to his house.

He was lucky to find that house. A friend of a friend of his cousin's bought it and wanted to rent it. Only a little over 400-square feet, the owner knew he could only rent it to a single person and for very little money.

Jacob fit the bill. He wasn't particular about where he lived; he had just wanted out of his parent's basement. A year after quitting college, his mom had started riding him hard about making something of his life. She'd tell him how handsome he was, and he had a charming smile and brains to boot. He could do anything he wanted in life, but J-Dawg liked his rowdy friends and wanted out from under the prying eyes of his parents.

Once he rented that house, he had the freedom to do what he wanted, when he wanted, and with whoever he wanted. The landlord never came around if the rent was paid on the first of every month. His friends were free to come and go and they all threw a few bills his way to help pay the rent and keep the raucous crank parties going.

He didn't always know where his friends got their money either, but he knew that they liked to case the houses around the neighborhood now and again. Yep, he and his buds had planned to make a lot of money from cooking and selling their drug of choice.

J-Dawg remembered that the neighbors tried to welcome him to the neighborhood and some old broad brought banana bread. He had no intention of being friendly with his neighbors. Except, one beautiful fall day, his attention latched onto a blonde goddess that lived across the way in one of the townhomes. He would see her come and go, and it looked like she had a couple of little kids. When she would watch her kids on the playground, J-Dawg made sure to wave at her. Once, she had waved back.

Oh, yes, he thought. One warm day, fueled by crissy courage, he wandered over to the playground to talk to her. She told him that where she lived was called Colorado Homeless Families and she was working hard to get on her feet. She had been on drugs, lost her apartment, and had become homeless. She was rehabilitated and had been clean for several years.

He liked listening to her talk and her kids were cute. J-Dawg smiled his enticing smile and told her that she was welcome to come over and meet some of his friends any time she wanted. As he walked away, he noticed a woman and a couple of men watching him from the office complex. He'd seen the woman before—she seemed to be in charge or maybe run the place. He paid them no mind, and lo and behold, one night the blonde goddess popped over to his house.

She only stayed a few minutes, and he introduced her to some of his friends. Being a gentleman, he walked her back home, gave her his best smile, and she invited him for dinner the next weekend.

He went, of course, taking a small gift of smack with him. *"Better than flowers"* he remembered thinking. He went back the next weekend. And the next weekend. And a few weekends later, she invited him and his friends, T-Crane, and Peaches. J-Dawg liked this beautiful goddess, but he always felt under the watchful eye of those living in the neighboring townhomes or those working in that office.

Several months later, the Sheriff's Department showed up with an eviction notice. Turns out his landlord wasn't using J-Dawg's rent money to make the house payments, so the bank foreclosed, and the property was seized. Damn. His new goddess of a girlfriend came and offered help and let him, T-Crane, and Peaches move in with her. He thought he found his soulmate and didn't even mind her kids. The only thing she asked was he be careful where he kept the drugs, so her kids didn't find them.

Without the extra money that his friends used to throw his way, and the customers unable to purchase drugs without her neighbors knowing, J-Dawg had found himself in need of money.

His goddess girlfriend loaned him what she could, but shortly after that, she was notified that she needed to leave Colorado Homeless Families. They claimed she wasn't paying her rent or taking care of her children. Looking across the way, his party house was completely boarded up, and now his goddess was being evicted also. Still, her neighbors were watching like hawks.

One of her neighbors had noticed a strange car parked in front of her townhome. They didn't know who the car belonged to, so their "watch group" called the cops. They found out one of his rowdy friends, Mad-Max, had stolen the vehicle in Colorado Springs and driven it to Arvada to steal some of their drugs in his goddess' townhome. Social services took her children, and they were officially evicted.

J-Dawg hadn't been in jail long when someone sent him a newspaper clipping. His party house had officially gone into foreclosure, and Colorado Homeless Families purchased the "drug house." He read that the house was evaluated for meth and torn down. It was now a garden area for employees and clients of Colorado Homeless Families. The newspaper article quoted the Executive Director, Connie Zimmerman, "Colorado Homeless Families is cleaning up the neighborhood. This is a celebration." He knew this was the woman who had kept a watchful eye over the people of Colorado Homeless Families. What Connie knew with certainty was written in Proverbs 15:3, *"The eyes of the Lord are everywhere, keeping watch on the wicked and the good."*

On a clear and sunny day in May, Louis Gomez sat on his brand-new deck and turned his face to the sun. He had just put the final touches on the deck in the backyard of his new house when he started to reflect on when he had hit rock bottom. Three years ago, he found himself legally separated from his wife of 20 years and needing to leave his home, lost his job, had no money, nowhere to go, and diagnosed with cancer. He had *less* than nothing, and Louis had discovered two new words firsthand: suffering and despair.

Louis had never been destitute and never thought he would be. He wasn't like the panhandlers he would see or those who slept in the parks or would sleep in the doorways of buildings. Now, he could see how someone could get to that place in the blink of an eye. A faithful Christian and a churchgoing man, Louis found that Psalm 69 perfectly reflected his despondency, with the sense of sorrow so deeply profound. This psalm mirrored Louis' overwhelming and terrible grief that was all-consuming.

The marital strain had begun years ago. Their two sons, Levi and Luke, were active and energetic, sometimes rambunctious, while his wife craved peace, quiet, and stability. When Levi was diagnosed as bipolar, his wife began a downward spiral, and their son's illness put an excessive and irreparable strain on their marital relationship. Finally taking its toll on his wife, she felt she could not care for them properly and wanted out of the turmoil. She filed for legal separation, and Louis was forced to move out of their home, taking their two sons with him to a small apartment. The legal separation aggravated Levi's bipolar diagnosis, and Luke began showing anger.

Unfortunately, Luke started to blame Levi for the separation causing strife between the boys. Luke was also showing signs of stress and experiencing headaches and stomach aches, causing him to miss school. Finally, Louis decided it was in his sons' best interest that he take 30 days off work to take care of his sons and help stabilize them in their new living conditions.

After returning to his landscape foreman job, Louis found the dynamics of his employment had changed. Some people had taken over his responsibilities, and management was pleased with the forced change, even though they had told him they were supportive of his absence to care for his family. He also found that clients were happy with their new contact, leaving him feeling like an outsider.

Louis knew that before he took his leave, the business was changing because of the downturn in the economy, and he had seen many of his crew of workers laid off during these times. Louis knew that caring for his family was the most important thing and that taking 30 days off with no pay would be a sacrifice, but it was one he was willing to take. However, within several weeks of returning, Louis found himself without a job. Management restructured and he was let go. This was a dire turn of events for Louis, as he was already low on money from the leave, and now he was jobless. Pouring over his bills, he found that it would not be long before they would have nowhere to live.

He applied for unemployment and continued to look for work. Looking at all his options in the landscaping industry, Louis decided to try to earn his commercial driver's license (CDL), which required getting a physical exam from a U.S. Department of Transportation (DOT) certified physician.

The physician found a suspicious mole and immediately performed a punch biopsy for testing. Within the week, it was identified as cancerous, and Louis was at once scheduled for a surgical procedure.

The doctor explained that it was crucial to remove it and the skin around it, so cancer would not spread beyond the skin and affect other body parts. This required surgical removal to cut it out, including a lot of the tissue surrounding it.

It turned out that more tissue needed to be removed than previously determined. The amount and depth of removal were quite substantial, leaving Louis in a prolonged period of recovery and unable to look for work.

By the time Louis was fully recovered from surgery, he had exhausted all avenues for finding employment and a less expensive place to live.

Max, an acquaintance from church who visited him while recuperating, brought him and the boys some meals. On one such visit, Max told Louis about the Colorado Homeless Families program. Max had heard the Executive Director, Connie Zimmerman, give a talk about this organization. She had referred to the "new poor," who were families that had never been indigent but were finding themselves suddenly homeless for various reasons like job loss, illness, or even broken families.

Louis thought to himself, "I am *all* of those!" His friend told him that Colorado Homeless families was a nonprofit program that provided transitional properties to house less fortunate families with children. Connie had expressed how proud they were to be a multicultural community that worked together and assisted one another.

The program was designed to provide a helping hand to those who can prove a willingness to help themselves, have specific goals, and show initiative toward bettering their financial and social situation.

The typical graduate takes about two years to gain self-reliance, and she spoke of hundreds of families that have turned their life around and moved on with better lives. "What have I got to lose?" Louis told his friend.

Louis contacted Colorado Homeless Families and moved into one of the HUD homes leased by CHF. It was a solid and genuinely nice home, and it even had a big yard for the boys to play. They spent many hours tossing the football and playing catch. Eventually, Louis had found a basketball hoop at a neighborhood garage sale and mounted it above the garage. He even installed a horseshoe pit in the backyard and taught the boys how to pitch horseshoes, something Louis used to do with his father and grandfather.

They were settled into their new home, and Colorado Homeless Families was the exact place they needed to be. Their family counseling sessions were helping them all cope with the impending divorce and the subsequent parental abandonment of the boys' mother. Louis attended the support groups and made some very good friends who were also single fathers. His case manager helped Louis map out a plan for his career after Louis was determined to stay in the landscaping industry.

He had two years of college education but had never finished as he had been anxious to get to work and get married; but his new goals included a short-term goal: find employment suitable to his skills; a medium-term goal: to finish his degree in business management and landscape architecture; and his long-term goal: to start his own landscape architecture design company. With plans in hand, hope for the future, and his boys thriving, Louis no longer felt Psalm 69 was his life.

While in the program, there were many areas where his skills were used. The grounds of the CHF complex were an enjoyable place for him and his sons to volunteer their time, and he continued to meet other families through this opportunity. He was also able to help with the upkeep and maintenance of the yards and landscapes of the HUD homes leased by CHF. Louis always made "giving back" part of his life, and he continued to do so gladly while thankful for being allowed to become part of this program.

After graduating with honors, Louis was invited to join a landscape architecture firm as a partner. For him, this solved many hurdles that he would face launching a start-up of his own. His biggest regret would be leaving the house he and his boys had come to love.

He met with Connie Zimmerman after their CHF family graduation celebration and was surprised at the offer she made to him. Connie was reducing the number of HUD home leases and was working toward consolidating most of the CHF families onto the centralized Colorado Homeless Families complex. To this end, Connie explained to Louis that she had recommended to HUD that he be considered for the purchase of the home he was currently living in. Louis jumped at the offer to work with HUD on the purchase since he would be able to take quick possession.

On this clear, sunny day in May, Louis Gomez sat on his brand-new deck and turned his face to the sun. He had just put the finishing touches on the deck in the backyard of his new home. After reflecting on when he had hit rock bottom, he had a new psalm. Psalm 145 perfectly reflected his hopefulness, with the sense of joy so deeply profound.

When Nina woke up, the throbbing caused disorientation.

Facedown in the brown shag carpeting, she could smell the alcohol and cigarettes in the air and taste the blood in her mouth. Through the roaring in her ears, she could hear the silence in the house. She didn't hear snoring, so the beast wasn't sleeping. No creaking floors meant the beast was gone. Shakily, she rose and made her way to the bathroom on wobbly legs. Once again, she looked at the face staring back at her in the mirror. Swollen eye. Dried blood around her nose. A loose tooth.

Carefully she peeled off her nightgown and sat on the floor of the hot shower. The water that pulsed on those places where the beast punched and kicked her made the throbbing skyrocket. As she bowed her head and let the water rain down over her, she silently prayed that the water would wash the blood, bruising, and pain down the drain. Another night of intoxicated, non-stop rage. Beast drunkenly pulled her from a deep sleep and made her sit on the sofa while he railed about everything wrong with his life, including how they were now losing their house because he had been fired from his job. Now that they were going to be homeless, what were they going to do, the beast yelled. And he made sure to scream at the top of his lungs that it was all her fault. She knew trying to get away would only make the beast angrier—and the shoving, slapping, punching, and kicking would commence. And it did. The last thing she remembered from early this morning was the slamming of the front door, the beast's truck roar to life, and screeching tires down the street. That's when she sank deep into the carpet and welcomed the darkness.

As Nina carefully stepped from the shower, she dried off as well as she could while softly patting the areas of the bruising and the soreness. Making her way to the bedroom, she saw the sheets tangled and pulled halfway to the door, where the beast once again had dragged her out of bed in the middle of the night. She gently dressed and caught another glimpse of herself in the mirror before she left the bedroom.

"*It's time,*" she thought, as she gingerly reached for her backpack and the small bag of clothing and toiletries she had hidden under the bed months ago. Deep inside one of the side pockets of her backpack was a card from Colorado Homeless Families. Nina silently left by the back door and shuffled down the alley to the back door of Ruth's house. She and Ruth had met one summer day while walking to the local farmer's market, and she and the older woman had become fast friends. Nina later found that Ruth's name is Hebrew for "compassionate friend." Ruth had become just that. Ruth understood what Nina could never say aloud. Now, here she stood on wobbly legs, five doors down from her house and hoping the beast would not drive by in the alley and see her. Nina knocked lightly on Ruth's back door and knew that this would be the day that her friend would help her to the light. Ruth had told her on one of their farmer's market walks that a friend is one who strengthens you with prayers, blesses you with love, and encourages you with hope. She began to help Nina with the start of a new life.

Ruth's previous career in social work led her to have many connections, one of which was for Colorado Homeless Families, which was the card that Nina held in her hand. Ruth also amassed friends, associates, and acquaintances through her tireless volunteer work in her church, battered women's shelters, homeless shelters, and crisis centers. Nina's history of domestic abuse with the beast had previously landed her in several battered women's shelters, but these were always short-term solutions and were not the long-term solution for self-sufficiency that she deeply desired.

Generally, Colorado Homeless Families was not an organization to take single people. They focused more on one- or two-parent families helping to keep their children off the streets.

It seemed easier for individuals to find housing, or sleep on a couch or fold-out, or even stay with a friend or family. With children, no one wanted to house families for very long. Ruth explained that, at the moment, there was a cottage home available at Colorado Homeless Families. It was available to a small group of women who did not have children.

There was one space available. Ruth helped Nina complete the application and the interviews. Nina applied to Metro State College to finish her degree in social work and Ruth helped Nina set up and pay for a post office box for her mail. Nina's grants and loans had come through and she had applied for a work-study program in the Financial Aid Office at the college. Nina also had a desire to help others; it was what she was born to do.

Today, as Ruth held Nina's hand, she wound through the streets of Arvada to the Colorado Homeless Families' center. During her interview, the CHF case manager had explained that Nina would be subject to all the requirements as the other families. Thirty percent of her income had to pay for rent. She had to be working, going to school, or both.

She was required to attend counseling classes at the CHF Family and Resource Center and volunteer her time somewhere within the CHF facility. Before the beast made her quit college, she always worked part-time at clothing stores, so she was looking forward to volunteering in the Colorado Homeless Families' clothing bank.

As Ruth slowed the car, Nina looked west to the Rocky Mountains and remembered a verse she had read in her Bible in the book of Psalm 121, *"I lift up my eyes to the mountains—where does my help come from? My help comes from the LORD, the Maker of heaven and earth."* Nina had to hide her Bible from the beast, but now she would be free to read it whenever she wanted.

As Ruth pulled the car into Colorado Homeless Families, Nina took a cleansing breath and felt a tiny ray of sunrise in her heart.

In 2010, The Democratic Republic of the Congo (DRC), formerly Zaire, claimed a population of over 68 million people living in an area roughly three times the size of Texas and having one of the highest growth rates in the world at 3.39%.[71]

Law enforcement and public order lie with state security forces of the Congolese National Police (PNC). The National Intelligence Agency (ANR) is responsible for intelligence, while the Armed Forces of the Democratic Republic of the Congo (FARDC) is responsible for external and internal security. There is also the Republican Guard (RG), and Directorate-General for Migration (DGM) that focus on border control. All these agencies have dissident elements, but the country is also widespread with combatants, rebel and militia groups (RMG), political-religious groups, community-based self-defense groups, and hundreds of criminal networks.[72]

State security forces act independently of civilian control and military command and continue to be investigated for human abuses, unlawful killings, disappearance, torture, rape, arbitrary arrests, and detention. There is also arbitrary interference with privacy, family and homes, and state security forces abuse and threaten journalists which contributes to the steep decline in the press and journalistic freedom.[73]

The law in the Democratic Republic of the Congo provides for freedom of speech and the press, however, the government restricted these rights in practice, and freedom of the press declined because the government intimidated journalists and publishers into practicing self-censorship. Following an assessment visit to the country in June 2009, Margaret Sekaggya, the UN special rapporteur on human rights defenders, said journalists and other human rights defenders, "face illegitimate restrictions of their right to freedoms of opinion and expression" and underscored that the country's, "defenders, in particular journalists, who report on human rights abuses committed by state and non-state actors, are killed, threatened, tortured, or arbitrarily arrested and their offices raided."[74]

Freedom of speech claimed that individuals could *privately* criticize the government, its officials, and private citizens without being subject to official reprisals. However, *public* criticism of government officials and government conduct or decisions regarding issues such as conflict and insurgencies, management of natural resources, or corruption sometimes resulted in harsh responses, often from the ANR.

Radio remained the most important medium of public information due to limited literacy and the relatively high cost of newspapers and television. With only three state-owned radio stations and three television stations, there were more than 350 radio and television stations that were privately owned and independently operated.

Free speech was not free, however, and there was a long history to prove it. In 2009, government authorities imposed an indefinite suspension on broadcasts by Radio France Internationale.

The broadcast signal was eventually restored, but government authorities informed foreign journalists that the military code of justice (criminal penalties, including imprisonment) would be applied to anyone who committed press offenses. Journalists expressed concern over the ability to report on sensitive subjects such as the conflict in the east and corruption. Later that year, a journalist with Radio Star was killed by bandits while on his way home from a wedding. His friend, who was present during the attack, escaped unharmed but was arrested.

In 2008, unknown assailants shot and killed a journalist for Radio Okapi. Two years later, soldiers broke into Radio Moto-Oicha and apprehended and beat a radio technician. A short time later, ANR agents arrested the director of RadioTelevision

Communautaire Mitumba and held him without charge for 11 days.

Later that same year, ANR agents sought a journalist who participated in a broadcast that criticized municipal officials for alleged mismanagement. Before the end of the year, this same journalist was injured in an altercation with ANR agents, was hospitalized, then released in the company of two unidentified individuals, and his whereabouts were never made known.

Radio stations that covered or reported on controversial topics often saw temporary interruption of broadcasts and faced harassment. One watchdog group reported a 16 percent increase in broadcast freedom abuses, such as murder, assault, arbitrary arrest and detention, threats, and illegal sanctions or censorship. This continued to make radio stations afraid to address sensitive topics as this freedom continued to be restricted.[75]

Ashina and Faustin Mbemba and their 18-year-old daughter lived as normal a life in the Democratic Republic of the Congo as they could. Ashina had been operating a Christian radio station for 11 years. The station was popular, their needs were met, and she felt safe in her community.

Darkness lay on the horizon, as a rebel army was beginning to build and gain momentum. It was only a matter of time before they were in her community, and when they finally did arrive, they laid claim to people's homes, food, and valuables. The more the people of her community fought back, the more intense the violence became with chaos, destruction, beatings, and even murders.

Ashina used her radio station as a platform to speak out against this violence and the trampled rights of her neighbors, however, the more she spoke out, the more acts of intimidation they brought against her. Within days, the intimidation intensified, and the rebels broke into her radio station and violated and beat her. They also threatened to kill her husband,

Faustin, if he refused to join their army. To save his own life and those of his wife and daughter, he left with the armed men.

The danger in her community persisted, as did the threat on her life. She finally had to decide to flee. Ashina, her daughter, and her sister's family fled to a refugee camp. It would only be a matter of time before she would be found there. Ashina and her daughter were given refugee status and permitted to go to the United States; her sister's family, which included her brother-in-law and their three children, had to remain.

After arriving in Colorado, Ashina and her daughter lived in the basement of a family that had also fled the Democratic Republic of the Congo. Knowing that she had to make a living, she began studying to become a Certified Nurse's Aide (CNA), and after she started working, Ashina sent most of her paychecks to her relatives still living in the refugee camp.

A very long three years later, her sister's family received permission to immigrate to the United States. Unfortunately, the family with whom Ashina was living would not allow five additional people to move into their basement. Ashina could not afford an apartment for all of them on her $8.00 per hour Nurse's Aide pay. She learned about Colorado Homeless Families through a co-worker, and Ashina and her sister's family were approved to live together in the transitional housing.

Although Ashina had learned some English, after moving into CHF, the adults quickly enrolled in all the ESL classes: basic, intermediate, and conversational. They also signed up for the educational courses to help them better adapt to their new country and attended support group meetings. Ashina signed up for counseling to help her overcome the brutality she faced, the division of her family, and the loss of her passion: her Christian radio station.

No longer fearing for her safety, death threats, and intimidation, Ashina once again became determined to continue to be a voice to speak out against the violation of human rights, brutality, and corruption in the Congo. She used local news, media, and of course, radio outlets to expose those things that many people face living in the Congo.

Never appreciating freedom until it is taken from you, Ashina volunteered her time in the community and always tried to find a way to help others living at Colorado Homeless Families. She thanks God each day for this freedom and plans to take advantage of all the wonderful opportunities she has to improve her life in the United States by getting more education to attain a better job, helping her family members get their education so they can get good jobs. Maybe even one day, they will be able to purchase their very own home.

Thanksgiving was something new for Lev and Anya Kozlov. Never in their own lives had they ever experienced a special holiday set aside to offer prayers of thanks. Seeing their new country set aside a day for celebrating the blessings and harvest of the year was something Lev, Anya, and their eight children were excited to do.

They learned that on this Day of Thanksgiving, it is tradition for Americans to share a family meal, and some even attend church services giving thanks. Their sponsor brought them an entire traditional Thanksgiving meal, and the Kozlov's were overwhelmed. "We feel like kings; we think we are in heaven," they said as they thanked God for their blessings.

The Kozlov's life in the strife-ridden and poverty-stricken area of southeastern Russia was also one of oppression. Their life grew more dismal each day, and the hardships were made worse by escalating political and religious conflicts. Lev Kozlov had worked long hours as a shoemaker that barely provided the family enough money to buy the very basics. Their home was only a small four-room house for their growing family ranging from 4 months to 13 years old.

The Kozlov's knew that coming to America was their only chance for a life free from poverty and political and religious conflicts. After dreaming of a free life full of possibilities, they arrived in the United States from Russia and settled in Denver. They had local sponsors and offers of aid when they arrived, however, the Kozlov's did not have a place to live. During the first month, they shared a small apartment with another large family. Leaving what little they had behind, they arrived with $100, five boxes of clothes, and eight hungry children. The uncertain future of what they faced in America was still tolerable because of the hope of what *could be*; that far outweighed the hardships they faced in Russia, knowing things *could never* get better if they stayed.

Nearing Christmas, a former Colorado Homeless Families client called Executive Director Connie Zimmerman to further inquire about housing a large Russian family that had recently arrived in Denver. They were currently living with another family but were eager to apply to get their own space. The Kozlov's had already spoken to the CHF case manager who was a sweet young Russian lady. There was a bigger problem. Colorado Homeless Families had no place to put a large family.

Not to be discouraged, little six-year-old Alina Kozlov, who spoke very little English, kept calling the CHF case manager: *"Please you have house for us?"* and, *"Please we need home."* The CHF case manager continued to work with Connie on a solution, but there did not seem to be anything they could do for this large family.

In what seemed to be insurmountable odds, Connie Zimmerman knew her God was bigger than any odds against them.

A house next door to one of the CHF-HUD properties had caught on fire earlier in the year and had been rebuilt by a developer. A local dentist, who Connie had met on several occasions, purchased the rebuilt home but was having a problem keeping the house rented.

The dentist, who Connie had learned, had been active in missionary work in India, knew about the CHF program, and offered the house to Connie to use for her transitional housing program. Unfortunately, the rent he required was too expensive for the rents that were set by the Colorado Homeless Families program. So, the house continued to sit vacantly.

The Kozlov family weighed heavily on Connie's heart, even though she had been told by the Lord that she could not help everyone who asked. At the same time, her mind would drift back to the vacant house, but knowing the rent was not something CHF could afford. She continued to turn this problem over in her mind, and although she knew the Kozlov's could not afford the rent on the vacant house, she told them that she would check on it.

One evening after Connie arrived home, she was reminded she needed to be true to her word and look into the vacant house for them. Before anything, Connie found herself praying, *"Lord, this family is so large. I cannot take care of these people with what I have, and You know that. So please let me know if I'm supposed to help them in some way."*

About 4:00 am, Connie awoke to a song playing in her head:

♫ I will bless those who bless my people
I will love those who love them too.
For this is my promise I have given to my servant Abraham,
I will keep my word. ♫

She knew it was a Jewish song but did not know the name of it or all the exact words, so she got up and wrote down all the lyrics that were coming to her. The next day Connie asked the CHF case manager to contact the Kozlov family and ask them if they were Jewish. The case manager said the family insisted that they were not Jewish but Christians. Connie wanted the case manager to verify if they were Jewish Christian because she felt strongly that God wanted Colorado Homeless Families to take in a Jewish family, and Connie needed to know this information.

The CHF case manager confirmed they were Jewish Christian. They relayed information that Mr. Kozlov's sister's family had been sent to Israel, but his own family was sent to America. Their mother was of Jewish descent.

Connie called the dentist and asked him if he would consider "missionary work" in his hometown by renting his empty house to this family. The Kozlov's only had $700 for rent, and Colorado Homeless Families would manage the property and oversee all the upkeep and maintenance. The dentist agreed and would send the paperwork to Connie's office.

When Connie met with the Kozlov's to complete the paperwork, she told them God had given her a song. She sang it to them, and they began crying. Lev and Anya said to her that they had been praying that God would give Connie a dream that would lead her to help them.

The Kozlov's continued to receive donations and assistance from local churches, schools, and volunteers, and they used the CHF program banks for furniture, dishes, household items, clothing, and food.

With every basic donation the Kozlov's received, they were extremely grateful. Lev received assistance with job training at a local trade school in diesel truck mechanics, and at the adult education center for English as a Second Language instruction. They joined CHF educational classes, which helped with their transition into American culture, and attended counseling to help them adjust to their new lifestyle.

The Kozlov's settled into their nice CHF home and placed their children in schools, where they quickly began to enjoy their new life. They began to thrive and excelled at speaking English. Both schools held a drive to collect food, books, and clothing for the family.

They have never known so many good things. The Kozlov family understood then that America was a much richer place for their family, better than anything they could have even dreamed of in Russia.

They entered America homeless, financially desperate, and in great need of help. They were overwhelmed by the generosity of strangers, and with the help of Colorado Homeless Families, they found a new life. After two years, they bought a new home. Their future filled with promise and possibilities.

Stella Towne waited at the bus stop and bowed her head in prayer.

Mr. Bridges had died today, and she was grateful that his family got to sit with him in his final hours. She had a lot of different tasks in her job, and today she organized and provided the Bridges family with the food cart of iced tea, lemonade, cookies, and various snacks while they sat vigil at their patriarch's bedside.

She never had an idea of a "dream job," and certainly working in the hospice industry would have *never* been her idea of the kind of job she might enjoy. After working there for ten months, she had recently realized there was no place she would rather work, and she received good reports from her supervisors. It was an emotionally difficult job, but she also knew Jesus, who told her she could do anything He called her to do. Mr. Bridges had been at the hospice facility for three months and was in amazingly good spirits when he arrived. He told her one morning that he had been a literature professor, so they bonded over their shared love of books. Especially the classics. She sometimes got to read to him when her daily duties were complete, and they had just finished *The Catcher in The Rye* two weeks ago.

Stella boarded the bus that began the 30-minute ride to Colorado Homeless Families. She and Jim and their three children had lived there for the past year, and she still pinched herself at what a miracle place this was. Several years ago, she decided to quit her job with a financial company. Jim had started his own painting company, "Paint the Towne," after having worked for another painting company for more than a decade. It was his chosen field, and he thoroughly enjoyed the work. Even before they got married, he had told Stella that it was his dream to have his own painting company one day. After they were married, he began taking some side jobs on weekends, including painting their church and some of their neighbor's homes, which earned them some added money to purchase their first home. Several years later, Jim felt that it was the right time to begin his dream of starting his own company, and within a couple of months, things were busy for Paint The Towne.

With her accounting experience, Stella pitched in and was able to help Jim. However, the busier he became, the more work she did at night after working eight hours on her own job. After several months of working until midnight, she and Jim reviewed their finances and decided it would be beneficial if she quit her job and help with their business full time. She never particularly liked her job, and there was no room for advancement anyway. Plus, she was hearing rumors of impending layoffs, so she resigned and became a full-time employee of Paint The Towne.

Still not her "dream job," Stella did like her job with their own company. She had a wide variety of duties and brought some much-needed organization, order, stability, and marketing efforts to the business. Helping Jim grow their business challenged her, and the greatest benefit is that she got to work from home. She also had the opportunity to volunteer some of her time at the local library, and she loved being home to take care of their three children.

Then the dream shattered. The call came from the hospital shortly after lunch. It was the emergency room, and the nurse told her that Jim had been admitted with severe injuries. Stella dropped the phone, grabbed her purse and keys, and fled out the door. After arriving at the hospital, she learned that Jim had started work that morning on a commercial job for a restaurant. The scaffolding collapsed, and he was unable to brace himself for the fall. A restaurant employee witnessed the collapse and called 9-1-1.

The doctor explained Jim's injuries from the forceful impact of the accident. After x-rays and scans, they found he had spinal damage, a couple of broken bones, serious internal bruising, and a concussion. Of chief concern was that the spinal injury would require surgery. Long-term effects such as pain and diminished mobility would require lengthy treatment, possible future surgeries, and physical therapy. Thankfully, Jim's injuries were not causing paralysis, but she knew his road to recovery would be long and tedious.

Jim had several consecutive surgeries on his spine and eventually went home. His broken bones healed well, and he began physical therapy to regain movement and help with mobility. Stella would sit at her desk at night after Jim fell asleep and open the stack of mail.

The medical bills were piling up, and the income they enjoyed from their company had come to a screeching halt. She spent day after day talking to the insurance company and working with their mortgage lender. Their savings were eroded, and Stella found that the economy had taken a sharp downturn, and it was a tough time for her to re-enter the workforce. Besides, she needed to help Jim with everyday activities like getting dressed and going to the bathroom.

She also had to drive him to his daily physical therapy appointments, make his meals, and ensure he took his medication and rested. She also needed to be there for her children since Jim was limited in his movements.

Finally, after selling everything she could like Jim's painting equipment and work van, and her car, they only had Jim's SUV left. Even after selling some of their household goods, her grandmother's china, and some of her jewelry, they could no longer make the house payment. Within 180 days, their lovely home entered foreclosure, and Stella sat at the desk and cried.

Stella asked the neighbors if they could spare some moving boxes, and she began to pack their belongings. Many of her neighbors offered to buy some of their things, and she knew they were trying to be helpful as she gratefully took their money for their items. She cried as she packed and had no idea what they would do when a neighbor offered her a brochure for Colorado Homeless Families. She made the call, went to the interview, and was put on the waitlist and told there was a delay in a new construction project, but CHF was planning on availability before the end of the year. She crossed her fingers as they had to be out of their home by Christmas.

Colorado Homeless Families helped her and Jim with the necessities of moving into a new place exactly one week before Christmas. They were the first family to move into the new townhomes built as the "Farm House Extension Project," the nearly one-million-dollar project to create seven new townhomes.

Stella moved most of their remaining things with Jim's SUV but had to shop the CHF furniture bank for items they had to leave behind or had sold. Through counseling and help from their case manager, she obtained her job with the hospice center. She volunteered her hours at CHF, helping with the reading programs and support groups, while Jim prepared for one final surgery on his back. He was working several hours each week, and after physical therapy, he was able to obtain a maintenance job with a university where he and Stella could enroll in classes at no charge.

Stella thought of Colorado Homeless families as a true gift, a miracle really, that was there to help her and Jim get back on the road to being financially stable. Soon she was scheduled to begin classes towards a degree in counseling. She was looking forward to moving up from her job as a hospice aide to becoming a counselor to provide spiritual and emotional support to patients and bereavement support to family members.

As Stella reflected on the honor of knowing Mr. Bridges through her job at the hospice center, she realized that through these circumstances, she did find her "dream job" after all. And it was not what she expected.

Karen Lucero made sure to leave her Certified Public Accountant (CPA) office in downtown Denver in plenty of time to make the 45-minute drive to Denver International Airport. She parked her new SUV in short-term parking and dashed to the nearest flight information display to check on the arrival time. It showed the flight had landed and listed the carousel where the bags would appear.

It had been three long years since she had seen him in person, and she was so nervous that she had butterflies in her stomach.

Although they communicated, sometimes it was difficult to speak between technology challenges and the time difference, with Kuwait being nine hours ahead of Denver. The 7,000-mile difference felt like he could have been on Mars. Karen settled into a seat near baggage claim carousel 12 and waited for her son Trey.

They had had their challenges, but she couldn't be prouder of Trey. The drug problems, legal bills, and ultimate divorce from Trey's dad had taken its toll on both of them years ago. Left with nothing but a stack of bills, a dead-end, minimum wage job, and a barely working car, Karen didn't know how she and Trey were going to survive. She had only been able to attend two years of college classes intermittently because Trey's father kept taking the money she was saving for school and spending it on drugs. When he was arrested, what little money they had left was cleaned out for attorney fees. He was sentenced to prison anyway, and he was still sitting there as far as she knew.

She had been working at a fast-food place during the day and took on a part-time job in which she cleaned office buildings at night just to make rent and get enough money to file for a low-cost divorce. Her husband had ruined her finances, reputation, credit, and her and Trey's lives. Desperate, Karen added a third job as a weekend telemarketer—the worst job she ever had. She would rather clean the fat vats for cooking French fries than to continually face rejection from irate, faceless strangers. Having faced enough rejection in her life, the telemarketing job got her yelled at, cursed at, and called names. It was more than she could manage, and she quit after six months.

Through all of this, Trey was a trooper. He was always a terrific kid with a very easy-going personality. He was quiet and loved to study, making him good in school. He was friendly, honest, dependable, thoughtful, and everyone who met him always said he was mature for his age. When Karen could not pay rent, Trey offered to help the landlord or the maintenance man by doing chores for them. One day, she looked out the window and saw him helping the landlord paint a railing. "He shouldn't have to be doing this," she cried to herself. Shortly thereafter, no amount of extra work that Trey did could pay for their rent, and they would need to move.

She laid bare her heart one night to a custodial co-worker while on their dinner break and told her they would be homeless the next month. She asked the woman if she knew of a safe, warm place where she could take Trey and stay. The woman made a couple of suggestions but told Karen to let her make a few calls first.

Later that week, her co-worker handed her a list of five places with phone numbers. Karen scanned the paper and saw several she had heard of and one she had not: Colorado Homeless Families. Karen began to call them on her breaks the following day, going down the list one by one. She was able to request applications and would hide in an empty office at night to complete them. She would always return them with a prayer for help.

After a week, she received a phone call from Colorado Homeless Families. They wanted to set up a screening interview. Trying to make an appointment to meet the case manager at an offsite location was difficult because of working two jobs. He offered to meet her at her fast-food restaurant during her dinner break. She was nervous and wanted to make a good impression and say all the right things. The morning of the interview, she began to feel uncomfortable with wanting to make a good impression. What she felt as though God was placing on her heart was Ephesians 4:25, *"Therefore, having put away falsehood, let each one of you speak the truth with his neighbor, for we are members one of another."* She knew that God was telling her to just simply tell your story and tell the truth.

Karen and Trey were moving into a townhome in the Colorado Homeless Families within two weeks. Trey liked his new school and was making friends in the CHF complex. He especially took an interest in helping some of the smaller children with whatever challenges they were having. He always pitched in to volunteer in the CHF complex even though minors were not required to do so. Karen and Trey found a local church, and Trey became active in his youth group. Karen attended all the educational seminars and worked with her case manager to set goals. Not knowing what area to further her education, her case manager suggested she make an appointment at the local college for career assessment testing.

Karen found these tests to be helpful as she deeply desired a career compatible with her personality. Her scores showed her as a "conventional" work personality that would excel in a career focusing on organization, numbers, records, orderly, attention to detail, and following a set plan. The career counselor recommended an educational path in accounting, finance, or mathematics. As Karen reflected, she was always good with numbers, and balancing the checkbook was a breeze for her—when they had money.

As the new semester at college began, Karen quit the nighttime custodial job to focus on night classes. She was able to transfer most of her credits from her earlier courses, and decided she wanted to become a Certified Public Accountant and someday own her own company. Partway through her first semester, she found a better-paying job; even though it was an entry-level accounting position, she liked that it was closer to CHF. Happy about the new job, she discovered the downside was that she never had to have an "office wardrobe" before.

Executive Director Connie Zimmerman encouraged Karen to use the CHF clothing bank to shop for a wardrobe more suitable for her new job. Karen learned to also shop thrift stores, resale boutiques, and consignment stores for affordable office attire and eventually created a beautiful and professional wardrobe.

After two years in the CHF program, Karen was nearing the completion of her education and planning to move towards accumulating the additional graduate credits to qualify her to take the Uniform CPA Examination. She had also moved up in her company and was a supervisor in the accounting department. She enjoyed school very much, and she and Trey would sit at the kitchen table and do their homework together, excelling in her classes and Trey excelling in his. As she put away his laundry one day, she saw the college applications in his bedroom, and she swelled with pride. She hoped he picked somewhere close and was confident he would get a scholarship with his good grades.

Arriving home one evening after class, Trey was sitting on the sofa. There was only a couple of weeks to go until his high school graduation, and he was beaming as he held a letter and a book in his hand. "Mom, I signed up for the Army today," he said as he handed her the enlistment papers. Needing to sit down, he explained to Karen that nothing was official until after the physical and the Armed Services Vocational Aptitude Battery (ASVAB), and then he would take the oath and sign the contract at Military Entrance Processing Stations (MEPS). He would then report to Basic Training shortly after that, then Advanced Individual Training (AIT) before even reporting to his first Active Duty Station.

Karen was astonished...and speechless. She did not expect this, but she also knew that his personality, sense of responsibility, and duty were a perfect fit for the military. Trey had turned 18 years old a couple of months before, and she knew that from a young age, he never made decisions lightly. She also knew one of his favorite verses was Psalm 82:3, *"Defend the weak and the fatherless; uphold the cause of the poor and oppressed."* Crying, she hugged him and told him how proud she was of him. Inside, however, Karen wanted to crumble, and she wanted to beg him not to go. Ever the thoughtful son, Trey handed her a booklet for the local chapter of Blue Star Mothers of America, Inc. Karen laughed, and they decided to go out for a celebratory dinner where she would make him answer all her 1,000 questions.

After Trey left for the Army, Karen began to pray Psalm 91, commonly called the Soldier's Psalm or Soldier's Prayer. She prayed this over him and his squad, and Trey would pray the same prayer of protection; she knew it had kept him and all his brothers-in-arms safe through all their missions in the Middle East.

The speaker sounded at Denver International Airport, announcing that bags on carousel 12 were arriving. She stood up and bent over to smooth out her work suit and looked up into the beaming face of her son, standing there in his Army fatigues. "Hi Mom," he said as he hugged her and picked her up to spin her around.

Karen knew that after settling him in at her house, she would treat him to his favorite restaurant. In the following days, Trey would want to stop by Colorado Homeless Families, as he did every time he came home. Wearing his "This We'll Defend" t-shirt, Trey loved to visit with the CHF staff and especially catch up with their former case manager, who helped them discover their road to overcoming.

"MASS LAYOFF" SET AT LUTHERAN MEDICAL CENTER IN COLORADO
BY THE DENVER POST
JULY 28, 2011

Exempla Lutheran Medical Center in Wheat Ridge is terminating 160 positions—6.5% of its workforce—citing economic weakness and the impact of healthcare reform. Management and nonclinical positions make up at least one-third of the reductions, but hospital spokeswoman Mo Sheahan said she couldn't provide specifics on the positions being eliminated. Lutheran President & CEO Grant Wicklund said the hospital is dealing with a number of challenges. "We are experiencing fewer patient admissions, increases in the number of uninsured and underinsured patients, and rising costs," Wicklund said. "To respond to these challenges and to support Lutheran's strategic direction to provide excellent quality care for our patients and community, we have identified areas where we can reduce expenses and realign staffing." Sheahan said Lutheran has 2,500 employees and just over 500 beds. She wasn't sure whether the number of beds would be affected.[76]

Jana Banks read the Denver Post article again and felt her face flush. She was one of the 160 positions, and doing the math, she was only .0406% of the workforce. The math made her feel even more depressed because it seemed that she was even less than one. The thing about layoffs, she thought, is that they provide you with the number of positions eliminated. They certainly do not provide the number of people affected—in her case; it was three. She and her two children, Holly, 14, and Jarrod, 10. What was sad was that her income, not even close to being considerable, was the only income they had, and it was going to zero.

She received her letter last week:

Dear Employee:
It is with regret that I inform you that you are being
laid off from your position...

She knew the rest. Human Resources had met with everyone affected and explained everything. She had worked in the hospital pharmacy for seven years and even had some seniority. In the end, that didn't matter.

The Denver Business Journal had published an article two years prior about the economic downturn. Health care in Colorado wasn't experiencing the downturn as much as other sectors of the economy were experiencing.[77] Things continued to take a downturn in all the areas, including health care. When she read that article two years ago, Jana remembered thinking that she was glad she was in health care, a seemingly stable field. She worked to fulfill her prerequisite courses at the local community college to prepare for continuing in the nursing program. When her layoff letter came, she finished her last prerequisite course and already had her schedule outlined to begin nursing school the following semester.

The one-two punch happened within three months of each other. The second punch came when she could not find a new job right away, thus unable to pay the rent on the townhome she lived in. She had no idea what to do, where to go, or to whom to talk. Five years ago, she had found this lovely townhome that she could afford on her salary and with the added benefit of being halfway between work and school where she had signed up to attend night classes. Within a few months of moving in, her kids liked the neighborhood. Her neighbors were friendly, everyone was helpful if needed, and they seemed exceptionally supportive of her and her family.

"Now what?" she sobbed to herself in the mirror. Jana cried tears of frustration each night, alone in her bedroom. She would bury her face in a towel or a pillow and cry so her children wouldn't hear her. Jana had worked so hard to stay on track with her goals, and now the dark clouds of devastation set in. She faced each morning with bleary, blood-shot eyes, still not knowing where to turn.

A friend invited her to lunch and suggested Jana apply for the Colorado Homeless Families transitional housing program. Jana had never heard of this organization, and even as her friend explained what little she knew of the program, Jana was skeptical. As her friend talked, Jana began to imagine they would need to share a home with other families or live in a motel-type location in a low-income or downtrodden part of the city.

Not knowing what to expect and utterly out of options, Jana looked up the phone number and called them anyway.

She completed the application and required paperwork and was approved after her screening interview and background checks. Within two months, she and her kids were moving into one of the brand-new townhome units that had just been completed the prior year. When Connie Zimmerman, Executive Director, showed Jana her new home, Jana was overwhelmed at how nice it was. She was also impressed at the well-maintained residences and buildings, and she found the grounds and surrounding areas were landscaped and wonderful.

When Jana settled her children into their living arrangement, new school, and the change in routines, she was quick to settle in herself. Assigned a case manager, Jana visited with the counselor and attended the required educational classes at CHF.

She found herself appreciating her new surroundings and was eager to begin looking for work; she had also been able to purchase her books to continue her coursework at the college to get her nursing degree.

With all the support and encouragement Jana received at CHF from both the staff and new neighbors who could relate to her difficulties, she found herself eager to support many on-site volunteer projects and openly welcome new residents. She even found herself attending a local church that she and her children enjoyed, where they made friends, and joined in numerous activities.

As they left the church that Sunday, she smiled walking to her car.

The message they heard on this day was from Psalm 30, "Weeping may linger for the night, but joy comes with the morning." There was no more crying into a towel late into the night.

After putting their 18-month-old daughter down for a nap, Joey Goodman sat down on the floor to play with her and Travis' 3-year-old son. She suddenly felt intense cramping and discerned immediately she was bleeding.

Not to alarm her son, she handed him the building block and told him she would be right back. In the bathroom, Joey *knew*, and began to shake uncontrollably. Twenty weeks along. Only 1% of miscarriages occur after 20 weeks. "Oh, Lord, no!" she cried and reached for the phone to call Travis.

Travis felt his cell phone vibrate in his pocket. He tried to check in with Joey every break he took, but he didn't always get a break since the used car company he worked for was understaffed.

He would sometimes go outside and pace the car lot to call her while he was out. His wage was only a little over $10 an hour. He made 25% of the dealership's gross profit on every car he sold, which would be about 300 dollars for him. The downturn in the economy in 2008 made for a slow upturn in car sales over the last three years. And he just did not have the "bulldog" in him required to be a good car salesperson. It was the only job he could get at the time when he so desperately needed a job.

He took Joey's phone call anyway and hearing her voice had him running for the car. He told his boss on the way out the door he had a medical emergency and would call later. Travis didn't even wait for an answer; he just jumped in the car and headed home, or rather, to his cousin's home.

Travis was in college when he met Joey. She was living with four roommates, working as a full-time waitress, attending classes as her money allowed, and trying to get into the engineering program at the university. It was a lot to handle, but the thing he fell in love with was her passion for making her dreams come true – even if she could only take one class per semester. Travis had put off college for several years, so he was older than most students. He graduated the year after he met Joey and asked her to get married.

They both wanted her to finish college because it had already taken her several years to get her general education credits behind her. Yet, Joey wound up pregnant after their first year of marriage, and she no longer wanted to pursue her college education. Travis was having difficulty finding a job, as he would start at a company only to experience mass layoffs.

This happened three times in three years. Then Joey found out she was pregnant again with their daughter.

Rising costs of rent in the Denver Metro area were outpacing the pay scales, and soon they could no longer afford an apartment of their own. Travis' cousin, Aiden, and his family offered their basement. Travis and Aiden worked nights and weekends to make the basement livable and even installed a bathroom. Travis and Joey were grateful for the roof over their head. Travis knew it was only a short-term solution, but with trying to find a good job and raising two small children, he and Joey didn't even have time for a conversation, let alone develop a plan.

After three months in Aiden's basement, Joey found out she was pregnant again. He also knew that they would soon need to leave Aiden's basement. Thankful for the space, it was not a place to raise two—soon to be three—small children. He just did not know what else to do. He found himself lying in bed sometimes, staring at the pipes in the ceiling, wishing time to stop. Or slow down so he could catch his breath and, hopefully, catch a break.

Taking only 10 minutes rather than the usual 20 minutes to get home, he found his daughter napping, his son quietly playing with his blocks, and Joey in the bathroom crying. "We need to get to the hospital now," she cried. Travis ran to the neighbor's house and asked Mrs. McKinney to watch his two children. She grabbed her jacket and ran with him to the house.

Travis and Joey raced to the hospital to be met with grim news. *Miscarriage.* The traumatic part was yet to hit them. Joey still had to give birth to the baby and would need to go through the labor process. Distressed and in shock, the staff explained the options as they tried to make appropriate decisions through a fog of grief. Joey was kept overnight for observation, and Travis brought her home the following day.

Tears of grief filled Joey's days, and Travis called in sick to stay home and take care of their children. He would bring Joey breakfast, lunch, and dinner in bed, but she wouldn't eat.

One afternoon after the children and Joey were napping, he found a local newspaper. There happened to be an article about Denver's Road Home (DRH), an umbrella organization formed back in 2005 to coordinate the community's goodwill efforts—soup kitchens, food pantries, and donated clothing. DRH was not providing the services; it was helping those who did by helping fund the hiring of outreach workers, opening shelters, and expanding programs.

At the end of the article was also a list of places that helped homeless families with transitional programs. He didn't consider themselves homeless, but he knew they needed to transition from where they were to something—better. Among others in that list was a place called Colorado Homeless Families, and "family" is what struck him. His entire family needed help. Travis called them.

Within a month, Travis and Joey were placed at the Colorado Homeless Families complex. They met with their case manager and attended the first several seminars. Joey was immersed in grief, always with a far-off, glazed look in her eyes, and Travis was trying to do everything else by himself to keep their family afloat. Finally, their case manager suggested meeting with one of the counselors that Colorado Homeless Families contracted with. The case manager felt that they needed a professional counselor to help with their grief before moving forward.

As they went into intensive grief counseling, they discovered that Joey felt guilty. May she had done something wrong, or God was punishing her, but she didn't know why. They both got to express that the word "miscarriage" did not properly convey the impact of their loss. It was a traumatic experience, as they reflected on the pain of labor and giving birth to an already formed, tiny, perfect baby. That experience just seemed more than a miscarriage, as they got to hold the baby in their arms.

Travis expressed that the process of giving birth to a baby they held in their arms seemed minimized by the word "miscarriage," and that the baby was too young to be provided a birth or death certificate seemed wrong. Several months of counseling and expressing their emotions helped them begin to heal the fractures they didn't even know existed.

Travis came to terms with the fact that he would never make it as a used car salesperson and began looking for a different job. He took a position at a local bank that was better suited to his personality, and he also picked up his long-lost passion for photography and began working part-time as a photographer.

As Joey emerged from her grief and met with the CHF case manager, she began to find that she wanted to pick up her education and continue forward. She found a part-time job that she enjoyed and still allowed her time to play with her growing children. She also helped other CHF mothers with daycare responsibilities.

They were able to graduate from the CHF program after two years, and Joey earned a scholarship to study engineering—in Amsterdam. Travis was also looking forward to continuing with his banking career and gaining experience in the international finance field. They also found that they were looking forward to expanding their family.

Melanie Hanson breathed a massive sigh of relief. She and her two teenage sons, Jordon and Sheldon, had just finished moving into their new townhome at Colorado Homeless Families. It was one week before Christmas, and she was thrilled there was an opening.

The last few years had been hell on their family. Their oldest son, Brandon, had graduated from college and was in the military stationed overseas. They didn't get to see him often enough, but it helped Melanie know he was doing well and liked his job.

Jordon was in his first year of college, getting excellent grades, enjoying his sports scholarship, and making new friends. He still lived at home, as he wanted to help reduce college expenses.

Sheldon was in high school and was busy with his studies, sports, and had just joined a band. They practiced every chance they could find and were getting very good.

She had quit her full-time job when the boys were in middle school because they were all so active in sports and school activities. Melanie had volunteered at their school and was an active parent class assistant. She wanted to raise smart, confident, respectful young men and give them the absolute best start to life she could.

The recent loss of her ex-husband's job brought angst and anger to their home, and Reed had taken in out on her. As bills slowly stacked up and Reed couldn't find another good-paying job, he got angrier and more abusive, and the violence escalated— always behind the closed bedroom door and always when their sons were not home. When his unemployment benefits ran out, and the bank notified them of foreclosure measures, Reed imploded on himself—and exploded on Melanie. If it were not for Jordon and Sheldon arriving home unexpectedly one evening, she was sure Reed would have killed her. They muscled their father away from her, shoved him out the door, and Jordon called the police. While Melanie was tended to by the medics, Jordon and Sheldon packed their father's things in boxes and threw them in the driveway. Within a couple of days, a restraining order was issued against their father, and he could not come near any of his family members, the house, or Sheldon's school.

Picking up the pieces of her life, Melanie began looking for a job. All she could find was a part-time cashier job at a local card and gift shop. She began to ask several acquaintances for advice or assistance. A volunteer friend told Melanie about Colorado Homeless Families. She called and started the application and interview process. It was a snowy day in December when she got a call that a townhome was opening up and her family had been approved to move in. She and the boys packed as many of their things as they could fit in two cars and a small moving van and headed towards the Colorado Homeless Families complex.

They entered counseling for the trauma they had endured. They also received counseling, both as a group and individually, to help them deal with the break-up of their family. Melanie filed for divorce with the restraining order still in effect, but she lived in fear that her husband would still find them.

Christmas was enjoyable, even under the dark cloud of recent events. Brandon came home briefly but had to leave after several days to return to his post. During the Christmas break, Jordon and Sheldon threw themselves into helping with the Colorado Homeless Families Christmas events and helping their mother cook Christmas dinner. Her amazing and intelligent young men understood the financial challenges and the impossibility of exchanging gifts. They all said they were appreciative to be together, enjoyed caroling, watching football, and laughing and teasing one another. As they cheered on their favorite football teams, Melanie looked on and smiled with pride in her heart, and she felt the dark cloud getting a little lighter.

The phone rang at dinner time on New Year's Eve. She and Sheldon had decided to stay at home and watch movies, while

Jordon had left for a ski trip with some friends from college. Melanie answered the phone, knowing it was probably for her son. "Mrs. Hanson, this is the Summit County Coroner. We regret to inform you that your son, Jordon, collided with a tree while skiing with friends. He was rushed to the local hospital where he was found to be unresponsive." Melanie dropped the telephone as she collapsed on the floor. Sheldon rushed to pick her up and grabbed the phone. The doctor told him that Jordon had crashed into a tree, and by the time he reached the hospital, there was nothing they could do, and he was pronounced dead at 5:00 pm. The coroner provided Sheldon with the additional details and the telephone numbers of who to contact.

Jordon's funeral was a week later, and all his high school and college friends attended and offered their heartfelt sympathies and support. Melanie didn't remember any of that day, or the week before, or the week after. She could hear Sheldon crying at night, and she would try to get out of bed to go comfort him, but her legs wouldn't move. Brandon was given military emergency leave to come home and make the funeral arrangements. She vaguely remembered a court officer asking for permission for Reed to be able to attend the funeral since the restraining order was still in effect. They did not speak at the funeral and the boys avoided him. He was obviously intoxicated.

Sheldon returned to school shortly after Jordon's funeral, but Melanie felt paralyzed with grief. Eventually, the CHF counselors reached out to her for grief counseling. She went every day to the counseling center, and by February, was able to resume the additional counseling needed to help her through both the family's old and new traumas. The Colorado Homeless Families' counselors continued to offer daily support and encouragement at each step and offered intensive counseling for Sheldon as well.

As Melanie began to understand that CHF was providing her a safety net, she began to resolve the emotional issues of her marriage and began the deep grieving process of her son. By late spring, the CHF case manager began to work with her to help her identify her strengths and move her towards full-time employment that was better suited to those strengths. Melanie was a little hesitant to begin full-time work so soon after Jordon's death but was thankful when she found that the job offered her support, good pay and helped surround her with a group of peers that ultimately helped her self-esteem issues.

Sheldon was able to lean on his friends for support and, through CHF intensive counseling, was able to begin to deal with his grief. The counselors also gave him support and some coping tools that helped him better focus on his schoolwork and return to the after-school activities and music that he loved. By the summer, Sheldon decided to get a part-time job to help Melanie with the living expenses. Connie Zimmerman, CHF Executive Director, was always quick to offer positive comments to Melanie on the hard work and determined focus of this family that had experienced such profound tragedies.

Sheldon graduated from high school with honors and began attending the University of Denver. His studies and schedule allowed him to continue to live with Melanie and provide her support and assistance.

After two years, Melanie was thankful to graduate from the CHF program, becoming entirely self-sufficient. She and Sheldon found a lovely rental house, and she found herself giving thanks that she could support herself and her son. As Melanie looked at her Christmas tree and the ornaments of her "three wise men," Brandon, Jordon, and Sheldon, she knew that Colorado Homeless Families was more than just a safety net at a time when she needed it. They helped shape the person she had become, helped make her stronger, and lifted her at the worst time in her life. Their guidance, help, and support would live in her heart forever, she realized, as she placed the stamp on the Christmas card.

Photo: 2013 CHF BOARD OF DIRECTORS
L. to R. Tom Faulkner, Treasurer, Tammy Prichard, Jan Wiens, Secretary, Gaye Andersen, Larry Zimmerman, Connie Zimmerman, CEO, Eileen Schneider, Aruna Kumar, Margaret Carpenter, Eric Kumar (Absent: Terri Taylor, President, attending a funeral)

Photo: Award winning Farmhouse Extension Project.

2016

FINISHING THE RACE

<u>Retirement</u>

"For she's a jolly good fellow, for she's a jolly good fellow
For she's a jolly good fellow, which nobody can deny
Which nobody can deny, which nobody can deny
For she's a jolly good fellow, for she's a jolly good fellow
For she's a jolly good fellow, which nobody can deny!"

Connie Zimmerman stepped up to the podium when the singing and applause stopped. She looked out across the hundreds of white chairs filled with attendees under the enormous white tent and saw all the white balloons. Knowing that the balloons represented goals, aspirations, and dreams in life, many faces that smiled back at her had fulfilled those dreams with the help of Colorado Homeless Families that began in 1987.

Hundreds of people who attended this party were homeless when she first met them, and many had shown up today to speak of how Colorado Homeless Families had changed their life.

Connie adjusted the microphone and cleared her throat of the tears that threatened to fall. "First of all," she began, "I want to thank Jesus Christ, my Lord and Savior, for giving me the burden of spirit for the homeless and the opportunity to answer the call....

"I am grateful for the CHF Board of Directors, the staff, donors, grantors, foundations, organizations, the volunteers, my family and friends for their support, encouragement, and many prayers in their part to help the CHF families obtain their goals and dreams. Putting feet to this one vision has elevated so many to a higher level of life.

"I am grateful for the opportunity to work alongside the Lord Jesus Christ, to feel His long suffering, compassion and love for homeless families and individuals and to see how He can miraculously provide for their needs."

Connie was now facing a new calling: retirement. Not retirement from helping others, but retirement from Colorado Homeless Families.

At Connie Zimmerman's open air retirement party from 29 years of work at the helm of Colorado Homeless Families, she handed the reigns to another director. Karen Allen became the Executive Director of Colorado Homeless Families.

Besides the many former CHF families who spoke, there were also past and present CHF Board Members, numerous staff and volunteers, city council members, foundation dignitaries who Connie had worked with for years, and friends and family who walked beside her.

Photo: *Larry and Connie Zimmerman at Connie's 2016 retirement festivities.*

<u>Awards</u>

Awards given to Executive Director Connie Zimmerman are numerous and were well earned as the founder of Colorado Homeless Families:

- 1993 HUD Award for Exemplary Progress in Program Improvement, Advancement, and Expansion
- 2001 Denver Post Season to Share Grant Award
- 2002 Jefferson County Nonprofit Recognition Award
- 2009 Jefferson County Commitment to Excellence Award
- CoNAHRD Affordable Housing Project Award
- 2012 Arvada Chamber of Commerce Woman of the Year
- 2013 Arvada's Woman of the Year in 2013
- Several special recognitions from the City of Arvada
- Special recognition, Colorado State Senator, Evie Hudak
- Several special recognitions from HUD
- Congolese Communities of Colorado Humanitarian Award

Presentation: Terri Taylor | President of CHF | Connie's 2016 Retirement

Reflections

Providing homes and support for the homeless, Colorado Homeless Families started with humble beginnings and grew into the successful and effective nonprofit that it is today:

- In 1989, began with six properties rented from HUD
- In 1992, purchased ten foreclosed properties
- In 1996, built 12 townhomes
- In 1997, built the Family Education and Resource Center, which houses the CHF offices, educational seminars, food bank, and community meeting space
- In 2003, built three duplexes
- In 2005, the farmhouse extension adjacent to CHF was purchased, and seven townhomes were built

HUD properties were the beginning foundation of Colorado Homeless Families, and many families were happy to have purchased them after graduating from the program:

- Colorado Homeless Families purchased a total of 75 HUD properties
- 31 HUD properties were sold at cost to homeless families graduating from CHF
- 39 HUD properties were released as CHF housing

By 2016, Colorado Homeless Families owned 40 transitional housing units with no mortgages. Under Connie's leadership, CHF accomplished the following:

- 503 families housed
- 420 families successfully became self-sufficient
- 161 families purchased their own homes
- 109 individuals graduated from Tech Schools, Colleges, and Universities

Photo: Connie Zimmerman, CHF newly-retired Executive Director and Karen Allen, Colorado Homeless Families new Executive Director

New beginnings

In 2016, Karen Allen became the Executive Director of Colorado Homeless Families and expanded the services to focus on a holistic approach to self-sufficiency.

In 2020, Colorado Homeless Families was rebranded to BeyondHome to reflect better the commitment to forward progress and possibilities that come with housing while being a place for safe, expectant transformation and growth with holistic supportive services.

BeyondHome offers a comprehensive approach for families to become self-sufficient for life, and families work hard to achieve personalized goals for their education, housing, finances, and family. https://www.beyondhomeonline.org/

EPILOGUE

Nehemiah was tasked with rebuilding the broken-down walls of Jerusalem, and Connie Zimmerman was tasked with rebuilding the broken walls of the homeless. There are important principles to be learned in rebuilding anything, whether it is BC 444, AD 1986, or AD 2022. Both Nehemiah and Connie Zimmerman experienced those principles:

Cause. Rebuilding needs a cause. Nehemiah was burdened that his fellow Jews in Jerusalem were living in deep distress and constant fear because their city wall had been broken down (Nehemiah 1:30). Connie Zimmerman was burdened that her fellow man was living on the streets with their children, and no one seemed to be helping them.

Cry and Confess. Nehemiah wept, mourned, fasted, prayed, and waited on the Lord (Nehemiah 1:4-11). Connie Zimmerman also mourned, prayed, and waited on the Lord, knowing that this cause needed to be embraced as she wanted deeply for someone to help the homeless.

Courage and Consent. God gave Nehemiah, a humble refugee, the courage to make his request to King Artaxerxes, the most powerful man in the world (Nehemiah 2:1-11). Connie Zimmerman, a retirement home employee, made her request to the Lord Himself, as well as to the many city, county, state, and federal institutions to partner in the rebuilding of broken lives.

Capacitate and Cheer. At Jerusalem, Nehemiah developed a team from scratch–encouraging, empowering, and working alongside them (Nehemiah 3). For Connie Zimmerman, the Lord equipped her to rebuild, but not on her own. Gathering and encouraging others to help while seeking guidance from professionals during the process to build Colorado Homeless Families.

Commit and Charge. Nehemiah's team worked with all their heart, laboring from dawn to dusk, facing ridicule, taunts, false rumors, and even physical attacks (Nehemiah 4 & 5). Connie Zimmerman and Colorado Homeless Families worked hard to rebuild lives, but not without constant testing and trials from both internal and external sources. God is the provider of strength at such testing times.

Covenant. After witnessing the mighty hand of God enabling Nehemiah's team to fortify Jerusalem in just 52 days, the people took an oath that they would walk according to God's law (Nehemiah 9:38, 10:29). Connie Zimmerman knew that once the task of starting the nonprofit that God sent her to build was complete, she and all who benefited walked with thankful hearts and would continue to tell the story of God's goodness and how He can re-build lives. In 2018, God prompted Connie to "tell the story."

Photo: 2012 Arvada Woman of the Year winner Connie Zimmerman shown with the selection committee. The committee includes past winners who were celebrated for having made extraordinary contributions to the City of Arvada.

Family Members at Connie's Retirement Party June 25, 2016
L. to R.: son Jason, granddaughter Caitlyn, daughter Jennifer, mother Betty, Connie,
sister Lorelie, granddaughter Yulia, husband Larry, and brother John.
Back row L. to R.: Virginia, niece Nicky, and great niece Ivory.

To Larry Zimmerman, my husband, and partner going on 51 years. Larry encouraged, supported, and volunteered his time on boards and meetings with me for 29 years to accommodate and assist in the enormous undertaking of housing and equipping homeless families with emergency needs. After he retired from Adams County, Larry also volunteered his time alongside me presenting educational seminars, support group meetings, and life skill classes to our families.

To my two children, Jennifer Graham and Dr. Jason Zimmerman, who volunteered their time during Christmas vacations to help deliver gifts and food to homeless families living in our community. Their friendships and acceptance of the families coming from various nations, cultures, and communities were an invaluable asset to making them feel part of the family community. I appreciated the time and effort Jason spent on cleaning up the community grounds in the summer and improving the landscaping. A special thanks to Jennifer for always being available to work alongside me for whatever job position was needed to be filled during her high school and college years.

To my mother and father, Betty and Emil Armstrong, who were the team leaders of our family of seven children. They orchestrated great examples of sharing, caring, supporting, encouraging, and reaching out to help others. My parents, who had 6 children which included myself and my 5 siblings, also adopted a young, orphaned boy from Cambodia. My siblings were an inspiration as well. My older brother, Ken, founded an orphanage in Cambodia, and he and his wife Pat adopted a Vietnamese orphan and raised six other children from Vietnam. Two of my sisters, Debra and Lorelie, adopted children as well.

To my grandchildren, Yulia, Caitlyn, and Caleb Graham, while volunteering their time during the spring breaks and summer months at [CHF], Colorado Homeless Families, I want to remind them of the picture of this legacy of homeless families which they had witnessed, living happily and peacefully in a transitional housing community and that they will have a desire and an opportunity to pass this legacy on to others.

The individual families in this CHF Community were diversified; there was respect, concern, and love for each of the individual families. The families came from different communities, cities, and nations, and different languages were spoken. The CHF diversified community had common goals that solidified and brought peace and safety to the community. All the individuals in the community were valued and had visions, goals, and dreams and were attending a college, university, or a trade school, as well as the adults were reaching out to serve others in the community.

The love, concern, and burden to help homeless families can only come from the Lord. I, by myself, would not be concerned for others. The Lord looks for people he can use to reach out to the needs of others, God is Love. These are the people God chose to use for CHF.

I am very grateful for the support and encouragement of Pastor Roland Taylor of Crossroads Baptist Church of Northglenn, Colorado, and his wife Gayle Taylor, who was board President of CHF for 2 years.

I'm so grateful for Pastor Kim Skattum and his wife Sheryl Skattum of Crossroads Baptist Church of Northglenn, Colorado. Crossroads Baptist Church in Northglenn has stood with CHF and supported our organization with food baskets for all our families for Thanksgiving and Christmas for 25 years. They allowed us to use the church building for special events and spaghetti suppers to raise monies for CHF. The church sponsored our homeless families and paid their rent deposits. They helped adopt our families for Christmas. They provided our children with school supplies. They have given CHF monies to help with the emergency needs of our families, to use for car repairs, pay electric bills, gas, etc. We are grateful for the continual support from this wonderful, caring church with compassionate pastors and staff.

We are grateful for the following individuals and agencies:

- Mr. Eric Kumar, President of CHF Board for 20 + years, and his wife, Aruna Kumar, CHF Board member for 20+ years.
- Mrs. Gaye Andersen served 20 + years on the CHF Board of Directors,
- Mrs. Terri Taylor served 15 + years on the CHF Board of Directors as Secretary and later as President.

- Mrs. Eileen Schneider served approximately 15 years on the CHF Board of Directors.
- Mr. Tom Faulkner served on the CHF Board of Directors for 10 + years as Treasurer.
- Mrs. Jan Wiens served on the Board of Directors approximately 10+ years as a board member and as Secretary.
- Mrs. Margaret Carpenter served approximately 6 years as a CHF Board Member and as Vice President.
- Mrs. Vicky Reier served on the Board of Directors for approximately 2 years and is currently President.
- Mr. Don Mathieson served on the CHF Board as a member of the Board and as an advisory member for approximately 3 years and volunteered his time as a realtor.
- Mrs. Tammy Prichard served on the CHF Board of Directors for approximately 6 years.
- Mr. Brad Hill, Real Estate Attorney, advisory board.
- Mrs. Brigit Davis, retired VP from Arthur H. And Helen K. Johnson Foundation, advisory
- Mrs. Kathy Larkins, Board member, 3 years
- Mr. Greg Garnett, CHF Board Treasurer, 3 years.
- Mrs. Lynn Campbell, Treasurer of Board, 3 years.
- Mr. Kent Sperry, Treasurer of the CHF Board, 2 years.
- Mr. Don Henke, Treasurer of the CHF Board, approximately 5 years, retired VP of Bank.
- Mrs. Eva Kennedy, CHF Board Member, 4 years.
- Mr. Gus Maline, CHF Board Member, 3 years.
- Mr. Lee Snyder, advisory and mentor, as well as volunteered as a CHF grandparent.
- Gary Snyder and Cathy Snyder served on the CHF Board of Directors for 3 years.
- Mr. Gary Hickmon, advisory, mentor and grandparent, and youth worker for many young boys and children at CHF.

- Mr. Steve Persichetti, a volunteer broker and contractor with signing contracts with HUD and RTC for buying foreclosed homes for CHF and assisted as a volunteer general contractor for CHF to build 12 units and the CHF Offices and Educational and Resource Center.
- Candace C. Leone was from the HUD Homeless Programs. She trained me on how to develop and manage a transitional housing program for about 4 years. She also helped me with obtaining additional foreclosed properties for more families to be helped.
- Nicole Kelso, HUD Homes Homeless Programs Representative was also very helpful in my housing training.
- Mr. Brian Bacon, a real estate broker friend, and advisor who gave many long hours to help us sell the outside homes so we would have the monies to build more homes within the CHF community.
- Mayor Bob Frie, City of Arvada, Colorado was an encourager and gave recognition to CHF Transitional Housing Program and helped us with good advice in obtaining an Arvada Grant to build our seven farmhouse units.
- Mr. Mark McGoff, Mayor Pro Tem and Arvada Council Member was a mentor and spoke at the educational seminars for the families living at CHF.
- Arvada City Council and Chamber of Commerce gave much support and recognition to me as the Director and CEO of the CHF Transitional Housing Program.
- I am very appreciative of Mr. Ed Talbot, Director of Arvada Housing, and the section 8 Program and for CDBG grants given to CHF to assist in building new properties,
- Carrie Espinosa, who is responsible and compassionate with our families as she oversees Section 8's housing vouchers with her assistant, Dina.

• We are very grateful for the Extreme Home Makeover Program with Ty Pennington building CHF a duplex for 2 families, with the assistance of HomeAid of America and Home Aid of Colorado and working with The Denver Nuggets and the Kroenke Sports Center to build CHF a basketball court. Sears also blessed us with 50 sets of dishes, cooking ware, towel sets, blankets, toolsets, and vacuum cleaners for 50 of the families living at CHF.

• Noel Lane III, CEO HomeAid of Colorado working with the City of Arvada and making it possible for the 3 duplexes to be built on the expanded land of CHF.

• Laura Brayman, Director of HomeAid of Colorado and Steve Prokopiak, Chairman of HomeAid of Colorado, The Board of Directors helped to build from the grants given to CHF, 11 more homes for homeless families to be able to live in their transitional housing program.

• Roger and Darlene VanWagner for their strong support, large monthly donations, and encouragement.

• The City of Westminster, nonprofit assistance by Mr. Ed Powers for CDBG grants which helped purchase 20 Hud homes in the City of Westminster for CHF and finished the basements in the homes that needed extra bedrooms for the children.

• Jefferson County, Jean Jacobus CDBG grants, Adams County CDBG grants, and Colorado State Division of Housing grants, Tom Heart, John Pallock. which helped CHF build and purchase properties in the extended community area in Arvada, Colorado.

• Mr. Blake Chambliss, coordinator for RTC Affordable Housing Program assisted me in obtaining 10 RTC foreclosed properties in Arvada, Colo for CHF.

• Rev. Frank Trueblood, President of Fellowship of Christian Inmates, who set up the tax exemption for CHF.

- John Parvinsky, Director of Colorado Coalition of the Homeless, a mentor, a valuable co-partner in giving CHF training, grants, and recognition.
- Susan Kiely, CEO of Women with a Cause, gave grants to women living at CHF and paid for their computers, childcare, and tuition costs.
- Bill and Ann Tremble, resourceful people and encouraging of CHF and supported refugees and immigrants fleeing poverty and war.
- First Bank located in Arvada, Colorado, on Ward Road, gave grants and extended customer service.
- Pastor Clyde Speas, volunteered his time, gave support and encouragement, and mentored many of our families.
- David Wilson Talmage, M.D. gave many small grants for emergency family and housing needs, including 50 turkeys for Thanksgiving, 4 new furnaces, and monies to support a woman at CHF who could not work for 3 months due to surgery for a brain tumor.
- The family owners of White Fence Farm Restaurant gave Thanksgiving meals to all our CHF families and case management staff several times.
- Christie Ward, Certified Speaking Professional (CSP) with the Impact Institute of professional speakers supplied CHF with highly rated speakers for the family and educational seminars, including volunteering herself free of charge.
- Foos Financial including Brad and his wonderful serving staff of six, decorated the CHF Office and Community Room for the Annual Christmas Family Party each year, where gifts and food were given to the many families living at CHF. Foos Financial also painted CHF houses, did landscaping, laid sod, and painted all at their own time and expense.
- Keppen Laszio, a doctor at Discovery Chiropractor, and his wife Jennifer have taken families at CHF on shopping sprees,

they have adopted other families for Christmas, and they have given free chiropractor treatments, and donated food and cash to CHF regularly.

• Ryan Wurgler owner of Waste Connections in Colorado purchased 100 bicycles to give to the 99 children living at CHF during Christmas of 2008. He later became a CHF Board Member for 2 years.

• Greg Pries donated and discounted his professional skills in repairing and replacing new furnaces in most all the CHF properties at wholesale cost.

• Dr. Tom Olschner donated approximately five years to give education seminars, support group, and counseling to our families who were needing direction in the success of their personal and family social stability.

• Sue Hamblin pulled together a group of ladies who gave free childcare to our families while they attended their educational and support group meetings every day for 3 years.

My valuable employees and team staff for 29 years consisted of the following individuals who were employed at different times:

• Elaine Nava, office manager
• Bonnie Russell, bookkeeper
• Heather Neill, receptionist
• Tonia Hamblin, later receptionist
• Ken Armstrong, the beginning case manager who also worked battalion chief and chaplain for North Washington Fire Department giving survivor and fire safety education training, saving lives until 2016.
• Norm Strasheim, head case manager, retired from Arvada Police Department.
• Kirsten Bayham, 2nd case manager, social worker, and informational assistance with international cultures

- Stephanie Parmley, 3rd case manager, social worker and manager of food bank and clothing store
- Bonnie Jane Mitchell, receptionist, and processor of homeless applicants
- Jamie Parmley, property manager, security and maintenance supervisor, and oversaw furniture donations and food donations.
- Andrey Russ, property maintenance, furniture, and food pick-ups.
- Don and Linda Coleman supervised the furniture and clothing giveaway on Saturdays at the warehouse
- Pat Armstrong, secretary, and receptionist at the beginning of CHF.
- Betty Armstrong kept up files.
- John Armstrong and Yuriy Demchenko, property maintenance and pick up and deliver donated items.
- Laura Armstrong, secretary, interviewed homeless families, and case manager.
- Marion Jump worked in a food bank and cleaned homes before families moved in.
- Katherine McCubbin grant writer in the early years.
- Jennifer Zimmerman receptionist and case manager at the beginning of CHF.
- Jason Zimmerman, yard and landscaper.
- Brian Thompson, case manager in the beginning.
- Kim Albert, secretary.
- Jess Ryan, Dick McGraw, maintenance in early years
- Bruce and Linda Foltz, CHF telemarketers for 10 years.
- Larisa Degtyar, case manager and ESL teacher for Russian and European refugees and immigrants.
- Larisa Schevchenko, manager, food/clothing bank
- Jillian Hochstetler, grant writer for seven years.

- Tammy Prichard, secretary and Darlene Ball, bookkeeper in early years.
- The CHF Summer Youth Program was directed by the following individuals: Gary Hickmon, Lilly Armstrong, Dina Armstrong, Ri Jr. Armstrong, Davy Armstrong, for eight years. Shon Ridenour assisted for approximately 2 years prior to 2014. The summers of 2014 and 2015 were directed by Brando Perez, Gabby Garneau, Gonna Garneau and Kevin Jang.

Last, but not least:

For the unique skillset, patience, and processing of this book, I especially want to thank Donnetta Wilhelm, for listening to the Lord and to my array of stories, organizing them with the copious documentation on hand, her diligent research to write down the story of CHF with her excellent understanding. And to the editor and chief of Capture Books, Laura Bartnick, for encouraging me to write this story, and for initially recording it, patiently editing with Crystal Schwartzkopf, formatting, and publishing this story. My hope is that this true story will help the readers know that every small thing matters. The history and background of everyone involved in such a project matter.

Our God is able to do exceedingly abundantly above all we ask, say, think, or do.

Photo: *Arvada Mayor Marc Williams (left) and Master of Ceremonies Jerry Marks (right) present the 2012 Arvada Woman of the Year Award to Colorado Homeless Families Executive Director Connie Zimmerman*

The writing of this book began shortly after the death of my beloved mom, who always pointed me toward faith in Jesus. I continued writing the story through the death of my dear dad, a man who always pointed me toward hope. The manuscript was completed after the death of the love of my life, my husband, who always pointed me toward love.

To those I lost who pointed me toward faith, hope, and love, I thank you, and I dedicate this accomplishment to you.

This book is solely the work of my Lord and Savior Jesus Christ. Through profound loss, I truly experienced, *"For with God all things are possible,"* as only He made the writing of this book possible. I am deeply honored and humbled that He chose me to give voice to this amazing story of what faith in Him can do, and how many lives are changed when we are obedient to what He asks of us.

A special thank you to my Bible study friend, Kathy Larkins, who recognized the writer in me.

Finally, to Connie Zimmerman. My own faith grew in unimaginable ways as I wrote your faith story. Thank you for inspiring, answering endless questions, and for your patience and caring during my darkest hours. I believe there is a special crown for you for running this race and keeping up with God.

Donnetta Wilhelm resides in Colorado. She enjoys poetry, writing, music, painting, and gardening. Her passion, however, is for Jesus and encouraging those who are on their spiritual journey. Other publications and her blog can be found at www.cbtpublications.com.

End Notes

1 https://denverchamber.org 2017/04/24
2 https://extras.denverpost.com › snapshot
3 https://arc hives.hud.gov
4 https://www.congress.gov/bill/100th-congress/house-bill/558
5 https://www.mainememory.net/artifact/103610
6 https://www.cambridge.org/core/journals/modern-american-history/article/cops-at-war-how-world-war-ii-transformed-us-policing/9BDE08E301171481539C25333E404115
7 https://www.nationalww2museum.org/war/articles/american-masculinity-after-world-war-ii
8 https://dailyutahchronicle.com/2001/11/01/russian-educators-visit-campus/
9 https://www.heritage.org/europe/report/preparing-america-the-wave-russian-immigrants
10 https://www.nytimes.com/1992/01/25/us/russia-with-hope-america-stay-special-report-seeking-shelter-us-after-soviet.html
11 The Poetry of Robert Frost: The Collected Poems, Complete and Unabridged Hardcover – January 1, 1979
12 The Collected Poems of William Wordsworth (Wordsworth Poetry Library)
13 Federal Reserve History https://www.federalreservehistory.org/essays/savings-and-loan-crisis
14 Congressional Budget Office https://www.cbo.gov/sites/default/files/102nd-congress-1991-1992/reports/1992_01_theeconeffectsofthesavings.pdf
15 Corporate Finance Institute https://corporatefinanceinstitute.com/resources/knowledge/credit/savings-and-loan-crisis/
16 The Silver Lining RTC Newsletter Spring/Summer 1993, Volume 3, Numbers 1&2
17 https://youth.gov/youth-briefs/foster-care-youth-brief/challenges
18 "1190 Immigration and Nationality Act". U.S. Immigration Legislation Online.
19 https://travel.state.gov/
20 FAM 502.6, U.S. Department of State
21 https://www.everycrsreport.com/reports/R45973.html#_Toc22660098
22 Instructions for the 2012 Diversity Immigrant Visa Program (DV-2012) Archived 2016-12-29, United States Department of State
23 https://travel.state.gov/
24 https://travel.state.gov/
25 www.migrationpolicy.org
26 https://ftp.iza.org/dp1231.pdf
27 https://cnnc.uncg.edu/congolese-refugees/
28 https://www.uscis.gov/sites/default/files/document/guides/M-618.pdf

* Nicaraguan Adjustment and Central American Relief Act of 1997 (NACARA) temporarily decreased the 55,000 annual ceiling to 50,000. Beginning in FY2000, the 55,000 ceiling has been reduced by 5,000 annually to offset immigrant visas made available to certain unsuccessful asylum seekers from El Salvador, Guatemala, and formerly communist countries in Europe who are being granted immigrant status under special rules established by NACARA. The 5,000 offset is temporary, but it is not clear how many years it will be in effect to handle these adjustments of status.

[29] https://www.trendwyoming.org/articles/biggest-challenges-after-prison-release/
[30] Bureau of Labor Statistics, U.S. Department of Labor, The Economics Daily
[31] https://www.hud.gov/program_offices/comm_planning/cdbg
[32] https://www.unfpa.org/sites/default/files/pub-pdf/MarryingTooYoung.pdf
[33] https://www.merriam-webster.com/
[34] Romans 8:6-8
[35] Romans 3:10-18
[36] John 15:18-20
[37] bakers-evangelical-dictionary/persecution.html, 2 Timothy 3:12
[38] Robert H. Krapohl, Charles H. Lippy, The Evangelicals: A Historical, Thematic, and Biographical Guide, Greenwood Publishing Group, USA, 1999, p. 163
[39] https://www.un.org/en/chronicle/article/humanitarian-response-2015-nepal-earthquake
[40] https://www.usaid.gov/humanitarian-assistance/nepal
[41] https://ec.europa.eu/echo/where/asia-and-pacific/nepal_en
[42] https://www.worldbank.org/en/country/ethiopia/overview#1
[43] https://www.thenewhumanitarian.org/analysis/2019/10/16/Abiy-Ethiopia-Eritrea-Nobel-peace-Tigray
[44] https://2009-2017.state.gov
[45] https://www.refworld.org
[46] https://www.helpguide.org/
[47] https://history.state.gov/countries/bulgaria
[48] CIA World Factbook and The United States Commercial Service, Pakistan Country Commercial Guide FY-2002,
available at http://www.usatrade.gov/Website/CCG.nsf/CCGurl/CCG-PAKISTAN2002-CH-10:-0049A7A0
[49] https://citeseerx.ist.psu.edu/viewdoc/download?doi=10.1.1.688.9999&rep=rep1&type=pdf
[50] https://citeseerx.ist.psu.edu/viewdoc/download?doi=10.1.1.688.9999&rep=rep1&type=pdf
[51] https://irp.fas.org/offdocs/911comm-sec12.pdf
[52] https://spl.cde.state.co.us/artemis/ucbserials/ucb4109internet/ucb41092004internet.pdf
2004 Colorado Business Economic Outlook
[53] https://www.bls.gov/opub/ted/2012/ted_20120405.htm?view_full#:~:text=In%202010%2C%20othere%20were%2010.5,was%20little%20changed%20from%202009
[54] https://www.homeaid.org/
[55] https://www.salon.com/2020/02/29/extreme-makeover-home-edition-hgtv/
[56] https://aspe.hhs.gov/topics/poverty-economic-mobility/poverty-guidelines/prior-hhs-poverty-guidelines-federal-register-references
[57] Lamentations 3:17, New Life Version
[58] 2 Corinthians 4:7-9
[59] https://www.hrw.org/
[60] https://2001-2009.state.gov/g/prm/rls/71565.htm
[61] https://www.hrw.org/sites/default/files/reports/thailand0912.pdf

[62] https://www.hi-us.org/refugees_in_thailand
[63] https://www.hrw.org/sites/default/files/reports/thailand0912.pdf
[64] https://www.hi-us.org/refugees_in_thailand
[65] http://www.uniteforsight.org/refugee-health/module3
[66] https://www.refworld.org/docid/5971a84f4.html
[67] https://www.sos.state.co.us/
[68] https://www.history.com/topics/crime/history-of-meth
[69] https://www.fs.fed.us/lei/dangers-meth-labs.php
[70] https://www.nar.realtor/meth-labs
[71] https://www.worldometers.info/world-population/democratic-republic-of-the-congo-population/
[72] https://www.state.gov/reports/2020-country-reports-on-human-rights-practices/democratic-republic-of-the-congo/
[73] https://2009-2017.state.gov/documents/organization/160453.pdf
[74] https://2009-2017.state.gov/documents/organization/160453.pdf
[75] https://2009-2017.state.gov/ 2010 Human Rights Report
[76] The Denver Post, July 28, 2011
[77] Denver Business Journal, Bob Mook, Apr 26, 2009

Made in the USA
Coppell, TX
30 July 2022

80638077R00203